Dreams,

Visions

And

Heroes

By Carolyn Smith Phillips

"Dreams, Visions and Heroes" by Carolyn Smith Phillips. ISBN 978-1-60264-647-6 (softcover) and ISBN 978-1-60264-648-3 (eBook).

Published 2010 by Virtualbookworm.com Publishing Inc., P.O. Box 9949, College Station, TX 77842, US. ©2010, Carolyn Smith Phillips. All rights reserved. No part of this publication may be reproduced, stored in a retrieval system, or transmitted in any form or by any means, electronic, mechanical, recording or otherwise, without the prior written permission of Carolyn Smith Phillips.

Manufactured in the United States of America.

Table of Contents

Introduction

Is God personal and intimate? Does He really see and hear all? Can anyone see, hear and feel God? In this follow-up to her compelling book *Michael An Endtime Sign* these and other questions are answered by Carolyn Smith Phillips. This book brings back childhood memories. Come take a journey with a six year old child that woke up one day at age eight with the gift of dreams, visions, angel visitation, seeing future events and witnessing them come to pass and discerning of spirits. Because of the time in history her gift remained a secret with her, her aunt and her daddy for years. She credited this book and her faith to her faithful Aunt Ellen and her Daddy, whom she says built her foundation of faith. Their strong trust in God and building God's character and nature into her left little room for doubt or fear, yet to be an eight year old child in a rural community without internet or assess to book stores she struggled and learned from the Bible to gain a deeper understanding of this gift she calls it. She dreamed about her own death, her marriage partner, and felt Father God in her Daddy's car.

This book is packed with wisdom, funny sayings, courage, faith, surrender, and a country lifestyle on a Virginia farm when family and community helped one another. Her Aunt and Daddy used every opportunity to teach her Bible values because both felt God had given this child to them to teach. A gift they themselves didn't understand but knew she wasn't the first one in the Smith family that was born with such a gift. The simple straight-forward truths were interwoven into this child's life that made her stand out in crowds. You will definably see a different look when looking from the inside out.

The author's 50 plus years in having dreams and visions along with her research on the subject and intense study of different Bible translations have accumulated an amazing amount of knowledge as well as her own personal experience hearing God, and seeing beyond the natural senses. You will know God as she calls him from a different viewpoint after reading this book. He comes a live in the life of this child and you grow with her as she grows up. You see from the inside out. Her Daddy's belief was that after Israel became a nation in 1948 Christ opened up the Holy Spirit and His gifts and poured them out on all who were willing to receive.

She says we all can hear God in our souls if we enter the silence of our mind and listen. This book is loaded with insights. Carolyn reveals God's personal and intimate relationship in such simple truths it gives us all a better understanding of the God within us.

Carolyn also shows us how to see Father God, Mother God Wisdom, in a different way, from a different viewpoint, one in which we will gain a deeper relationship in understanding our Creator. She shares with her readers how we all can enjoy and have that same intimacy with our Creator. Carolyn again shows that she goes against many conventional beliefs in presenting God in such an intimate and loving way, one whom she has dedicated her life and work to come to know more deeply herself.

The fear of death and endtime events just vanishes after reading her books. She lived a strict yet free life in the presence of God daily and claims He talks to her daily, even now. All God shares whether in spoken word, dreams or visions or angels she lines up with the written word, the Bible from many different translations. She says if it doesn't line up with the written word then trash it.

In the end I loved the story for the story's sake. It is a page turner for sure with each short chapter ending in a way that begs for you to read just one more page. You cannot put it down. You will read it in a single long sitting... Again, the story stands on its own. But whether anyone gets everything or even anything on the first read through or not, on a subconscious level I believe it will make a difference to each individual's adventure.

Dedication

I would like to dedicate this book to my Daddy, Henry Smith, A World War II Purple Heart hero. He came home a wounded solder with many metals and purple hearts. He said, "Any honors, metals or money should go to the families of those solders that didn't come home." Daddy, you refused to talk about your bravery but your children always knew they were blessed and special because of you. I love you and hope I have made you proud. I hope to give a glance of how special you were to us and to your grandchildren and future heirs and how firm and strict you were as well in a good way. I feel so honored to be loved so much that you would take the time to teach me Jesus' Character and nature to live by and live in.

To my Aunt Ellen, Ellen Tune Smith, who was a hero in the Smith family. The greatest prayer warrior and Bible teacher The Smith Family ever knew. Thank you for taking the time to be our Mother, our hero, our family glue and giving me the real wealth to live by, God's holy word by example. I hope to pass down just a little of your wisdom to all future generations for one book couldn't do you justice. I hope many will see how very special you really were to give your life to teach children. Thank you for your visits from time to time since you've crossed over. I hope you inspire and help me to share only what you would want me to share in my books concerning you. Now with your blessing I shall pray the prayer you prayed over us many times for all our families and readers. You and Daddy loved the Jews and as you said, so many family members gave their life in World War II to help set the Jews free. I feel this prayer is your way to honor all mankind Jew and gentile alike. You and Daddy said, "All that is born of Jesus Christ is a Jew."

"The LORD blesses you, and keeps you; The LORD makes His face shine on you, and be gracious to you; The LORD lifts up His countenance on you, and gives you peace. Amen. (Aaronic Blessing, Numbers 6: 24-26)

About the Author

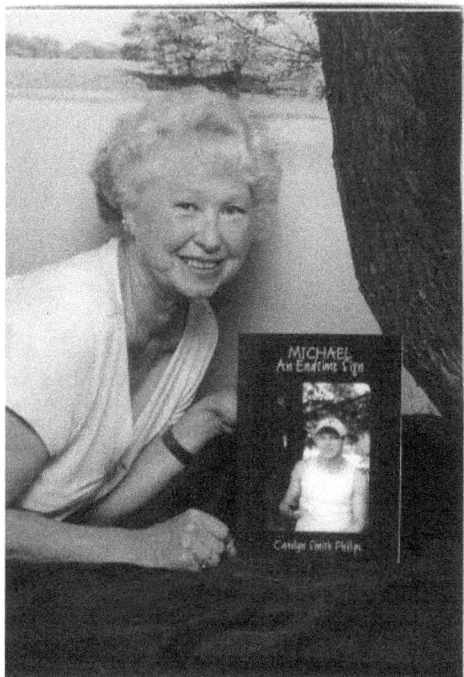

Carolyn Smith Phillips

C arolyn Smith Phillips of Halifax Virginia is a wife, mother, stepmother, grandmother, a Toy-Chinese Chihuahua Breeder and a published author. Her latest book in print is *Michael, An Endtime Sign*.

Before her disability and retirement she was a real estate investor, paralegal, a counselor who worked with unmarried pregnant teens and abused children for the Southern Baptist Association of Jacksonville Fl. She had her own radio talk show for six years. A regular guest on several local Christian Television shows, a very talented and yet time to pray and help others. She now resides in her hometown.

The Author attended Halifax County schools where she graduated and continued her education at Keysville Community College, Keysville Va., Danville Community College, Danville VA., and, Old Dominion of Virginia, in Norfolk VA.. Her subjects were real estate, law, finance, appraisal, physiology and sociology, as well as the Century Twenty-One School of Real Estate. She attended W. V. Grant Ministries in Texas where she received a minister's certificate, and The First Superet Light Branch Church of Washington, D. C. where she finished a twelve lesson course in Spiritual Light and received her instructor's certificate. The author continued her love and studies with the Institute of Children's Literature where she graduated. She also continues her studies of the meanings of Jesus Christ words and follows the leading of the Holy Spirit, God's power within her. She believes we live in the greatest age of all ages as she studies the news to compare it with Bible Prophecy. She speaks out boldly and with full confidence concerning what God has showed her over her lifetime to date in the secret place of God her Creator.

The Family Picture

**Geneva, Henry Smith-Thomas (Tommy), in front,
Shirley Mae beside Daddy and Carolyn Ann, the biggest girl.
1955, the year they lost their Mother.
Less than a year later they lost their Daddy, also.**

Chapter 1:

Humble Beginnings

According to a marriage license and birth certificates, Mama and Daddy were married December 1, 1945. They had their first child, Shirley Mae, March 1, 1948. *(May 1948 Israel became a nation but remember it was degreed in 1947, like Shirley Mae was conceived in last part of May or beginning of June 1947 around the same time Israel became a nation on paper but not announced, a key fact in the end of time for people who study the endtime signs.)* She was a tiny petite little thing with green eyes like Daddy and blondest brown hair. Daddy named her after his niece who had passed away and she was the apple of his eye.

Then September 30, 1949, Carolyn Ann was born *(that's me, and I was conceived between Thanksgiving and Christmas of 1948 seven months after Israel was declared a nation).* I was told I was born at our Evington Virginia home with a mid-wife and house doctor. As you know back then parents didn't have the luxury of scans and had to wait for an emergency before the house doctor showed up and the birth to find out the sex of the baby. Therefore when Mama went into labor and the doctor realized I was coming feet first they didn't expect me to live. They said my mama almost died giving birth to me and vowed not to have any more children if she lived through this delivery.

After I was born feet first they said I was so blue I looked shiny black and not breathing, dead. So I guess the devil already knew he had his hands full if I lived and decided to wipe me out at the start of this race. According to family stories the mid-wife wouldn't give up even after the doctor said I was dead. She dipped me in cold water then real warm water, breathing into my mouth and praying over me. Could a near death experience be the reason I have dreams, visions and heavenly visitors? Some call that seer, prophet, prophecy.

After I started breathing on my own my color began to change, crying loud enough for the neighborhood to hear me. Mama said the midwife stated she believed she had a singer on her hands. They said my mouth never stopped after that and neither did my feet. They said when my feet hit the floor I never stopped running. Always on the go, keeping Mama, Great-Aunt Lucille, Aunt Elsie and Daddy busy keeping up with me. As I got older Daddy and Aunt Ellen confirmed that I stayed on the move, multitasking, always doing something while thinking of something else to get into. A real handful so I was told. Now you must realize these stories came from family members and what parts are true or false I haven't a clue. I guess daddy didn't like the birth control back then so Mama conceived again.

By October 21, 1951, Mama was giving birth again. (*That means she conceived around Christmas in 1950. As we can see they enjoyed the holidays back then very much.) S*he learned her lesson and went to Lynchburg General Hospital to have this one. It was a boy and they named him after Daddy, Thomas Henry and called him *Tommy.*

Where did that leave me? Shirley Mae the apple of Daddy's eye and his baby boy that came after me? In the middle that's where. With Shirley being so small and petite and a very sickly child she got a lot of attention. Then Tommy being the baby boy got the rest of it from Mama and Daddy. So aunts and uncles and my grandparents spoiled and gave me most of my attention.

Daddy always said Mama was the most beautiful woman he had ever seen. He bragged on her cooking and cleaning as well as everything else she did. Mama was a housewife while Daddy worked on the railroad as a cook. Daddy would leave very early on Monday mornings and return home late evening on Fridays. While Daddy was at work and all three of us were not old enough to attend school yet Mama would go walking with us. Sometimes we walked and picked blueberries or blackberries. Sometimes we picked apples and pears. Some days we walked to town and window shopped Mama called it. On those days before returning home we would go in the drug store or little café on Main Street in Gretna Virginia and get something to drink. I don't remember ever eating there unless Daddy was with us. Some days Mama would spot a dress in the window bouquet and we got to enter. Mama would ask the lady if she had two and gave the sizes. If the lady said yes then we got to try them on. If they fit us then Mama told the lady to hold them until Saturday. Mama loved dressing Shirley Mae and myself like twins. We never bought Tommy any clothes in that bouquet, but I do remember when Mama and Daddy went to Lynchburg they always came back with clothes for him while we stayed with Grandma Falls. Then some days we walked the railroad tracks and Mama would find the neatest little objects and money. Now, you must remember I am seeing all this through the eyes of a child so not every detail will appear. Only the ones I remembered, or were told, or the ones that touched my heart.

I can say I only remember happy times with Mama and Daddy up to the day Mama left us, which was in September 1955. I remember the date only because we were in school and it was right before my sixth birthday. From my childlike eyes, we seemed to be rich. We had a nice home, nice furniture, a car, and a truck. I remember our clothes came from a dress shop, not a cheap store. We always had plenty of food and shared with others. Mama dressed like a movie star, and Daddy dressed in fine clothes. Not like some of our family members who wore rags Mama called them. I remember pretty hair bows in our hair and Mama always smelled good. I even remember the nice people we visited at various times and they all lived in clean and nice homes. They dressed well and were clean also. I do remember some family members that lived in not-so-nice homes or wore not-so-nice clothes so I knew we were well-off. I also knew because Daddy would say for us to never make fun of people, no matter how they lived or dressed; that not everyone was as blessed as we were, but that didn't make us better. Mama and Daddy always seemed to be in love so deep, they showed it every day they were together by hugging and kissing, that I felt nothing could or would separate them. Daddy also said God had blessed him with a beautiful wife and mother for his children. That he had eyes only for Mama and that she had stolen his heart. She was a good mother.

What went wrong? What caused Mother to just pack up and walk away from her family and not look back? I know from a child's viewpoint she was happy and well cared for. I also know from her mother and family members that Daddy was good to her, a good provider and a peaceful man. The only answer we ever received from Mama was she was lonely during the week while Daddy was away and it just happened.

All I can tell you is a man started visiting us while Daddy was at work every day. I don't remember what month, but it appeared to be around spring. But once he started coming he didn't stop. When we told Daddy he defended Mama. He said he was just a friend and he trusted Mama and we had nothing to worry about. Fred was a kind man, very tall and some days we would go riding in his car up to Leesville Lake. I know the name because Mama would ask us if we wanted to ride with the nice man up to Leesville Lake. Of course we wanted to ride to the lake. What kid wouldn't want to go? I remember after he started coming to visit we didn't take as many walks down the railroad tracks or to town. Mama seemed to be happier with him coming by every day and taking us places. The days seem to go by faster also. Some days he would stay at the house and would give us money to walk to the store to get some candy.

On the way from the store we would stop in to see our neighbor. I don't remember her name but she was a short, fat little lady with a big smile. We always enjoyed visiting her because she gave us cookies and milk. She always had candy or cookies or something good to eat to give us. Sometimes we ate lunch with her. While we ate she would ask us questions. Mama said she bribed us with candy to learn the latest gossip. Well, it must have worked because, being little kids, we told all we knew. Sometimes she gave us a toy she had bought when she went shopping. I remember once she gave Shirley and me a tiny little pink doll in just a diaper with a tiny little baby bed. She gave Tommy a little blue dump truck. Those toys fit right into our little hands. We thought that was the neatest thing. She always wanted to know everything Mama did and who she saw while Daddy was at work. Nosey old lady we told her is what Mama called her. She would just laugh and keep asking until Mama called us to come home.

We were never allowed to cross the road without Mama. Sometimes a kid just got to do what a kid has got to do. We had been outside on this particular day a long time and we had gotten hungry. We had knocked on our front door and told Mama several times we wanted to come in and eat. But she always said go play. Across the road straight in front of our house stood this huge mansion and a nice elderly lady with cookies, candy and Pepsi just waiting for us. Before Fred started coming over we would go visit her at least twice a week. Whenever Mama needed to call Aunt Lucille she would use her desk phone and we would go more. She and Mama would sit on that big white porch talking while we ran all around the house. I loved playing on that big porch that wrapped the entire house. Sometimes she would ask us to stay for dinner and we would get to eat at this huge table with a fancy tablecloth. A nice lady with a white laced apron always served us and we didn't have to help with dishes. Once Fred started coming over to visit we didn't visit her any more. After he came over we wished we could go visit her and play on that big porch. Some days we would get real close to the road and stand but chicken out. I knew if Mama saw us it would be me that got the whipping. Mama always said I was the ring leader. One day we got near the highway and Mama didn't call us back so I grabbed Shirley and Tommy's hand and ran across that road. I could see the elderly lady sitting on the porch watching us. As soon as we stepped up on the porch she asked if our Mama knew we had *crossed the road*. When we told her no, she was busy with the nice man. She had sent us outside to play and told us not to come back in the house until she called us. Well we hit the jackpot with that news. That lady's face lit up like someone had turned a light on inside of her. She smiled and said, really, as she led us in the house and to the kitchen to get homemade sugar cookies and a coke. I knew it was a coke because it came in the same little bottle like Daddy drank. We got our own that day. Sometimes she gave us Pepsi in a glass but today we each got a bottle of coke. Then she led us all back to the porch where she sat down in her rocker and asked all sorts of questions while we ate. The more we talked the more cookies we ate. After about an hour I guess she told us we had better cross over and get on our porch before our Mama realized we were gone. She walked us to the road and told us when to run across and also told us not to tell our Mama we had come to visit her.

I remember it wasn't long after that day that Mama decided to leave us.

I've shared only a little of what led up to Mama abandoning us and that was from the eyes of a child. As a child I often wondered if Mama got afraid of Daddy finding out after we told the elderly lady and that was why she left. I also wondered if the little fat lady told mama we told. I do remember Mama telling Fred on some days that The Smith's were not the sort of people you pissed off. That if she ever left Henry she would have to leave her children also. But when we asked her if she was leaving us she would hold our face in her hands and kiss us and say no way. She said she loved our Daddy.

That Henry had always told her she could leave anytime she wished but she had better not take his kids. She said she would never leave unless she could take us with her. She warned Fred on many occasions that the Smith's had a lot of pull in that town. That Henry was friends with judges and she would never win if she ever took him to court. Just grown up talk we thought. I remember asking Daddy about some of that and he always said she was right and added she wasn't going anywhere. It was just mouth talking.

By the end of that summer Mama did get up the nerve to leave us. I remember it as if it was yesterday. If you want to read all of the glory details then purchase my book, '*A Daddy but No Mama*'. But for now let's move ahead and see if Mama's leaving had anything to do with dreams, visions and heavenly visitors.

The same weekend Mama left, we went and did as if Mama was still there. Her leaving us crying on the front porch the night before didn't seem to bother Daddy in the least. Daddy bedded us down for bed after supper and then washed up dishes. Saturday morning he cooked breakfast and washed up the dishes then got us all dressed for Saturday morning like Mama had always done. He said our first stop was to pay bills. He asked me if Mama had laid away any clothes in the dress shop. But when I answered no, he proceeded to tell us, after bills got paid we would go get groceries and then go to Grandmother Falls to visit. I remember Daddy being so sad and quiet that day. When we asked him if Mama was coming home, he would say, "If it be God's will." What does that mean I asked? All he would say was what I said.

We loved going to Grandma's on Saturdays because there were always kids to play with. The house would be full of her kids and their kids and Grandma let us do whatever we wanted. Grandma always had big hoe cakes on the table, real apple butter and Kara Syrup. On the stove cooking would be some kind of meat in a big pot, cornbread, turnip greens, pinto or great northern beans. Grandma allowed us to run through her house and she laughed all the time at everyone. We would see Mama get mad and fuss and other family members but we never saw Grandma mad or fussing. Daddy said if Grandma got mad people moved out so I always looked for that big smile. But that Saturday Grandma wasn't smiling so we went next door to Lucille's, Mama's sister who lived just across the driveway. When we asked why Grandma was sad she said it was because of your mama. Five o'clock came and went and Grandma didn't call us to eat supper. We sneaked in the front door and heard all the adults in the kitchen so we went to the dining room and got a cold biscuit and apple butter but Grandma heard us and told us to come to the stove and get our food. She reached down and kissed each of us and said it didn't matter what our Mama did we were still her special little angels. That and her smile told us things would be alright and we dug in to eat.

Before we knew it, two weeks had gone by, and Mama had shown up every day at school with Vanilla Wafers and sat with Shirley and myself all day but she hadn't moved back home. At recess she asked us questions about Tommy and Daddy. Mama was very sad, and she cried a lot. She said she wanted to come home but was afraid of Daddy and what he would do. I asked her every day when she was coming home, but she never answered me. I remember that she cried a lot, especially when school was let out and we had to leave. She cried so hard that the teacher told her she had to get herself together or not come back to school.

The first weekend after he paid bills, we went to Grandma's to visit a little while, and after dark we went to visit his brother Press and family. It was nice having Daddy home but sad, too. We whispered and asked each other questions and cried among ourselves, but we tried not to let Daddy know we were getting afraid that Mama wasn't coming back to us. When we asked Daddy when Mama was coming home, he always said whenever she wanted too. She didn't ask him when she left so she didn't need to ask if she could come home. All she had to do was come home.

At Aunt Ellen's I remember there was a big farmhouse and many animals running around in the yard. Chickens everywhere and she let us chase them while she laughed at us. I remember Aunt Ellen said there was a lot of work to do with such a big house and farm and asked us how we would like to come and live with her and help her do her daily work. Work was something we didn't know anything about, but we got excited about moving there. I remember asking what about Mama and she replied Mama wasn't coming back. That Daddy needed help with us kids, and if we moved in with them she could help our Daddy with us.

The next weekend, without Mama, Daddy moved us to the home house where Uncle Press and Aunt Ellen lived in Nathalie, Virginia. I remember it was a warm fall Saturday morning, and my sixth birthday had passed. Mama had forgotten my birthday. When I asked her at school she said she would bring my gift the next week. But I never got that gift. A big flat bed truck pulled up in our yard right to the front door. A tall man got out and other men following behind him in a hurry. They walked right passed us who were standing in the front door, pushing us gently as they told us to get out of their way as they entered into the house. They acted like they knew what to do and how to do it as they discussed among themselves what to put on the truck first. We ran in behind them and to Daddy to ask where they were taking our stuff. Daddy said they were there to move us to the home house. I felt the fear right then. I knew somehow without knowing that my life was falling apart at that very moment. I felt my belly sink as I looked up at Daddy and asked, but what about Mama? She won't know where we are. She won't be at school Monday. She won't see us at school every day? Daddy we can't leave without Mama. But I was pushed out of the way like all of a sudden what I felt didn't matter anymore. Children are to be seen and not heard I heard one of the mean men say. I began to cry and when I did, Tommy and Shirley started crying also. A tall dark skinned man said, "Now look at what you did. Shut that fuss up and get out of our way."

Daddy said Mama was gone and not coming back and for us to shut that crying up before he gave us a real reason to cry. That he and Aunt El would be raising us now.

But Daddy, I replied. Before I could get another word out, he said, take Tommy and Shirley Mae outside to play and stay out of the way.

I did as Daddy asked, but we didn't play. We all sat down on the bottom step near the ground on the side of the house far away from them and just cried. After drying our eyes, we just watched them load up that big truck with our stuff. The thought of Mama being gone made me feel sick to my stomach. I held my stomach to afraid to tell. I saw Shirley throwing up and crying she wanted Mama. Little Tommy just sat with his cheeks in his little hands like he didn't have a clue as to what was going on but he wasn't going to cry any more. He just sat there and watched us cry. Mama not knowing how to find us made us so sad. My stomach hurt like I had swallowed a big ball. I began to cry louder but when I saw and heard Shirley and Tommy both crying louder I knew I had to stop quickly or Daddy would be out there. He wasn't in a happy mood and I knew if Daddy saw that I would be in trouble. Grabbing both of them we got up and ran to the little short fat lady next door and I told her to tell Mama where we went. She promised us she would. She knew we were upset when we refused her cookies. Instead I told her we had to get back or they might leave us too. We went to the bottom step and just sat and watched the grown-ups load up our stuff.

Leaving our home and going with strangers to live and they were like strangers to us. We had been to their house before and we knew they were family but that's all. They didn't spend much time with us when we did visit. They spent their time laughing and talking with Mama and Daddy. I don't ever remember them coming to visit us. I remember Uncle Press came and brought us apples and oranges from time to time. Can you imagine how it felt for a seven year old, a six year old and a four year old not being told anything and yet watching our life as we knew it just vanish before our eyes?

I remember my one last pitch to talk to Daddy. We asked Daddy about Mama not knowing where we were if we moved. But before he could answer this tall big man with a strong voice said she's not coming back and we would never see her again. That she chose another man over her children and lost all her rights to see us or come back. Now stay out of our way and go play. Later we learned that was Uncle Jesse and not someone you make mad or ask questions to. We noticed Daddy didn't say a word to him as to how he spoke to us. That was strange. I remember not liking Daddy at that point. Actually, it made me a little afraid of Daddy like he was afraid of these men, too. He acted like one of us when they spoke. He did exactly what they said. Who are these people telling my Daddy what to do? Daddy and Mama never raised their voice at us. They didn't allow anyone else to do it, either. But Mama had left us and now Daddy allowed these men to do it and get away with it. I decided not to like them at that moment.

Later in the morning a familiar face walked up on the porch with a warm and friendly smile. We ran to greet Aunt Ellen before she got to the steps. It felt good to see someone nice and friendly since all the men acted like they were mad at us. She smiled all the way up the steps and hugged us. Telling us as she walked toward us and reaching for a hug to come and help her pack our clothes so the men could put them in her car. She said we were going to live with her for awhile. Later we learned the men were Uncle Jesse, Uncle Press and Cousin Johnny and the big boy was Clarence.

When they finished we all loaded up and left, leaving the house empty and clean. I remember looking back as Daddy drove off as long as I could with a feeling we would never see that house or Mama again. I remember Daddy telling us to turn around and stop crying. I remember the silence for a long time in the car with only a few sniffles from time to time. I remember seeing Tommy sitting in the front seat just looking out of the window. I remember Shirley's sad face as she looked to me for answers in which I had none. It seemed like a long trip and on the way Daddy explained to us that life would be different. He said much more but I don't remember what his words were; only the sinking feeling I felt inside. I remember Shirley and Tommy crying and him telling us everything would be alright.

Soon we arrived at the home house and drove around to the back to a little house where they pulled the flatbed up to the door. As all the men got out and began unloading our furniture Aunt Ellen asked us to go with her and help with lunch. Gladly as I followed behind her up to the big house and she shouted back for Tommy and Shirley Mae to come on. I didn't like any of those men. They were just too bossy and even bossed Daddy around.

Being in the kitchen helping Aunt Ellen was a real treat because Mama never allowed us to help her. While Mama cooked we ran around playing and running through the house and acting like kids until time to eat. Aunt Ellen asked many questions. She told us she knew how we felt because she lost her Mama very young and had to live with her aunt. She told us stories about how family help each other, and sometimes have to live together for a little while. As she moved around doing stuff, she showed us where the plates, glasses and silverware were teaching us how to sit the table. Soon she went to the back door and yelled lunch was ready. Then told us where to sit and showed us where the others sat.

When the men came in they were laughing. The whole time as they ate they were happy and talking to each other, making jokes with us and passing the food. Boy what a change of attitude at the table I thought but I liked it much better than the bossy one.

I remember Aunt Ellen with a warm smile but a very serious attitude, looking straight at Daddy and saying, "Henry I have one rule and that is church comes first. We go to church every Sunday regardless if we have company of not. And we go during the week if there is anything going on." I saw Daddy agree as he dipped into the cream potatoes. Then she went back to eating and listening to the men talk like we did.

After lunch the men went back to work and Aunt Ellen cleaned up the kitchen and started supper as she told us to go play outside with Clarence for a little while. We had learned at lunch that

Clarence was a foster boy they had took in their home like us. "Foster boy, what did that mean"? I asked. Uncle Press answered that it meant when your parents didn't want you any more you became a foster child and lived with other people.

"Am I a foster girl?" I asked.

Aunt Ellen laughed so hard her belly shook as she said, "No, you are a Smith. Now go play before you become a foster girl."

The way she said *I was a Smith* made me feel like an important and special person.

Outside we asked Clarence lots of questions about living there as we swung on the tree swing in the front yard. He told us about having to work in the fields of tobacco, the huge gardens, the wheat fields, corn fields, orchards, feeding the animals, getting in the wood in winter time, and many other chores that needed doing on such a big farm. He ended by saying, "Mrs. Smith was real nice to him and we would like her. But watch out for Press because he could be mean at times."

Several weeks went by and we had learned a lot of stuff. During that time Aunt Ellen had contacted all of Daddy's brothers and sisters and asked them to come down and meet us. She, Daddy, Uncle Press and Johnny were busy cleaning and getting everything ready for a family reunion in fall they called it. They were real excited about it and Aunt Ellen cooked lots of food, like a country ham, cakes, pies and all sorts of stuff. There was so much food it would feed an army I heard Daddy say. She was also busy cleaning up the upstairs and putting new linens on all the beds and taught us as we helped her along the way. She was a very pleasant lady and everything she did she would teach us to do. The way she taught made me want to learn even more. Tommy and Clarence had to hang with the men and learn what they did. Just us girls had to clean, wash clothes, sew, and cook she said. The Sunday arrived and we had returned from church and people were already there and regularly coming down the driveway. It seemed like a hundred people or more and all were happy, smiling and hugging everyone. Everyone talked loud and gave out a huge laugh when another answered them. Each one was introduced to us as, "these are Henry's kids, Shirley Mae, Carolyn Ann and Tommy." Each one rubbed us on our head and introduced themselves and told us how much we had grown since the last time they saw us.

Later after everyone left we learned that the fall reunion was about more than just meeting Henry's kids. They were also seeing

Daddy off as he had planned to leave that following Monday for Canada. How long they didn't say but it meant we would be left there with Aunt Ellen and Uncle Press while he went to that far away land to work. Fear gripped our hearts so tight to learn that we would be there without a mama or daddy. Both had left us. We really were foster kids. Our parents did just like Clarence's did. After that weekend and Daddy left the four of us stuck together like glue.

School also had been introduced to us during those two weeks. Like Daddy stayed around just long enough to get us settled before abandoning us like Mama did. I remember meeting our first grade teacher by greeting Aunt Ellen with, "So these are the kids without a Mama." An instant dislike from me began at that moment and I answered her very angrily, "We have a Mama." I was mad at the world after Daddy left and didn't care who knew it. But I learned very quickly she was like the men at home mean and very bossy. So the remainder of my first grade year weren't happy ones. I got my hand paddled several times a day with her yard stick. Shirley was timid and shy, so I fought her battles and took her hand paddlings by putting my hand over hers and letting the ruler hit me. The teacher said that meant I got twice the amount. Being the new kids meant lots of name calling and fights from the kids, also. I wanted to hit anyone that crossed me and just waited for someone to start something. Tommy was too young to attend school and would sneak on the bus with us. Aunt Ellen would come and get him around lunch time every day. That went on for a few weeks until Uncle Press found out. Then he sent Johnny after him and that afternoon we were told by Uncle Press if we took him to school another day we would get the belt on our behinds. So after that we got on the bus with Tommy crying and screaming for us. Every afternoon he stood at that barn with the biggest smile and waited until the bus stopped then he was at the foot of the steps as we stepped off.

After Daddy left I began having nightmares. Aunt Ellen said it was because of my nerves after Mama and Daddy both left us. She started tucking us in at night and taught us the 23rd Psalms to say every night out loud.

"The LORD is my shepherd; I shall not be in want for anything. He makes me to lie down in green prosperous pastures; he leads me beside still calm waters. He restores my soul to life. He guides me in paths of righteousness for his name's sake. Even thought I walk

through the valley of the shadow of death, I will fear no evil, for you are with me; your rod word and your staff, the Holy Spirit, they comfort me. You prepare a table of plenty before me in the presence of my enemies. You anoint my head with the oil of joy, my cup within overflows. Surely goodness and love will follow me all the days of my life, and I will dwell in the house of the LORD forever". Then she made us repeat this prayer, *"Now I lay me down to sleep. I pray the LORD my soul to keep. If I should die before I wake, I pray the LORD my soul to take. God bless Mama and Daddy and every body I love. Amen."*

I felt better when we prayed but began to cry once she got up to leave. I felt peace when she prayed with us but it didn't last long. We cried ourselves to sleep every night. Missing Mama and Daddy each day and all the changes in our life became easier as time passed. Our hearts hurt for Mama and Daddy yet our mind was filled with confusion. The pain was still there inside like a big boil just waiting for someone to touch it and make us cry. The first few months any little thing and every little thing made us run and hide and cry. After awhile we didn't speak of Mama to anyone but Aunt Ellen after Daddy left for Canada. It just made us cry more when Uncle Press said bad things about her. I remember Clarence shooing us many times on that old front porch to stop crying before someone heard us. After the first year and Tommy had turned five he stopped crying and like Shirley and I accepted what we couldn't change. Clarence, Shirley, Tommy and I talked about our parents' way away from the adults and became like a little pack, looking after each other. Johnny started calling me, "Cry Baby." He would tell everyone that all he had to do was pull my big toe and I would cry for hours. That's not what my school teacher called me though. She called me 'Lil Johnny'. She said I was every bit as mean as he was when he went to school. That made Johnny and Uncle Press both happy. They said it just proved I was all Smith.

Thanksgiving and Christmas were both happy and sad for us. The energy in the air was full of zeal as they all worked and prepared for the holidays. You could tell everyone looked forward to these holidays, all the family coming in and hunting season. It meant lots of preparation, laughter, planning, and work, which started the 1st of November. You could smell the fruit cakes smelling up the house all the way up to the end of the driveway, as they cooked, cooled and were stored in the seller, along with sweet potato pies, and all sorts of cakes and pies that could be stored or frozen. The entire Smith family came in for Thanksgiving and Christmas and that meant turkey, ham, beef and all its trimmings. The men to deer hunt while the women helped with food and cleaned up. Everyone helped. Kids couldn't hang around in the kitchen or get in the way; it was help or get out of the kitchen. I always wanted to help so I could hear what they talked about. If I kept my mouth shut they talked like I wasn't even there so that meant I always had a secret to tell the others. As soon as I forgot and asked a question I was sent outside to play with Shirley Mae. They would stop and look up as if they had forgotten about me then wondered what they had said that I might tell. Their expressions seem to tell me how big the secret was. If we wanted to play and not work that meant outside and stay until called. There were plenty of kid cousins to play with and help with chores. It was like a vacation for us with lots of laughter and hugs. Everywhere would be talking and laughter. Some would spend the night and leave on Saturday nights while others drove back and forth just to hunt together for those few days. It was the event of the year outside of the June reunion.

With each passing month we learned how blessed we were to have such a family as the Smith's. At the Smith home house where Grandma and Grandpa had lived and raised their children there was plenty of peace, love and joy to spread around along with the neighbors.

After the first year, 1956, we had learned that Uncle Press wasn't all that mean but just very stern and strict. He had a certain way to do things and you had to learn it the right way or his way the first time. He had a gentle side about him when he wanted to show it so we watched for that. Later we learned it had to be that way to survive. After World War II anyone that still had land and family had to work like slaves to build it back up. So much had went undone during the war that it would take years before you saw a real profit according to the adults. The lack of money was a problem also which meant not much for clothes or anything we could do without. All this was new for us because Daddy worked for the railroad and whether we had plenty of money or not we lived and spent like we did. But it was a whole different way of life on the farm. Money was very important for buying seed to plant and feed for the animals. They came first before vacations, new clothes and such. Borrowing money was only for seeds and crops not for luxuries. There seem to be such an appreciation in the air so strong you could feel it. Aunt Ellen said it was because people were so glad the war was over. Everyone had to pull their weight even the children and animals because World War II had took a lot out of people and cost many families their homes and livelihood. In order for a family to survive it meant everyone work and help each other.

While Tommy went to the store most every night with Uncle Press and Johnny, she would use some of that time to read Shirley and me Bible stories, especially those about dreams and visions since I was so curious about them. Johnny and Clarence had become big brothers and Uncle Press was just Uncle Press. He had won me over by teaching me how to drive the tractor. He would say if we went out in that field whatever the work was and did our best he would let us take turns driving the tractor later. We had learned how to please him so he wouldn't get so mad with us. Aunt Ellen said some days Press didn't even like himself and on those days stay away. We didn't like him fussing and the threats to whip us. When he got to ugly Aunt Ellen would say, Press that's enough, and he would shake his head and walk off. Everyone may have thought he ran the house but we knew Aunt Ellen did. She didn't cross him and walked in peace and taught us to do the same. As long as we didn't talk back to Uncle Press he would be nice. Aunt Ellen said we had him wrapped around our little finger after we had been there a year.

We all saw how proud Daddy was also when he returned from Canada two years later and realized how much we had learned. The time had passed rather quickly once we got the chip off of our shoulders and didn't pout and complain so much. It took awhile to get all that spoilness out of us and learn to keep the peace but it sure was a better feeling once we did. Teamwork was an enjoyable time to fellowship as well as work after we had learned not to complain and just get it done. We have many good memories that could fill volumes of books at Aunt Ellen's house we called it. We had come to understand how blessed we were to be able to learn and work. So much we all learned during those first two years without a mama and daddy. Being real was a blessing to everyone not just family but everyone. Being a blessing to each other and neighbors was practiced every day. We had learned how important God was also. If you were too sick to go to church you were to sick to watch television or play. It was stay in bed all day. We didn't get sick for church or school because we hated staying in bed all day. They believed Jesus Christ God's only living Son had spared them from death and poverty during the war and worshipping him was an honor. Being baptized in the local creek was also important if you planned to live for God. Aunt Ellen took the Bible very serious and helped us to understand the importance of studying it and applying it daily. She said the Bible was not a book we learn to read but one we learned to apply. Her consistency sowed the Bible into us daily just like they sowed the seeds into the fields on the farm. She had become our mother in every sense of the word. She filled that empty spot within us that longed for Mama. She did everything all our friends' mothers did. In our hearts, she was Mama. She had taken the time to teach us many things. How to sew, cook, bake bread and cakes, how to plant a garden and so much more with a good attitude, she always had a good attitude always. She said God didn't receive any pleasure out of our deeds if we didn't do it with a cheerful heart. She taught us how to go to the Bible for every answer we needed. She had a real thick book called Strong's and it showed us where the word was and what it meant. She taught us to ask for God's inner peace by reading the words of Jesus. That he would take missing Mama out and put joy back in us so we could be happy. She said when she was troubled in spirit she would read Jesus' words until she felt at peace within. Asking Jesus what it meant was a short cut if we really didn't have time to study.

Johnny had won Tommy over with a pair of cowboy boots. After he got those boots Johnny was his hero.

Left: One year old; *Right:* Six years old.

Chapter 2:

A Six Year Old Mama

Can you even imagine what it's like to be six years old and have to learn how to be a mama to two children? I had two years training before Daddy came home. Once we moved out when I was eight years old and on our own it was me just me. Look at your children and grandchildren at age six and see if you can imagine such a task. Not many can.

Daddy had gotten a job running a store with Mr. Billy Younger. The job came with a log cabin behind the store for us to live in that worked out beautifully. Daddy could work and watch us closely at the same time. We had to learn a new way of life again. A single dad was almost unheard of back then. Even divorce was rare in 1956. Tommy had started first grade and Shirley and I were in third grade. Daddy had put me in charge since I was the biggest that was the only qualification needed, even though Shirley was the oldest. Aunt Ellen had made us aprons like hers and told us we had to be the ladies of the house for Daddy. It was time to show Daddy just how much we all had learned since he was away. It was a little scary at first but fun to think we wouldn't have all those bosses. Just one boss, Daddy and that should be a piece of cake. We knew unless Daddy had changed in Canada he was not hard to please at all. The school bus ran and stopped right in front of the store so that meant no playing hooky. We would go in the store every morning for inspection and a treat. Daddy liked us to be clean and dressed nice.

One of the highlights of living behind the store was seeing all the people that stopped and all that visited the Younger's. Plus we had the run of the place most of the time and that suited my curiosity just fine. One Sunday this lady and gentleman came to visit Mr. and Mrs. Younger. They saw me hanging out clothes with my apron on standing on a little foot stool that Cousin Johnny had made. They visited often and each time asks about us. When I asked Glenn how they knew our name he said they know every body. They were rich. He then told me they had nicknamed me 'Little Mama' because every time they came to visit them I was hanging out clothes.

Years later our paths crossed again. They told me why they nicknamed me Little Mama. It was like Glenn had said. They thought I was the cutest thing hanging out those clothes standing on that little stool with that apron on. So smart to care for sister and brother while our daddy worked. Alice said she never saw us get in trouble and never heard about us getting in trouble. She thought that was unusual for kids left alone to raise themselves while their daddy worked. After that we remained close friends. I ended up helping Julian pass the real estate exam and taught Alice the Bible from a different point of view than her religion. We became life-long friends and it was told that Alice was very jealous of Julian and I was the only woman she allowed him to spend long periods of time with without her. Julian always said she was a jealous woman. One day while we worked in her flowers I asked her about it. She laughed and said she was jealous of Julian. He was a handsome man and lazy women were always looking for a rich man to support them but it wouldn't be her man. Then I asked why she wasn't jealous of me. She stopped planting that yellow flower in her hand and looked straight at me and said, because you love God so much. You don't just go to church on Sunday. You have a real relationship with Jesus where he talks and walks with you. I reached over and hugged her because that was the sweetest thing anyone had ever said about me. I laughed as she went back to planting and asked, so you don't think I am a miss goody two shoes? She said well if you are just be proud of it. Alice was so inspired with the different translations of the Bible and so eager to learn that she asked many questions. Our two hour real estate training turned into an hour of Bible and an hour of study on Thursdays. She was amazed and inspired with my dreams and visions that we used them many times as our lesson to find the Bible verses for them. When we worked in her flowers sometimes I would share the Bible lessons my Aunt Ellen had taught me when we worked with flowers together and later looked the verses up.

The last time I saw Alice she was shopping for clothes to give to some needy children she was helping. Something she and Julian did together at least once a week. They would go to Richmond or Lynchburg looking for sales and eat lunch out. That day she was shopping here in town. She told me she would be leaving for Italy the next morning to visit her family. Also something she did every year. When she returned from Italy she got off the plane sick and Julian took her to Duke. She never came home. Julian missed her everyday. He was lost without her and depended on me more. He would go by the shop and visit with Sam and tell him to stop work and go eat lunch with him. If Sam refused he would tell him he was calling his wife and inviting her to lunch. We met at Golden Coral many times for lunch and talked about Alice. One day he paid Sam a visit to tell him he had some good news but didn't have the heart to tell me. He asked Sam to tell me he had a fast acting cancer and had about two months to live. Sam came home and told me right away. I couldn't get over to his house fast enough. But our visit went as all the others had except he was excited that he was going to Alice. I laughed and asked him what was I gonna do? All my rich friends were dying and leaving me behind. He laughed and said you have to make new rich friends.

Just two short months later he went to Alice. I had visited him every day but that day I felt led to stay at home and pray. His son-in-law Dick called me and told me.

I still to this day drive by their house at least once a week and look to see if I can see Alice working in her flowers and Julian in the field on his tractor. Alice had told me after my first child was born that I was called to be a mama because I did it with such ease. She said not many women see every child as a gift from God. She had witnessed so much abuse and it just broke her heart to know little children were abused. She said we that lived in America were so blessed and yet so few appreciated it. It was like they had forgotten the great price our men paid in World War II so we could live, work and enjoy life in such a beautiful country. The name *Little Mama* meant more to me after knowing what it meant and knowing the two people that had gave it as friends. I remember one day I was sharing with Julian a problem I had with one of my children and his answer stuck in my heart. He said some children need more love than others. Just keep loving them.

I guess in so many ways I was Shirley and Tommy's mama since I helped them dress and did most of the work around the house. Daddy depended on me to watch out for them everywhere we went. He always said he had to be able to trust me when he wasn't there to care for them. A trust that only grew stronger with each year.

Over my lifetime to present I had three children of my own. I helped raise six other children plus my first two grandchildren for their mama to finish college. Then mothered twelve little toy Chihuahuas. So yes I would say that Alice was correct. My calling must have been to be a Little Mama.

During the time Daddy had been away I had learned how to put God, church and God's word first in my life by Aunt Ellen. I had learned to enjoy life and whatever task was set before me just to be content. I had asked Jesus and the Holy Spirit to come inside of me and make me a new person. I had been baptized in the muddy creek to wash my sins away so they said and participated in church activities. I had come to depend on Jesus and his word for almost everything I wanted since Mama and Daddy had left us those two years. Sometimes I had to try it my way then later crawl to God to fix my mess and guide me in the right path again but at least I had learned where to go. We all had learned how to make the best out of every situation and do it with a good attitude. We use to make jokes and say the only one allowed to throw fits was Uncle Press. We had learned many of our lessons the hard way, like complaining. When we first went to live with Aunt Ellen and Uncle Press we were spoiled little kids. But it didn't take us long to learn to get tough. Crying, complaining, and pouting didn't work for them. It was a sure ticket to a behind whipping. When we didn't like a certain food it only meant you had to eat a double portion if you complained. It didn't take us but once to learn to ask for what we wanted and not to ask for deserts until we had eaten all we had taken upon our plate and not to complain at the table. Aunt Ellen taught us that and many other secrets on how to get around Uncle Press and not set him off. He wasn't a mean man but a huge man and spoke very sternly so most little children were afraid of him until they got to know him. When he spoke he meant what he said and backed his words up with the belt or whatever was handy at the time. Aunt Ellen loved him with a passion so he couldn't have been as mean as us kids thought. Besides that was the way it was in the 50's.

Life long lessons I have lived by all of my life. I realized how easy it was to teach children good daily habits while small. Living them daily and applying daily made being a mother such a joy. I've watched people spoil their children rotten, giving in to every tear and scream only to hear those same parents later say they hate their own children or abuse them. It wasn't that they hated them but the way they acted not realizing they had trained them that way. Like the Bible says, *train up a child in the way he should go and he will return to it.*

Emotional and spiritual issues go hand in hand. By the time Daddy had come home from Canada I had my anger issues under control. I had learned how to forgive and how hard it was to have a good attitude with an unforgivable heart. Once I had forgiven Mama and Daddy the good attitude just showed up. I had learned where I could go to find my peace within. I had learned in the Smith family that responsibility came with many rewards and much praise. I learned to enjoy the responsibility and the more I enjoyed it, the easier it became. I learned people liked being around people who were happy and enjoyed being around a little kid like me when happy. I learned not to take the teasing personal but go with the flow. When Aunt Ellen said to write down your blessings for the day and thank God in Jesus Name Yeshua for each one before bedtime I didn't realize for years how important that lesson and all the others were. They were life living Bible lessons. When I had a complaint about someone she would give me a piece of paper and a pencil. She told me to write down everything I hated about that person. Then write down everything I liked or loved about that person. Once I was finished I had to count each row. Which one is greater she would ask. If it was blessings she would say well forgive and move on. No one is perfect. If it was more hate she would say, well, we really need to pray for Cowtail. I would ask every time, what about the person who hurt me. Pray for them as well but first clean up your own house before snooping around in someone else's home. Daddy would say clean up your own closet before you snoop in someone else's. Their heart belongs to God it is his responsibility to work in that heart not you.

Now I find myself thanking God for all of my family and the lessons each one taught me. I can see how people thought I was conceited now. In a way I guess I was because I had been taught so well that the lessons were rooted and grounded in me which made me bold and confident. I wondered many times if any of these lessons were the reason I had heavenly visitors, angels, dreams and visions. We were not supposed to wonder but just ask God but I would do it anyway. Stubborn, Uncle Press would say, stubborn as a goat. Could it be the lessons planted within me, rooted and grounded and growing with me each day along with my physical growth be the reason? The Smith's believed in a balanced life as well as a balanced meal. Could that be the reason?

It wasn't long before almost everyone teased Daddy about me being the boss in the house and that was why he didn't need another wife. I was his 'Lil Bossy Mama' around there people would say. They would say when they saw me walk in the store, "Henry, here comes your boss." They all had plenty of belly laughs over that. Daddy played along. If it ever bothered him then he kept it to himself. Years later Shirley would get so mad when she asked Daddy something and he would reply, "Let's see what Cowtail has to say about that first." She always told him he couldn't do anything without asking Carolyn first. Daddy never argued with her either just went along but didn't make a final decision on anything unless we all had discussed it and agreed first. Daddy always said, "Family business requires every family vote." That meant four out of four or we waited and gathered more information or Daddy decided with himself.

I have often wondered if my childhood had anything to do with me receiving the gift of discernment as most preachers called it. Most preachers said insight was just discerning emotions or paying close attention or some other off the wall answer. Some didn't even believe in the Holy Spirit or His gifts. I got my biggest laughs from so called know it all preachers and teachers. They wanted knowledge. Aunt Ellen said I didn't have anything but a big dose of the Holy Spirit and it was the Holy Spirit that showed me the future and everything else. Of course I agreed with her and Daddy over everyone else. They told me to laugh with them or just walk away and pray for God to open their eyes that they may see. I got called hard-headed and stubborn a lot because at first I would argue with a fence post just to prove I was right. Another lesson I learned the hard way, keeping my mouth shut. Sit in silence and allow them to be ignorant. My job was to only teach the ones God sent to me. Stop trying to save the world they would say. But unless you could prove it to me from the Bible I wouldn't listen.

I remember this one Baptist preacher who hated the Church of God teaching. He would throw in a judgment every Sunday about the little Church of God knowing it would go out over the radio. Well I had Church of God family and it made me mad every time. I remember telling Aunt Ellen one Sunday I was walking right up to that preacher and give him a piece of my mind. She would laugh and say another lesson coming Cowtail's way, Henry. But we had family in just about every religion and we weren't allowed to speak evil of any religion. Why could this preacher do it on the radio and get away with it? Besides when our family that went to the Church of God had special Sunday all of the family would attend out of respect for them was what I was told. I had been slapped in the mouth for saying some of those things. Therefore, I didn't like hearing it from a grown man supposing to be smarter than me preaching from the pulpit. After Aunt Ellen had laughed so hard she was crying we prayed and asked God to tell me or show me who was right. Before that preacher finished his sermon one Sunday I heard the inner voice within me speak very loud, *"I am the same, yesterday, today, and, forever. I change not."* When that sermon was over I got up and went straight to that preacher and told him what The Holy Spirit had said. He didn't change so I changed churches. Maybe that's why some people called me conceited, hardheaded, stubborn and bossy. What do you think? Do you think its ok for an adult to tell an elder to shut up or speak bad about people especially preachers? If adults want respect they should give it back right?

Sometimes in a dream when I saw bad things like someone fixing to die or wreck or what appeared to me from my viewpoint as bad I felt the spiritual gift that had been developed within me was a curse instead of a blessing. It would tear my nerves up for days and cause me to have nightmares if I slept. Most of the time I would stay awake, read my Bible and pray for God to change his mind for days without sleep and when I did go to sleep I dreamed about it. Sometimes God did change his mind or I should say God would get through to that person's heart and it didn't happen or got delayed. It wasn't God causing the accident or whatever but choices made by that person and it was the consequence Aunt Ellen would say.

Sometimes when I walked into a house and felt the spirits in that house, for example, an angry spirit, and the people were smiling and acting like all was well I would get upset. Upset because I hadn't learned the lesson to be silent. Sometimes in my own arrogance I would tell them they were lying. Their actions weren't lining up with their energy. Sometimes I kept silent and repeated peace under my breathe trying to leave peace like Jesus told us to do. If that didn't work I would just leave. Sometimes I tried to explain what I was picking up in the spirit realm but most of the time I got called a know-it-all, or none of my business or I was a liar. Sometimes I could feel the gossip energy and knew what they had said about me before I got there. I wanted to slap them. But I would wait for an opening to fuss or let them know I knew what they said. Sometimes I just smiled at myself knowing and watched them. That became my favorite game, smiling and watching. And sometimes I would be nice and get out of there as quickly as I could. Then there were the places where they suggested I stay and eat but if I had heard ugly things in the spirit before I got there I wouldn't eat. God said it was better to eat alone than eat from a selfish and begrudging table. I have actually left and be getting in my car and hear one of them say I am glad they didn't stay. More for us and I can take the leftovers to work tomorrow. I would smile and thank God for protecting me. Daddy had taught us not to eat at the table of a greedy person also. He said they would come later expecting more from you and think you owe them. Just to name a few experiences in hopes you could get a mental picture of what a child was going through with the gift of discernment. At first it wasn't enjoyable at all but mostly scary. It always made me feel like I was different after I learned most people didn't want the gift.

When I was a child and went somewhere with Aunt Ellen or anyone and felt bad energy I would ask if I could go outside. Sometimes if I stayed in their presence very long I got physically sick. Sometimes I would shake all over like I was having a seizure or muscle spasms. Embarrassing is what it was. Daddy and Aunt Ellen were the only ones that knew that about me and would allow me to go. When someone else said I couldn't go outside I would sit there and think in my mind, *Jesus loves me this I know for the Bible tells me so. It worked too.*

From "Cry Baby", to Little Johnny, to Lil Mama, to Cowtail, to all the other nicknames given me over the years, Cowtail stuck longer than all the others put together. Why I don't really know. Some said it was because I liked being late and giving myself that grand entrance. Some said it was because I never got in a hurry. Others said they couldn't forget the day the cow slapped me in the face with her tail. While others said it was because I wouldn't milk the cows until Uncle Press went out there and tied up the cows' tail. Daddy and Aunt Ellen said it was because I was the only child in the family that had Press wrapped around their finger and that was a great job in itself. When Uncle Press was in the Veterans hospital one year I learned he had listed me under daughter and that was why I never had any trouble getting information from the doctors. Aunt Ellen said that was a great honor for Press to consider me his daughter. She never told them any different.

I learned as a child that the more responsibility I had meant also more trust. More trust meant more freedom and control. I liked that feeling of freedom and being in control. It got me my way many times and I liked that too.

I loved Aunt Ellen's gentle spirit. Sometimes I would get upset with her because I felt she just let people run all over her. She would laugh at me and put me in my place. When she did that I would ask her why she didn't stand up to that mean person like she did me. She laughed and said, "Cowtail, you can catch more flies with honey than vinegar." But I would come back with my smart mouth, "we're not catching flies. She would laugh louder and say "you catch a mean-spirited person the same way you catch flies with kindness and love." Another thing I appreciated about her was her patience. I would ask so many questions and she would answer them all. She was forever teaching me and never seem to get irritated. Sometimes she would have to look up the answer or ask someone else but she always tried to give me the right answer. She remained our second Mom even after Daddy came home and we moved into our own house. As long as she lived we were there with her on Mother's day and every other holiday. We made her number one in everything we did. It was appreciation for all the years she was loyal and faithful to us. She was the greatest wealth in the Smith family in our eyes. She certainly was my hero.

She taught me a lesson in everything we did. I don't say that in bragging but just as a fact. She was always saying she wished all her other children were as eager to learn as I was. She had one child of her own, John whom we called Johnny. Yet she helped raise nineteen children I believe was the last count. She cared for foster children until they could find a home for them so there may have been more. She kept, Clarence, Wayne, Roger, Larry, and the three of us. Wayne, Roger and Larry were brothers. She wanted a home found for all three of them so they could stay together. She didn't want them separated. They never found such a home. She gave them all a piece of land to build a house. Some took it and some didn't. But she wanted to make sure they all had a home all of their life. So you can see where I got Little Mama from and why I cared for all children and their welfare as if they were my own. She taught me that it was easy to love your own flesh and blood but could we love a child like God did. All children were gifts from God and all were precious. She believed God had a special place where he punished people who were cruel to children. She believed only Satan's children could and would abuse a child. She also believed that no children were born evil but taught by adults how to be evil. She believed those adults would be held accountable by God Himself. Children were to be loved, honored and respected from moment of conception and forever.

So who really should have had the nick name Little Mama? Little because of her humble spirit, Aunt Ellen had twelve of the most important spirits any human being could have. Her surrender to God's will and her willingness to be God's servant, her obedience to walk away from all of her own family wealth to follow the voice of God and teach the Smith family, Her sincere heart towards God and humans, and her truthfulness that was as pure as any heart. Her straightforwardness and honesty amazed me but her unselfishness of her time and self put her far above any other human being in my eyes. Her faithfulness to God's word, church, and people in general gave her such a strength and confidence that you couldn't help but be affected by her. The way she saw people in general, as an impersonal person, such as treating a stranger well because he may be an angel or treat a child well for he may be the next Prophet Elijah. She looked for the good, and would say, it's in there somewhere, as she smiled to seek deeper into a person's soul. She so wanted to believe that all in all were good. So you ask me why she is my hero that's why. In all of my years I have met many that had some of those qualities but not all. I bet if a survey was taken there would be only a few in this world. It made her far richer than any wealthier person with only material wealth. That's why I believe she had friends like Governor Bill Tuck of Virginia and Senator Howard P. Anderson. And they cherished her friendship as well. She called them Cousin Bill and Cousin Howard.

You would be ever so wise to learn and teach by example a few of her golden nuggets. She and Daddy received the attention and respect of senators, governors, attorneys, judges and many others. It didn't matter if we were talking about past family members or present ones she would give me a golden nugget. She believed we were a whole person and needed to feed the whole person. From our minds to our spirits, a well-balanced meal in each area of our true self. When the eyes are full of Christ then the whole body was full of Christ, she would say. When you have been blessed with ears by God then you should appreciate God enough to listen to His Son's words and the inner voice. Control the mouth and you can control your whole lustful self. A mind full of God's word cannot sin and when your consciousness is pure before God it is pure before all men. How can we have forgiveness from God when we cannot forgive our neighbors or our brother and sisters she would say?

We became best friends over the years. I became the daughter she never had she said. She was the one who taught me never to show fear. She said if I showed fear whether I was riding with Johnny driving fast or him making me touch a live electric wire, in which we had many on that farm, he would continue to do it, if I showed fear. She said fear was the only enemy God had and the only spirit that Satan could use for his evils. If I was afraid to never admit it to another human being. Admit it to God and pray under my breath the 23rd Psalms or the Lord's Prayer. She said God would make them stop. Between her and Daddy they were right most of the time and most of the time I listened. A few times I just had to test the waters and see what happened. She always said nothing wrong with that as long as you were willing to accept the consequences without complaining or blaming. She was my first spiritual mother. A spiritual mother is someone who teaches you Bible truths and doesn't form opinions but gives it to you raw and allows God to give the understanding. Who is yours? Everyone needs a spiritual father and mother.

They said God had his hands upon me before I was ever conceived in my Mama's belly. I just agreed with them. It just wasn't normal Aunt Ellen said to be so hungry for God's words at such a young age. Maybe the two parents that were supposed to protect me caused insecurity so I turned to God for that security. There are many ifs but I know my life could have just as easily turned to do evil and harm. I see it every day children and teens blaming parents or something in their past to abuse themselves and others.

Then there was the dream about the ladder I had. I felt every experience in life was like a ladder and each experience was leading me to higher ground in God. In my understanding I believed the ladder was a symbol like the step ladder Jacob saw in the Bible. Every step on that ladder is for each individual's walk in life whether they believe it or not. I have a painting hanging in my living room now of the vision of the step ladder I saw. I was walking up higher and higher and with each step there was another lesson that had to be experienced and learned before I could climb to that next step. The higher I stepped the brighter the lesson. I just blended in the atmosphere until I couldn't be seen any longer on earth. With each step I blended into the light until I was one with the light. I just walked up into heaven until I was no more on earth. God received me into heaven by drawing me upward and upward, like he did Enoch. Enoch in the Bible walked with God until he was no more. That's what the dream meant to be.

Every word, every promise in that Bible is for every individual to receive. Like having a bank account and never withdrawing any funds. She said the bank account would get fatter and fatter but the human doing without was getting weaker and weaker. Then one day that human would starve to death and leave the fat bank account on earth for an heir. What that heir did with it was up to that heir not God. What sense did that make she asked? Don't store your treasures on earth for someone else. They may waste it. Store your treasures in God's storehouse. Those are eternal. She said we would be amazed at the preachers and people who give all they have to churches or preachers thinking they will receive that money or riches in heaven. "What does heaven need money for she asked? Earth is where we need the money. Invest it here. She didn't like the way churches preached the tithe. She said if they invested a portion of that money they received, the church could run and support itself. Also if the people pooled their money together and bought stocks and bonds they all would have a nice nest egg for retirement. That God's business was a business and should be treated as such not supporting preachers and buildings. Investing a portion of the money for missions and church activities but there would be money in the treasury for every project without having to beg all the time. She believed the churches that turned God into a beggar. Giving money to a church was like a bottomless pit. It never got enough. Always one more building to build or one more mission to support she would laugh and say. When I asked her why she didn't address the church with her ideals her answer was it wouldn't do any good. They believed the old fashion way.

That's why I felt to share a little of my childhood and those who helped to mold and shape me. What about you? Are you hungry for common sense truth as Daddy called it? Where did common sense go? No where. It's exactly where you left it when you laid it down and decided to pick up old ego man or college to experience awhile? When you get tired of being confused then turn around and head back to that step on your ladder where you laid down your common sense or sixth sense some called it. When you get there, bend over and pick it up. Ask God to forgive you for abandoning your common sense and your imagination. Then thank him for keeping it safe while you ran the ego fields awhile. You see lust, sex, adultery, drug use, alcohol all and every flesh habit is the fruit of your own ego. You had to choose to be there and usually that means you needed to experience something in order to learn a lesson in life. Otherwise you wouldn't be there. So look around, do you see who you are supposed to help? If you see no one, then look for your teacher, for you are the one that needs help. Life truly is one choice after another and we are always learning even when we teach. Now smile and say, Thank you Lord.

Sometimes the Holy Spirit would just shut my mouth so I couldn't speak at all for awhile. Like the time my brother Tommy was stabbed. After I prayed for him and God showed me in a vision his outcome, the Holy Spirit shut my mouth and wouldn't allow me to speak for six hours. Shirley, her husband Dennis, my husband Bernard and Aunt Ellen were on our way to Charleston S.C. Navy hospital. They all thought I was in shock and asked the nurse to allow me to see him first. As soon I walked in ICU and stood over him, the Holy Spirit spoke through me, *"you will be alright. You hear me Tommy. You will live and be all right. The Lord says so."*

He was stabbed in five major organs I believe is what they told us. I know the doctors had no hope of him surviving. The news from his commanding officer sent Daddy to the hospital with a heart attack. John and Clarence went with Daddy to the hospital while Aunt Ellen went with us. I know Tommy saw two angels and testified to me in front of two nurses. *He said he saw them while in the rescue squad, two angels. One angel was dressed in black and surrounded in fire. She said as she led the way, 'come.' The other angel was dressed in all white with gold sparkles surrounded in rainbow clouds and she also said, 'come."* He said he begged God to forgive him and called on Jesus to save his soul right there. When he did the black angel in the fire left him. So when the Holy Spirit spoke through me, *he said, I know. How I don't know. I told them to call you Carolyn. I would be alright when you got here. I know I will live and not die. But how I know I don't know.*

So you see God was working on both ends and needed me to keep my ego filled self shut so he could bring forth a miracle. That was the first time the Holy Spirit shut my mouth but it wasn't the last. Many times over the years God has closed my mouth. You see, sometimes we can speak forth something out of our ignorance that will stop a blessing or miracle. Ignorance just means we don't have understanding or enlightenment about something yet. For an example I am ignorant when it comes to medical stuff. Why because I haven't learned or been to school for medical. I am smart in many other areas but not medical. We learn just a little sometimes and that's dangerous.

I had a special gift from God they called it and I had to keep it a secret until God said it was time to reveal it. Everyone had special gifts. Some just hadn't been awakened to theirs yet. Aunt Ellen said there was no way to share it without ego getting in the middle of it. Once ego got involved it meant pain and heartache from heartless and ignorant people including our own selves. She said most preachers stood in the pulpit with the learned word and little faith and had no idea what the spoken word meant. That religious people were my enemies by their own choice but they couldn't help themselves. It was out of their own ignorant spirit they made the decision to not accept certain treasures. We all do she said, and that was a lifetime work and then you hoped you overcame. She and Daddy both said bragging and competition showed weakness and that's all egos were good for. That God wanted to use us for His purpose and that meant we had to be willing. She said we needed to be sensitive to the Holy Spirit within surrendered to Jesus' heavenly Father at all times. They said God loved obedience and a sincere heart and could work through such a person. She said truthfulness would get me a long way in life but also cause me much pain. She said I would need courage and humility to stay in a good attitude and not allow people to steal my joy. That being impersonal meant to love the person and hate their evil deeds or learn not to acknowledge the evil deeds. When it came to family it was hard to do sometimes. It required a pure heart, a pure conscious and unselfishness every day on our part. It was all about daily habits and what we decided to do with each moment of the day. She said weak people blame God but a pure heart could see and hear Jesus. The Bible was full of examples. Whatever God did for one in the Bible he will do for all. That he had to, to remain impersonal himself. She placed high marks on honesty and eye to eye straight forwardness. Staying faithful to the words of Jesus Christ was a daily task and required study of the meanings of every word. She gave me this example: She took a little flower seed and planted it in some dirt in a jar and then sat it in the window for sunlight. When she saw it had sprouted she asked me how much water did it need. Then she asked where should we plant it outside in the shade or in the full sunlight? When I didn't know the answers she gave me a flower book and ask me to look up the flower. When I ask her what the name was, she replied, you must find a picture of the same plant and see what the name was. Then look that name up in the index. Once she walked me through that process from start to finish even planting the sprout. She added that is the way we study God's holy words. She said she liked to take one word that might be burning in her heart and she would set as her homework to look up and find the meanings in the dictionary. Then she would find every verse in the Bible and write down every verse that had that one word in it. Check in the Bible everything people tell you see if it was in the Bible.

That's just one of many lessons they taught me daily. There's no way I could write them all in one book but I feel you get the idea as to how I grew up with the insight to see into the spirit world. I feel that Aunt Ellen and Daddy were the only two in my family that believed it was their responsibility to teach me daily. Almost like they were driven for me to learn everything they could cram into my heart and mind. The amazing part is that I didn't like games, sports, dating or anything in the hobby department like most kids did. My hobby was hanging out with adults who would teach me. It didn't have to be the Bible it could be anything from building a house to fixing the plumbing. As long as my mind wasn't idle.

Aunt Ellen said unity and concentrating on what the Bible said by feeling what the person in the Bible was feeling meant I had entered into their space. She said we judge by analyzing ourselves and we wouldn't have time to judge another nor make fun of another if we analyzed our self first. That every person was from God but not everyone knew that. She believed the breath of God was in every individual. It was our job to awaken them out of their sleep so they could obey God and do good deeds. Sleeping people don't work. God didn't like us mocking him and when we disobeyed him we were mocking him and acting like people still asleep. When we mocked and made fun of his other children we were only mocking God.

She said we could keep the stars in our eyes by keeping our mind clean and our hearts pure. Then we would own something worth blessing others with. That it wasn't about all this stuff you leave behind on earth when you die but the real stuff was what you could take with you. That you had to give of yourself to give a real gift because you are the real gift, all other gifts were worthless. By blessing others with eternal gifts which were ourselves that God would bless us. She said when we have a problem we are to take it to Jesus' cross and leave it there. That meant pray and ask God to work it to good. Then once we had surrendered it to our Heavenly Father we were to get busy working doing our own chores or helping someone else with a problem and give God time to work it to good. God always works it to good for those that love him because he couldn't do any different than what he is.

Some of the other lessons Aunt Ellen and Daddy taught me were not to listen to flattery. They said it was only the devil tricking me. Flattery was just building up and increasing the ego and ego wasn't very pretty. That beauty is as beauty does. That inner beauty was the greatest beauty of all. We couldn't be beautiful unless we walked with God daily. And last but not least both of them said our sex organs were sacred and holy and were to stay that way until after marriage. For me to not sell myself short or exchange my eternal home for a little temporary pleasure.

A few years passed before I learned Aunt Ellen had a college degree and came from a very wealthy family. She had chosen the way she lived her life and added that each individual has to choose or Satan would choose for us. She didn't believe wealth was a sin or anything like that. She just believed that what she was teaching and lived herself had more eternal value than money. She said money couldn't touch eternal wealth. For me not to spend my energy chasing after money, if I did, I would reap a whirlwind.

All through this book you will discover golden nuggets that were taught to me by those two people and others. There's not a day that passes that I don't think about them and feel the warmth of their love. In every daily task they are there, sometimes stronger than others. In every sickness and heartache they have been there with me. I hope you will believe that we are never alone. We are always surrounded with whoever we want to be there. I hope you start your little book of blessings and write each person's name you saw that day at the top. Then list every good deed they did for you or spoke over you for that day. If you can't find one then I pray you will pray for yourself because you are so pitiful not to be able to see one little blessing in each individual. Their nose may be clean or their mouth full of chocolate and it reminded you of a delicious cake or pie your grandmother made you in days gone by. There's your blessing-he reminded you that you are loved, for love is one eternal gift, we take with us. Receive your blessing today. Be blessed today to be a blessing.

Chapter 3:

I Dreamed My Own Death

B y the age of eight Uncle Press was in and out of the Veterans hospital in Richmond Virginia a lot. With each stay Aunt Ellen became more worried about him and his soul and would ask me to pray for him. At first when I prayed nothing happened. At least I didn't think it did because I didn't receive anything or feel anything or see or hear anything. She told me to ask God to forgive me for my sins. That I must have sin in me unconfessed if I wasn't receiving. A blockage she called it. I became upset but obeyed. She said we had to repent daily sometimes a thousand times a day because we had hidden sins in us that would block our communication with Christ. I didn't understand but trusted her. So off to the chapel in the hospital I went to pray. Sometimes she went with me and prayed also. But as time went on and his trips to Richmond became shorter in between Aunt Ellen became even more worried and that kept me upset. Seeing her cry made me cry. One night after being so sensitive to her feelings and picking up on her fear I really became afraid. I wanted to help her feel better so that night I asked Jesus if Uncle Press was going to die. I ask Jesus to please show me so I could tell Aunt Ellen because I didn't like it when she was afraid. I told the Lord that Aunt Ellen said I was a show me person so I asked Him to show me.

In a dream that night God did show me. He showed me Uncle Press was coming home in Johnny's 1955 Chev. The next morning at breakfast I told Daddy what I saw and asked him to tell Johnny when he came up to the store before he left for Richmond. That Uncle Press would live and come home in a few days.

After that with every hospital visit Uncle Press had, I was asked to pray for God to show me if he would live or die because every hospital stay seem to put him a little closer to death. After awhile Daddy and Aunt Ellen both began to see a pattern of answered prayers through my dreams. Only if they came to pass were they of God she said. One day they decided it was time to set me down and tell me about my Aunt Ruby. They said my Aunt Ruby was Daddy's baby sister. She had been placed in Lynchburg Training Center in Lynchburg Virginia for saying she could see and hear God. That scared me. I asked if they were going to make me go there. They said no but I needed to keep the gift a secret. They made me promise not to tell anyone but them about anything God had showed me or told me. For three years the only dreams I had were about Uncle Press. If he would live or die with each visit to the hospital and told no one but them. That's because I didn't pray for anything else at the time. I didn't know I could ask for myself. What do kids know unless someone teaches them?

At twelve years old I had the first dream about me. I saw myself lying in a beautiful lavender and white casket trimmed out in gold on the outside. I looked to be around thirty years old and so beautiful with long blonde hair. I could see my long eye lashes and soft hands. The inside lining of the casket was the purist baby pink you had ever seen. It looked so soft and warm you just wanted to wrap your precious baby in it. I was dressed in a flowing ice blue gown. As I continued to examine I didn't see any jewelry, flowers and no pictures in the casket with me. Just one beautiful bouquet of baby dark pink and blue roses in my hand, one for each one of my children and grandchildren I heard someone say. The pink were for the girls and the blue were for the boys. I thought how odd? I didn't literally count them so I have no idea how many there were but it looked like twelve. They were wrapped in pure white lace with a white pearl pen to hold them together.

I could see we were in a beautiful room surrounded by beautiful flowers of every color and size. It must have been late summer or fall by the color of the flowers. Beautiful rose bushes with roots that made the whole room smell like a rose garden, with just a touch of spices and other sweet smelling aromas that you would have thought you were in a perfume factory.

I saw the lights were dimmed and even some candles sitting on tables with flowers burning as I looked around the room. There was also a candle opera at my head and feet all lite up, like a wedding chapel. They made the whole chapel look and feel very warm and romantic. The front looked like a wedding was about to take place.

As I continued to look around I saw my family walking pass my opened casket. Some I knew and some I didn't know but all were crying. Some blew their noses like Daddy and Uncle Press while others talked to the people behind them or in front of them. I saw a few reach down and kiss my forehead as they walked by.

I heard comments like she was so young and beautiful. She was such a good mother and mothered children all her life. She was born to be a mama because she loved all children with such deep compassion. Some said I was a good worker and loved to work. Some said I was a good worker but so bossy. That comment made a few of them bust out in laughter. Then another would say, "If you knew what was good for you, you knew better than to cross her. She could out-smart you every time and be way ahead of the game. Like she was born with eyes in the back of her head I heard one person say. I heard them laughing again as they continued walking down memory lane.

Then I heard Johnny say, one thing I know for sure Cowtail had Daddy (Press), Uncle Henry and my Mama tied around her little finger. They jumped when she spoke, so that's what made her so bossy, they all spoiled her rotten. And it wasn't just them it was the whole Smith family. She must have had some dirt on them and threatened to tell all if she didn't get her way." Everyone laughed at that but Aunt Ellen and Daddy. They kept silent and just let them talk.

Then Jesse said, "Hell, she had me wrapped around her little finger. That I know for sure. If you really knew her, you just couldn't say no to her. There's not one in this bunch that could say no to her. It didn't matter what she asks us to do we all jumped to please her. That's why she was so spoiled, just plain rotten to the core." Then I saw the tears begin again and heard the silence as it filled the room as they walked by.

There I stood in the spirit in a flowing white ice blue robe among my family and friends and they didn't know it. It was my own family night memorial and not one in the room could see me or hear me. How sad was that? I felt the sadness rise up within me. That made me sad. Only the ones that were already in the spiritual realm that had stepped out of their own physical bodies could see and hear me. Why Lord? Why can't they see me? Didn't they learn anything from me? Don't they have just a little faith? Did they believe anything they read out of the Bible?

I also noticed when I began to cry those in their physical bodies that couldn't see or hear me cried also. Why Lord? Can they feel me crying?

Then a tall black headed man slim in built said, "but they can feel you. Look when you cry they all cried. When you stopped they stopped."

I said, "I see that. Why is that?"

He said, "Feelings are vibrational energy and energy can be seen, heard and felt. That's what we are energy or vibrations and they feel your vibration. Just like you could feel the spirits in a room while in your physical body, they can feel them also. They just don't know it yet or afraid of what people might think. They think they are causing the tears and some of them are caused by them."

I asked, "You mean all humans can feel spirits."

"Not only can they feel us, but see and hear us, if they really wanted to," he said.

I started moving among the crowd and it was as if some could feel me as I brushed by. Some thought they had a tickle in their ear when I whispered 'I love you'. Some burst out in laughter when I tickled them on their side. Some thought a bug or flea was flying around their head when I blew in their hair. But none knew I was there even when I did all that to get their attention. How sad I thought?

I stood back and watched the crowd after that. Some inspected my body and straighten the wrinkles out of my gown. Some checked out my make up while another fixed my hair and made the comment, "you know how funny Mama was about the way she looked when she was in public." But I couldn't see them clear enough to make out what they looked like.

I could feel every heart that was full of love and grief at the same time. I could feel appreciation as they made their nice comments. I thought how nice it would have been to have heard those nice comments while still in my physical body. The ones that acted like my children or called me Mama I didn't even know. They were strangers to me. I recognized Daddy, Johnny, James and other family members but the very ones that called me mama I didn't know. I could even hear the tears behind their words, even the jealousy behind some of them. That also made me sad. These people that talked and acted like my children had spent a lot of money to put my body away like a queen yet they themselves were strangers to me. How sad? Why would they spend so much money on a body that was going back to dust I wondered?

Then Christ put his arm around me and led me to another place of the memorial as he said, "It's not your fault. Don't be sad. They choose not to know you and that's why they feel like strangers to you now. Come follow me."

Christ led me in the chapel where gospel music was playing and the room was full of love energy. The Lord danced me around the room like we were at the opera. Swinging me and laughing as we whirled around and around. I could see my ice blue gown blowing in the wind as he whirled and whirled me. Laughter and joy filled the whole space and the Lord asked with a huge smile, "Do you like your going home party?

Its home coming for you my child for I am well pleased with the work we accomplished while on earth among these people." I was so full of love I couldn't even response.

It felt so romantic dancing with my Lord. I could see it was dark outside and asked what time it was. The answer came before I got the question out. Seven o'clock. The sky was full of stars. The air was clear and brisk like a fall evening. It felt almost like Thanksgiving. Later I noticed there wasn't a family night. All of it was done in the same night with the casket left opened while the people walked and talked.

At eight p.m., everyone sat down and a preacher stood over the opened casket and said a few words. There was crying and some laughter as he talked about me like I wasn't even there. I shouted at the speaker, "Tell them about my Lord. He is the hero. It is He, who did all that good, not me. Tell them about the good news, the new beginning, the awakened, and the abundance of life. Tell them there's no such thing as death. We live on somewhere." My own yelling drowned the crying but none heard me.

Around 9 p.m., I saw the people getting up and leaving as they put on their jackets. They were chatting about going over to the church for food and fellowship. I thought that's a good idea.

At the church it looked like a nightclub, the band was setting up and soon the music began to play. People were walking around filling their plates and faces. The leader of the band announced, that we would worship the Lord and if anyone felt like dancing or shouting then do so. I thought ok, finally a party full of life. While everyone was having fun eating and singing I flew back to my body at the funeral home. They were preparing it for cremation. I said my goodbyes and blessed the body that had carried me on earth all those years. Then I flew with my Lord back to the party at the church. It was clear my Lord was my husband as he stayed with me and led me from place to place with such compassion. No tears but full satisfaction that it was finished. It had been announced that there would be a private graveside service at a later date for me. I liked that.

It had been a glorious day and evening of family and friends celebration. The Lord called it my graduation day. All the praise, all the good deeds, appreciation, loyalty, respect, love, kindness, laughter and joy had been poured out one by one. They were the golden nuggets I would be taking with me to my eternal home I heard someone say. I gathered each one into a beautiful white basket trimmed out in gold lace. It looked like a basket a flower girl would carry full of flowers for her bride. With each nugget as I carefully placed them in the laced basket I noticed the basket was full and some had began falling out. I reached down to pick them up but my Lord said, *"Leave them for the gleaning."* So I continued to walk like a bride would walk up the aisle for her groom as the golden nuggets fell out on the royal purple carpet. I gathered every pure word, praise and every good deed, like small flakes of paper to place in my basket. I pressed them down as far in the basket as I could but many still fell out and were left behind to be collected by those that remembered my good deeds and shared them with others.

Later I learned my cup was full and running over with good deeds to offer to my Lord. The overflow remained behind for those who would carry out the good deeds on earth that I had sown in them. They would remain behind to grow and multiply and give God glory on another day.

I also saw the comments of hurt, jealousy, greed and ignorance, like dark pieces of dust, as I walked by. But before my foot actually touched them on the ground beneath me they flew away. The Lord said they were the dust particles that attached itself to my physical body but had no place in me. They would remain behind on the earth. I saw them fly away like small flakes of burnt paper as I breezed by with my Lord. My Lord walked by my side as if he was the father giving me away.

We continued to walk up like we were going up a beautiful staircase full of white lights. The steps were shining like gold and the stars danced around us like humming birds. With each step the beauty became clearer and more beautiful than the step before. I heard glorious singing and saw the cloud of witnesses all dressed in white robes. Some were trimmed in gold, some in silver, some in rainbow colors and some were purple and gold. When I looked back the cloud of witnesses looked like a bridal train that followed behind me as well. I was overwhelmed by the homecoming my Lord had prepared for me. The ice blue gown I wore shone with all colors of light dancing in it as it flowed around me. My face glowed like the sun with my eyes as bright as the stars.

Soon we were at a golden archer at the front of the chapel. As we entered hand in hand the heavens were breath taking. I saw multitudes of angels and all my loved ones standing in all smiles. I heard all of heaven singing, "hallelujah, hallelujah is the Lamb of God, for He has taken his bride from the earth. Hallelujah, hallelujah, to the Lamb of God, He has given the Almighty His bride from the earth. Hallelujah, hallelujah, glorious is His name." I saw from above the altar a most glorious bright light and a voice came from the light which said, *I have received your bride as my own. Great and mighty is her name.* Then His light shone so bright it blinded all around for a few seconds. It felt like the light consumed me into itself and I was overwhelmed with joy.

I saw angels dressed in gold, silver, blue, yellow, green, purple, pink and white and each one was just as beautiful and glorious as the other. They bowed as we walked through the long train they had made with themselves like the people would bow to a king and queen. Then I saw the most beautiful black angel being I had ever seen. It shined with a huge star from within its belly that made the angel glow all over. Someone said he represented the humans that hadn't awakened on earth yet. Then I saw standing beside this being other beings that appeared like black pearls full of light. They had a golden glow around them. One of the archangels said they represent the humans on earth full of God and had overcome sin and evil deeds but didn't overcome the physical body. Now they walk in the fullness of God day and night. Their hearts and minds were married to God but not their physical body. They allowed their bodies to do all sorts of deeds that were displeasing to our Lord. Some were called prophets, preachers, pastors, teachers and some were mothers, fathers, brothers, sisters, children, and friend upon the earth. To the humans around them they appeared to be pure but in truth they all committed sin behind closed doors. They battled with their own self while they helped others awaken to salvation. With each battle they stood and prayed for strength but didn't apply what the living word gave them. They gained ground in some areas and lost ground in others.

"Why so many, I asked? Because there are many who haven't manifested God in and through their physical body on earth yet. They fill the pews every Saturday and Sunday but deny the power within them. They play word games and pretend they each have the truth when in truth they deny the power of the resurrection. They sing songs to our Lord. They dress nice and witness the living word to others and even confess they are born again, saved, and love the Lord but they keep some of their physical desires. The earth is full of these people even in your own earth family.

Then we moved past the beautiful black pearls full of light stars to a place of radiance. I felt the question arise within me, who are these? But before I could ask the answer came. These are those that surrendered all of their heart, mind and body to our Lord. They repented daily and developed their soul by good deeds daily. They walked in unity with God's laws daily and even in hardship and pain they confessed Jesus is Lord. King of Kings, Lord of Lords. I will not bow to this pain but to God only was their testimony. They said what they meant and meant what they said. They lived in the living voice of God within them and obeyed. Their good deeds were the praise and worship to their Lord. They sacrificed themselves and their own comfort for the souls of others. They loved the unlovable and blessed the ones that abused and used them. They prayed for those that mocked God and through it all they kept praising God with good deeds.

Oh how stupid and ignorant and naked I felt in their presence. My heart became grieved as I began to cry. But the Lord said, "Follow me." So I walked with him, wiping back my tears of shame, on beyond these beings of radiance. With each step forward I began to feel enlightened and awakened again, more than before and the ignorance and tears left me. It felt like I was being washed inside and filled with joy. The cleansing that took place within was as fresh as a spring rain.

Then I saw what appeared to be the earth of darkness. It was far behind me yet the planet earth felt so close. I felt my feet connected to the planet earth and I saw a silver cord that connected me to both worlds. I felt the people loving me like a loving husband loved his wife. I felt the intimacy as they embraced me. I felt the love vibrate from them to me. I felt myself blend into the light with them. It was like we became one light. Like I was in a huge ocean but had blended with just a few drops of the ocean and became one with them. Each of us was an individual yet we felt like a whole. Then I woke up and realized I had been dreaming.

Once awake in my physical body I realized I must have been sleep-walking. I could see Daddy following behind in his baggy white underwear with a worried look on his face as I walked around in the room. I could hear him call my nick name, "Cow Tail, Cow Tail." It sounded like it was coming from a far away place, barely faint it was. I felt so far away from Daddy yet seemed so close I could touch him. Like slow motion yet I could feel an energy pulling me from this far away place closer and closer to Daddy. I moved around in the room as if I was looking for a place to land as I heard him call me again and again. Then suddenly I was wide awake. I felt my feet touch the floor like I had just landed from the ceiling. I realized instantly I had been away and had just returned. I was back in my room on earth. I could feel my skin as I squeezed my arm and starred at daddy standing there in his white briefs with a look of fear. Boy what a sight to see after seeing heaven. Immediately I asked, what are you doing in here Daddy?

Daddy said, Are you awake now? You have been sleep walking, talking all crazy stuff in your sleep again. What did you eat for supper? Did you watch any scary movies? I told you not to watch that stuff. He sounded almost irritated with me. It's late. Go to bed and try to get some sleep. I have to work in the morning."

"But Daddy," I said. But he came back with, "No buts. Go to sleep. We will go see Ellen in the morning about this. There's got to be something she can give you to stop these crazy dreams of yours." He led me by my right arm to the bed, covered me and walked on out, cutting the light out as he pulled up the door.

"Sleep." I thought as I laid there in the dark. I could hear Shirley snoring in her bed but still felt I was all alone. I pondered over what I could remember and wondered what it all meant. Does he really think I could sleep after that dream? I got up, turned the light on and got my notebook and began writing the dream down. I saw Shirley turn over and thought, *O Lord, if she wakes up, she will tell Daddy I had the light on after bedtime.* I didn't care as I brushed back my long blonde hair and continued crossing my legs in the middle of my bed like an Indian so my lap would be my desk. I was afraid and confused as I wrote the dream on that white piece of paper. Am I going to die I thought? Teach me what the dream means Lord. I saw you with me and the place you prepared for me so why am I so afraid. I began to cry yet after remembering I had children in the dream I realized it had to be years down the road before I actually died. It had to be years before I died because I was going to college to be a lawyer. Daddy and Aunt Ellen both said I was going to be an excellent Philadelphia lawyer because I could ask so many questions. The judge would let me win just to shut me up, they said with lauger.

After awhile I saw the sun coming up through my window but waited until daddy called to get up and fix breakfast before I actually got up. I was hoping he would have mercy on me and cook himself but that didn't happen. He acted like he was still mad with me for keeping him awake. He asked if I got any sleep. When I answered no, he continued in his grumpy self, he didn't either. Wonder why he said as he looked at me from looking up above his coffee cup sipping it.

I starred back like I couldn't help it as I grumbled the same old routine every morning. In the kitchen I turned the stove on while Daddy got the bacon out of the refrigerator. *Daddy do you realize we live like I am your wife and do everything a wife does.* As he put the bacon in the frying pan he said, *yes we do live that way. Maybe you will think twice before you get married and do this for some other man.* I made the biscuits for the oven and replied I am never getting married and never having kids. Then once he finished with the bacon and had that cooking. He sat down in his chair at the end of the table to enjoy his coffee, while

I finished getting the table set and went to call Shirley and Tommy to get up and eat. They came in about the time I was cooking the eggs all dressed for school. I never ate breakfast and would dress while they ate. I really wanted to talk about the dream but he was too grumpy. It was Friday and most Fridays we went to Aunt Ellen's anyway. At least I hoped we would after school this Friday.

After school Daddy did take us down to Aunt Ellen's. We loved going to Aunt Ellen's and I knew she would feed everyone and I wouldn't have to cook supper. As she worked around in the kitchen she asked Daddy if he was staying to eat or going back to the store. When he said he was staying it was like Aunt Ellen knew he had something on his mind. She told us to go outside and play until she called us in to set the table. But I stayed behind with Daddy in hopes we would talk about my dream. Shirley was yelling, "Come on, Carolyn that means you too. You think you are so grown but you aren't. Aunt Ellen said *you kids*. That includes you too so come on. "

Daddy spoke up and told Shirley to go on and play and leave Carolyn Ann alone, that he and El needed to talk to her anyway. Shirley went on out of the back door telling Clarence and Tommy that I was in trouble again. Aunt Ellen got Daddy and herself a cup of coffee, and then she sat down and asked what was going on. Daddy proceeded telling her that I had kept him up most of the night, sleep walking and talking in my sleep, again. Aunt Ellen took a sip of her coffee then asked me if I remembered the dream. After I answered yes I did. She asked for me to share it. When I finished telling her about the dream she looked at Daddy. Silence filled the room a few minutes as they sipped their coffee. Finally she asked me if I knew what it meant. I replied I didn't other than I was gonna die at the age of thirty and have a beautiful casket. Jesus was coming after me and I was going to heaven. Jesus and I both would be at my funeral but no one would see us or hear us.

Aunt Ellen laughed and said, well you know if that is the case then you had better start living a cleaner life, stop being a tomboy and stay out of fights. Then she looked at daddy and asked him if he knew what it meant. Daddy replied no and then asked Aunt Ellen if she thought the dream had a meaning. She answered by saying that I had dreamed the meaning. What she wanted to know was how were they going to deal with this? He looked confused and worried and answered what do you think we should do, El? What do you mean she dreamed the meaning? Aunt Ellen replied that she felt it was time for them to explain to me about Aunt Ruby's gift.

"Gift." I got excited when I heard the word gift. What gift? They looked at each other then started laughing like they were teasing me. Again I asked what gift?

Again they just laughed harder and finally Aunt Ellen said, "Cow Tail that curiosity spirit is going to get you in trouble one day." Then she proceeded to tell me about my Aunt Ruby. I stopped her by saying I had already heard that story about Aunt Ruby. She said you haven't heard all of it. She shared that Aunt Ruby was daddy's baby sister and she lived in Lynchburg. I said I know that. I went with you to see her, remember. I've already heard this story, remember. She stopped me and continued that Ruby had dreams and visions and some people were afraid of her and sent her there to live. She claimed she could see and hear Jesus too. Have you heard that know it all? She asked.

You see, she said, every dream has two meanings or more. I'm not smart enough to tell you the meanings of the dreams. I know there were people in the Bible that God used. They had dreams and visions and God gave them the meanings of those dreams Himself, He will give you the meanings also. Later I will read some of those stories to you in the Bible. But for now I feel you need to put this on the shelf and leave it there in your mind. You see, you are just twelve and in the dream you are thirty. You still have your life to live and according to the dream you will be a mother and grandmother. Thirty will be awfully young to be a grandmother so the age must be wrong and it can't be wrong or it means something else. If the age is wrong then I feel there is nothing to it. Why don't you go play now? Let me and your daddy talk while I finish up supper before your Uncle Press gets here.

But what if it is true and I do die? Suppose I have a baby real young and that baby has a baby real young? She said you have to get married first and that means you have to be eighteen and if you got pregnant at eighteen your baby would be eighteen and that would make you thirty-six. So it's not possible. Go play. But what if I do?

She said, "Well then, if I was you, I would live each day and fulfill my every wish. I would go to church, read my Bible and pray for God to keep my soul. I would go to school and get married when I grow up and have babies. I would live life to the fullest every day. That's what I would do Cow Tail. Now go play.

Well what's the other meaning, I asked? She said, well it could mean you will die to self like Jesus told his disciples to do and pick up your life and follow him. Or it could mean you would die to the life you know and begin a new life. Either way, do everything for the glory of God and speak and think kindness. Either way you are assured you will be with Jesus in heaven. She then asked, do you know how many people on this earth are afraid of death? Even in your own family there are people afraid of death. You can help those people to not be afraid. You can live doing good deeds and helping people to understand the afterlife. You can encourage them to do good by doing well yourself. In your own dream you saw people in all radiance. Maybe God wants you to stay on earth and help others as well as help you to do good so you will be one of those people in all radiance. You couldn't be good nor do good by yourself so that means you will have to let Jesus inside you be the good one. Now for the last time you go play.

I thought about what she said and in my heart it felt right. I looked at her and Daddy and said, "You know what? I see those people like I saw in the dream that looked liked black pearls. Sometimes when I am around people I don't see their body. I see the beautiful star inside of them and it draws me to help them no matter what they are doing I just want to help or at least stay in their presence a while. You know some times I see them and they look like an angel, like Mrs. Jennings."

Aunt Ellen asked. How long have you been seeing this Carolyn Ann? I thought I was in trouble when she called me Carolyn Ann so I didn't answer. But she asked me again. How long? What do you mean you see Mrs. Jennings and she looks like an angel? I figured I had better answer her this time especially after seeing the serious look on Daddy's face. Yeap, don't you see it when you see her? She is like a light bulb all shinny and everything. I love going to her house. It doesn't matter whether she has work clothes on with an apron or her Sunday clothes on, she always shines, like an angel. Not like some people who are dark. Some people have a dark light and they feel nasty even when they have on Sunday clothes. I won't touch them. Yuck. Yuck. Yuck I said as I grabbed a biscuit and ran out the door to play. I didn't want to share any more.

I ran out of the back door yelling for Clarence. He, Shirley and Tommy came running from around the front. What did you do? Did you get a whipping? No I didn't get a whipping. They wanted me to talk about the dream because I kept Daddy up all night. Clarence said you better stop that. If he gets mad like Press he will whip you. He won't whip me I said back at him. Before we got the chance to play we heard Aunt Ellen call to wash up. Press was coming down the drive way. We ran fast to wash up and get to the table before Uncle Press got there. She always gave us a warning so he wouldn't fuss at us. He believed if Aunt Ellen was in the kitchen working we were suppose to be there too. He always drove around to the back of the door so we had plenty of time. I was the first one at the table wet hands and all. Aunt Ellen said, Cow tail, let's keep the dreams between us okay. Then I saw Uncle Press walk through the door and knew immediately she meant him. He stopped in the middle of the door smiling; well I see we have rug rats to feed for supper tonight. How's everything going Henry? I wondered where you were when I didn't see you at the store, as he continued his way through the door taking his hat off and proceeded to wash his own hands.

After supper Daddy and Uncle Press went back to the store and stayed until 10 o'clock. The store closed at nine but he always had to fill up the drink boxes. We helped Aunt Ellen wash dishes and then she got her Bible and read us the story of Joseph. When she finished reading the story she said, some people were very jealous of Joseph because God spoke to him in dreams. Some of them tried to hurt him. Joseph didn't know he was suppose to keep God's secrets and told everyone in his family. His own brothers tried to kill him but God wouldn't allow it. But they did sell him to some strangers and he went away from his family to live with them.

I knew immediately she was talking about me too. I looked up and out of fear asked, is that why Aunt Ruby lives with strangers? She said yes, because no one told her to keep her secrets to herself and only tell the people she could trust. Clarence spoke up full of excitement like he had just heard a horror tale. I'm not telling any body about my dreams, but Carolyn did. She kept Uncle Henry up all night. Suppose Uncle Henry had been like those brothers and killed you, he asked me? I frowned at him so mean and said, my Daddy wouldn't kill me. You're crazy. Then I hit him as hard as I could on the arm. Well the fight was on. Aunt Ellen scrambled to get out of our way, laughing. She knew that was the end of the discussion about dreams. She went on in the kitchen and while she baked a chocolate cake for Saturday the four of us were all over the place wrestling. Secure that Aunt Ellen was watching for uncle Press and warn us before he caught us fighting in the house.

Daddy showed up a little after ten to pick us up to go home. The den was all straightened up like there hadn't been any playing around in it. We asking why we couldn't stay all weekend, and he replied, we would move in with El if he let us. That meant get your stuff and get in the car. We got home and ready for bed when Daddy came to the door and said good night. Sleep well and don't let the bed bugs bite. He didn't mention the dream at all.

After praying we dropped off to sleep. My last thought was getting to sleep before Shirley. We shared the same room and she snored and I hated it. I prayed for my own room every night I laid there awake listening to her snore.

How long I had been asleep I don't know but I woke up with Daddy standing over me again. I looked up and said, "I was sleep walking again, wasn't I? Daddy said, go to bed and try to get some sleep with a worried tone in his voice. Without even asking he knew I had had that same dream. He knew Aunt Ellen had told us before according to the way she understood the Bible a one time dream or vision could be changed. A two time dream or vision could be changed but just a little harder. But a three time dream was settled in heaven and couldn't be changed or she hadn't found it in the Bible yet.

The next morning when he called me to get up and fix breakfast he asked me about it before Shirley and Tommy got up. I told him it was the same dream. He looked worried and reminded me to keep it to myself. About that time Tommy and Shirley walked in with Shirley saying she wanted fried eggs, not scrambled. During breakfast Daddy gave us the list of things he wanted us to do by noon. If we finished by lunch we could go to El's. Either he would take us when he came home for lunch so be ready or if he got tied up he would send Johnny. But Daddy never got that tied up that he wouldn't come home for lunch when we were there. If we weren't finished with chores he would send Johnny after us around 2 or 3 pm. either way we would go to Aunt Ellen's on Saturday. Very few Saturdays we didn't go.

The third dream came the third night and Daddy became more worried and more protective over me. With each dream I saw and understood a little more of it. It gave me a strong hunger for the words of Jesus Christ and the New Testament. I didn't like to read very much of the Old Testament because it felt more like death. But I loved reading about Abraham, Joseph, Jacob, Enoch, Elijah and Elisha. I hated the book of Job. I felt that book was a lie. I couldn't bring myself to believe that God would stand by and allow Satan to do all he did to Job and his family. Other than Job any one else that talked to God or God talked to them I was drawn too. I would read their stories over and over especially what the Lord said. Some of it didn't make sense to me because I couldn't pronounce the big words. Some didn't sound like God so I would ask God what it meant. Sometimes the verses would light up and get real bold and it felt like God was talking right at me or to me and I would understand and sometimes I just skipped right over them. Seeing Daddy more concerned about me and seeing some of the verses full of light and bold were just a few of the changes I noticed after the dreams.

I realized another change after the three dreams of my physical death was being in a hurry to live. By the age of thirteen I wanted to date. Before then I was the biggest tom boy you ever saw. Fighting and sticking like glue with Johnny wherever he went. It certainly wasn't boys. I was going to college and be a lawyer. I remember asking Daddy if I could date and the surprise on his face made him choke. He cleared his throat and replied I had to have a boyfriend to date. I looked at him like he thought I was stupid and said I will get one of them. Can I date? He answered when I got one of them then we would talk about it. Rest assured Daddy told the whole family and they all teased me about one of them boyfriends. Johnny said he felt sorry for any boy that dated me because if he didn't act right I would beat him up. I had learned the first year that you had better have a good attitude with that family or the teasing alone would make you want to kill them. They loved teasing better than any family I have ever met and looked for any little thing to needle you with. I can't tell you how many times I stomped out of that house and pouted on that front porch swing, just blessing them all out. Didn't they know this boyfriend and dating business was new to me also? I had to get on with my life just in case the dream was true.

I noticed also that I loved being around small children and the elders more after the dream. I would sit for hours and listen to the elders talk and tell stories. Babysitting J.P. was my delight then Wanda Gail was born, another living baby doll for me to baby-sit. I acted just like their mama. They were Aunt Ellen's first two grandchildren and she spoiled them rotten. I enjoyed watching her play and talk to them, like her heart was wide open flowing love and joy into them. I would sit with them as she read the Bible to them like she had to us. I watched as she stopped whatever she was doing to help them, hold them and feed them, whatever it was at the time. I felt they had given her new hope and a renewed joy. I noticed when family came to visit they saw her joy and Uncle Press's also. The house was always filled with love, peace and joy but these two grandbabies had made it overflow. They certainly were the apple of her eye. I would sit for hours and listen to J.P. and the elders talk and not be bored. Strange! It was like I could feel their every word. Like energy was coming from their mouth or something. Since I was a big talker myself that wasn't like me to listen and I usually became bored after five minutes and start talking or just walk away. I was usually the one doing all the talking and being told to shut up and give my mouth a rest. Aunt Ellen said JP and Wanda had hypnotized me. I noticed I watched their expressions as they spoke and what tone they spoke in, every detail of their expressions and words. Then I could repeat every word, gesture, tone and expression just like the person had said it. Aunt Ellen said she believed I had a photo static memory. I became interested in my past generations also, a strange interest. I asked many questions about them we even went to visit Cousin Mildred who had kept up with families for a hundred years or more. I even asked Daddy and Aunt Ellen if they ever felt their ancestors hanging around. No answer was given, only a smart answer in teasing me.

Soon Aunt Ellen caught on and decided to use my new interest to teach me further. Since she and Daddy wanted me to be a lawyer she decided to see how interested I really was and started carrying me with her to see her banker, lawyer and other important friends. Business friends she called them and we did go to their office sometimes but went to their homes mostly. Several times we went to this big house to see a big man who lived on the other side of South Boston. He looked like Daddy and dressed like Daddy but she called him, Cousin Bill. She picked out a pretty dress and helped me dress. I felt like a princess in it. Then while helping me fix my hair she said when we got there, if they offered me anything to eat or drink for me to accept and say thank you. She said when they got ready to discuss business for me to stay outside and play. She asked me to keep quiet and not ask any questions. Then she asked if I could do that for her? I agreed to her terms and on the way over I asked her many questions just to get them all out before we arrived. But all she said was he was a real close and good friend of hers. He was a very good man and did much good for the state of Virginia. But he had to remain our little secret because he was so important.

I remember, as we drove up to this big house and got out, a tall big man with a hat on came to the door before we could knock with a big smile on his face. Then he took his hat off as he reached to hug Aunt Ellen. He looked down and asked who that pretty little girl was? Aunt Ellen said, "She's Henry's daughter." "Well does Henry's daughter have a name?" He said. "Carolyn Ann but we call her Cow Tail." He just laughed a great big belly laugh and said, come on in Ellen. It is so good to see you. Let's see if we can find some lemonade for you ladies." He said we will go out and sit on the back porch if that's alright with you, El.

She replied that was fine as we followed him to the screen door where he opened it for us. Outside the porch went all the way across the back of the house and painted white. Even the chairs and table were white. I noticed a swing in the yard and some pretty flowers as I sat and sipped on the lemonade and as they went down memory lane. Asking questions like how this one is and that one and they would answer and move on to the next name.

After a little while Cousin Bill asked me if I would like to go swing while he and El discussed some business. I shook my head with a yes and went to get up when Aunt Ellen corrected me by saying, "That's, Yes Sir, Carolyn Ann." I went to reply when Cousin Bill answered, "That's all right El. A nod is just as good."

At that I proceeded to walk down the steps and off the porch and out to the swing. I was close enough to see them sitting on the porch talking and laughing. I could hear them talking but couldn't make out what they were saying. When they finished their business he walked her off of the porch and yelled for me to come on like he had known me all his life. As he walked with us around the house towards our car he said, "El, you bring this pretty little lady back to see me. Maybe next time we will have some cookies or candy to give to such a pretty girl." Then he bent down and held out his hand for me to shake hands with him. They hugged and he said he hoped he had helped. If not to let him know and he would see what he could get done.

After we left I asked many questions but she gave no information. She asked me if she could trust me and not tell anyone where we went or who we saw. She promised to take me again if I kept her secret.

She did take me back to see Cousin Bill many times after that first trip. He did have cookies and candy each time after that also. He made us feel right at home and always laughing. I loved the way he laughed with that big cigar in his mouth. He was a very nice man and not only looked like Daddy but his mother had died when he was thirteen years old and was raised by his daddy, just like you he told me one day. He loved to tell us stories about the places he had gone and things he had done. He told them in such a simple and plain way that I would sit as long as they allowed me and listened. After we got pass the first few visits I was allowed to ask him questions and he answered every one of them. He talked a lot about flying so much so when I got older I went to the air shows at the William M. Tuck Airport down at Wolf Trap. One day I asked him if he had any children and he replied one, Lester. He said his wife was sick a lot and he moved on to another subject. He did tell me to tell my Daddy he was going to stop by his store one day and eat some pickled pigs' feet. Sure enough he did. When Daddy came home that day he said a friend of yours said to tell you hello, when I asked who, he said Cousin Bill.

Sometimes we visited him at his office, Tuck, Bagwell, Dillard, Mapp and Nelson. Sometimes while there Mr. Mapp would give me candy or chewing gum. I knew he was a very special friend of Aunt Ellen's by the way he treated us. Aunt Ellen said he was rambunctious but when I asked her what that meant she just replied he moved around a lot for many years until Eva took sick. After that he moved back to the home house where he was raised by his father. He was just a good ole country boy that loved the south as much as we did. He was never to busy or to important to not see her though. I knew it was a pure friendship by the way he talked about his lovely wife he called her. A very strong respectful energy flowed in his house, stronger than in any other home I had ever entered. Being a child I had picked up on many things that most adults wouldn't have Aunt Ellen said. That impressed me and her all our life. I never told anyone until years after Aunt Ellen had passed and only then when someone asked me about it.

After I married and had children I learned Cousin Bill was actually Governor William M. Tuck of Virginia. The 55th governor and was a democrat. Whether he really was her cousin I never found out. It was 1975 when Aunt Ellen called and asked me to take a ride with her the next morning. I asked bring Tammy or Jay or drop them off at the sitter. She replied get a sitter that a very good friend of hers had passed and she wanted to go out and see the family. Sure enough we went to Cousin Bill's home. He greeted us as friendly as he always had. Aunt Ellen started her conversation with how sorry she was to hear about Eva. We proceeded to the kitchen and then the back porch as they talked about her. He had watched me grow up, and with each visit said I was getting prettier and prettier but this day he didn't. His heart grieved for his lovely wife.

We only visited Cousin Bill one time after that. We had stopped to see Aunt Dee I believe Aunt Ellen called her and she told us Cousin Bill had had a stoke. It was 1976 the same year my last daughter was born Penny Dawn when we rode out to see him. But a lady came to the door and said he wasn't seeing visitors that day. Aunt Ellen asked her to tell him who she was but the lady said he knew you were coming Miss El but he's not up to see you, (housekeeper Aunt Ellen said). Later in the week Aunt Ellen said his stoke was worst than she thought. Cousin Bill passed June 9, 1983. We didn't go to the funeral but to the graveside at Oakridge Cemetery after the funeral. When I asked why we didn't attend the funeral she said there were more important people that needed to be there than her. All she said at the grave as she put her small bunch of flowers was he was one of a kind. Rest in peace Bill, you certainly made history and put South Boston on the map. She brushed back a tear and placed a small bunch of pink roses on his beloved wife Eva's grave and said almost the same thing except she added it was an honor to know you all these years and you are missed. Through all the years she never told me what type of business they discussed or what he helped her to do. Just that he was a very important person and I needed to stay friends with him, but now he's gone and Aunt Ellen is sad.

Another one of Aunt Ellen's friends she took me with her to see was a Virginia Senator. From those childhood visits our friendship grew along with Aunt Ellen's. Even though I couldn't tell anyone I always felt special to be able to visit him with Aunt Ellen and call him Cousin Howard. Over the years he became one of my closest court house friends. He remembered when Aunt Ellen use to bring me with her to visit him and his wife. He always asked me about her as well as my Daddy. That always impressed me after I found out who he was. I learned good people are just good people regardless of their title or income like Aunt Ellen had said.

I remember years later he found out a project I was working on and decided on his own to help me behind the scenes he called it. That built my confidence up at least by a ten. Over a period of time he helped me in many ways. He said one day when he passed a note to me in the court house after helping me find a certain deed, that he thought what I was doing for those young people was a great thing. That it would go down in Virginia history. He said El and Henry would be proud to know I had learned the secret of success. If you want to know more about either of these honorable men visit the South Boston Virginia Museum.

Aunt Ellen and Daddy both had many such friends as the two I mentioned that she carried me to visit. For some reason our relationship grew closer and closer after my dreams began. I felt honored that she would share her secrets with me like I had shared mine with her. That made me feel special and the trust she had in me I tried real hard to honor.

Several years passed before I had another dream that felt like they were from God. I was actually glad. I had dreams but they were different and Daddy called them 'too many hotdog dreams'.

Chapter 4:

I Dreamed My Own Husband

I had gotten serious about dating by age thirteen but Daddy ignored me when I brought it up. I should say he laughed at me and told me I was too young to be dating. Thirteen years old he would say and want to date. When I mentioned a few friends my age that were dating he said they weren't his daughters. That made me mad. Then I reminded him that they didn't have to be the wife for their daddy either. I had kept house, cooked, washed clothes, and been a mama to Shirley and Tommy since I was eight years old. Anything that was done around the house I had to do it and help them with homework, fix their hair, patched them when they got hurt. I survived his and Mama's desertion and kept Shirley and Tommy alive. I worked in tobacco and made my own money. I knew I was mature enough to date. You know so much to know nothing he would say. You think you are mature but you have so many things to learn about people before you go off with some boy. He asked me who the boy was I wanted to date. What kind of family did he come from? I told him I didn't have one yet that I wasn't going to date just any boy. He laughed and made more jokes like he did when I asked him about dating at twelve years old. That always sent me stomping out of the house and to my favorite place in the woods to pray. They teased me about praying so much too. Daddy shouting at me, that's right, run off to that hiding place but you better be back before dark. Johnny said I couldn't go to the poop house without praying.

After I finished fussing to myself walking down the dirt road I would start singing. Singing always made me feel closer to Jesus and gave me peace within. "I come to the garden alone, while the dew is still on the roses, and the voice I hear, calling on my ear, the sound of God is ringing, and He walks with me and he talks with

54

me, and he tells me I am his own., and the joy we share is beyond compare," making up words as I went. I didn't like the feeling I felt inside when I got mad and could never stay mad long because of it. Whatever came up out of my spirit I sang, even some I made up. When I got to my circle in the woods that were hidden among the trees the mad feelings would be gone. It was just a perfect place for lying in the sun and talking to God and then laid there in the silence and waited for God to talk to me or for the angels to show up. I had run away from home down in those woods one day and found it. It had such peacefulness about it I thought maybe it's a place like God used when he talked to one of those Bible people. I took some bushes and swept it clean. Then I drew a circle around a tree and called it my holy ground. I remembered when Aunt Ellen use to read the Bible to us, every person that had dreams from God had a special place where they talked to God and God talked back. This was my special place. I noticed after that first day when I swept it clean that it stayed clean. I wondered sometimes why there were no leaves or bugs or anything inside of my circle. But I figured God's angels were always there guarding it from such things. Whatever I discussed with God stayed in the circle just like Aunt Ellen's living room. I would tell God everything I wanted and that day it was to start dating. I remember asking God to show me what the boy looked like that he wanted me to date. I told Him I really didn't want to date so I asked for a boy that would fall in love with me, marry me and be the father of my children. I wanted four or more children and I wanted them to love and serve God. I wanted my husband to work and make enough money so I could stay at home and be a wife and mother. I wanted a brick house in town or near town and beautiful furniture and curtains. I wanted him to show up when God wanted me to meet him and get married. Also to change Daddy's heart about me dating. Then I just laid there in the circle waiting for God to talk to me or I was filled with great joy. Once God spoke or filled me with peace and great joy I knew He had received my request. Then I would skip and whistle all the way back to the house.

It was spring of 1963 and I was thirteen years old going on fourteen when I dreamed about this dark black headed boy with blue eyes. I saw him washing a car windshield and smiling a great big smile. He had a dark suntan and just as cute as he could be. I didn't tell Daddy or Aunt Ellen about this dream but only my best friend. She teased me by asking how I knew it was from God. After hearing my answer her curiosity got the best of her and she asked me to pray for God to show her a boy, one she was suppose to marry. I did pray and ask God to show her but I don't remember if he did then or later in her life.

I was riding the school bus one April day and when it stopped at the stop sign I looked to my left and there he was. He had black hair and was washing a windshield and smiling. He worked at the Halifax Texaco in Halifax. I punched my friend and told her to look. That's him. I told her the boy from my dream. Remember the one I saw in my dream with black hair washing a windshield. She looked and said, *"That's him? That's the one? He looks too short. Are you sure that's him?"*

We laughed at how short he really was and wondered if he was the one in my dream. Maybe he isn't the one in my dream but he sure does look like him except he is just too short, we laughed and joked.

That afternoon riding the bus home a black Ford with that same guy driving was behind our bus. Barbara yelled for me to look. When I did and saw it was him I yelled for Ann to come to the back of the bus and see him close up. Barbara suggested we write a note and put it to the window for him to read. I wrote, 'what is your name?' we could see him moving close up behind the bus as he could to read it and when he did Barbara yelled laughing, *that's Bernard my cousin.* He followed the bus to our stop which was Daddy's store. When I stepped off I made sure I twisted my butt for him to see as I glanced back over my shoulder to make sure he saw me. Then I smiled right at him and went on in the store with Shirley and Tommy. He kept following the bus.

The next morning on the bus Barbara handed me a note from him. She said he had followed the bus to her stop and asked who I was. When she told him, he asked if she thought I would go out with him. She said she told him, maybe, call her and ask. Then she said he wrote his name and phone number and gave it to her and asked her to give me the note and tell me to call him at lunch time. I got so excited I couldn't sit still. The bus driver yelled for us to sit down in our seat. As we got closer to the stop sign I had gone to the side window to get another look as we stopped at the stop sign. With the bus stopped I figured I would wave at him but he wasn't out there.

When I got to school I ran to the phone booth to call him (that's right no cell phones). He answered the phone and we chatted about five minutes before I had to go in. That was a long morning before lunch waiting to call him again. That afternoon he was washing a windshield and looked at our bus and waved and smiled as we passed by. Ann asked me if I thought my Daddy would allow me to date. I knew I had to ask but whether he would allow it or not I just had to wait and see.

When Daddy came home after closing the store I told him I needed to ask him something. When I asked him about dating and told him I had had another dream. I shared the dream all but the part of marrying him. Then I told him I had seen the guy that was in my dreams and knew his name. Then I showed him the note and told him I did call him from school. That he had asked me out on a date for that following Sunday to go to Tuck Airport to an airplane show. Daddy said no.

When Wednesday came I asked Daddy if we could ride with Johnny from the store down to Aunt Ellen's and he pick us up after he closed. He said yes. I knew I had to talk to Aunt Ellen and talk her in to talking Daddy into letting me date. Aunt Ellen listened very carefully when I shared my dream and then told her I had seen him. That he had asked me out but Daddy had said no. Then I asked her to talk to Daddy for me. At first she said no. But when I commented about not trusting me to date hurt my feelings. That Jesus trusted me enough to give me dreams and credit enough to do what was right and know right from wrong, why couldn't they? By ten o'clock and Daddy was there to pick us up I had convinced her to at least talk to Daddy. Now the key was to get them together before Sunday to have that little talk.

Friday morning I asked Daddy if we could go to Aunt Ellen's on Saturday around lunchtime. Also if he saw Johnny could he ask him to pick us up and take us down if he didn't want too or couldn't find anyone to watch the store a few minutes? After he had agreed then I asked him if he would stay for lunch when he dropped us off. I could tell he was getting suspicious. He didn't give an answer about lunch but he stayed when he realized lunch was ready and all he had to do was sit down and eat. After lunch Uncle Press and Johnny got up and said they had work to do. After they left Aunt Ellen asked Daddy if he had a few minutes to talk to her about this dating business. He agreed and to make a long story short Aunt Ellen did convince him that I could be trusted enough to date. He did take Shirley and me to the airplane show. That was daddy's string to take Shirley with us or not go. BC didn't mind at all. We married Christmas Eve of 1965 but more on that in another chapter.

Another dream had come to pass. Daddy didn't want us to marry so young but since he was leaving for the army January of 66 he agreed. Whether the dream played a role in it or not, I don't know. Back then getting married young was the norm. I could see his point for I had just stopped being a tomboy a year back. Daddy never spoke of it other than he wished I hadn't had that dream. He felt my life was moving too fast and I agreed with him but it was almost like someone else was pulling the strings and all I was doing was following.

After that, the dreams stopped for awhile. Daddy and Aunt Ellen both said it was a good thing. That I needed a break and just enjoy a little of my life.

Chapter 5:

Surrounded By Love

But before I get ahead of myself and go into my marriage I want to share more of our happy memories as children with the Smith family.

As I think back and remember how we watched Oral Robert's on television every Sunday along with a few others before leaving for our little Baptist church I don't remember one preacher teaching on dreams. Maybe God had it planned that way so I would learn to be totally dependant on him and not get involved with religion.

Aunt Ellen read it to us straight out of the Bible until we could read ourselves and taught us to accept the Bible as it was written. She said as we grew up we were to study the meanings of every word Jesus spoke right down to the buts and ifs. She told us to never take one preacher or another as the total truth. They were men just like all humans and misunderstand things and to judge them. The best way to know truth was to hear it from God for ourselves and then check it out in the written word because Satan could come as an angel of light to deceive us. Satan may speak many Bible verses but Jesus' words he wouldn't speak. When I asked her why she said his words were like fire and would burn him up. She wanted us to study and learn the truth for ourselves. I remember II Corinthians chapter 4 where it said for us to look at the unseen. When I asked what that meant she said we were to seek after things from above in the heavens. That time and everything in the physical was temporary and would fade away one day. Look for the invisible things she said for they were the reality and for us to keep our minds fixed on the living word. I remember she dropped a spool of thread about that time and let it go. When Clarence jumped up to get it she said let it stop running first. Once it stopped running it would be easy to get it back. She said this physical world was like that spool of thread always running down hill. So many fools chase it and find themselves far far away from living right. Once they catch it, it's not what they thought it was. Then if wise they would turn around and start the journey back home where their Creator is. You see God will let you chase the world but he won't run after you. He will wait at home until you return.

I remember Elisha and Elijah both seeing an army of angels. I can still see and hear Aunt Ellen as she reads with such force, *"Open up our eyes Lord that we may see. Let us see into the unseen realm."* I found that verse in II Kings chapter six one day. She would ask us what we thought something meant and Aunt Ellen would be amazed sometimes when I shared with her what I saw. She would hug me and say, girl you amaze me sometimes and sometimes I would like to put a sock in that mouth of yours. Then she would take her pointer finger and gently touch my lips and add, *"I hope you give that mouth to God for Him to use for His glory. Then it will work for good, Cowtail. Don't allow Satan to use it to talk about people and lie okay."* I could tell she was speaking that over me like she was praying over us.

Aunt Ellen could see our house, each room, smell the air and see the walls but when I told her there was an angel in the room or one standing beside her as I described the spirit to her it was like she knew who I was describing. She claimed she couldn't see him. When I ask her if she could feel the energy in the room? She claimed she couldn't. But her calm sweet smile told me she either saw them or felt them. She knew I felt safe and secure with the angels being all around us and I could see them.

It was confusing for me sometimes because I didn't understand why the angels were there but never seem to help. I guess they were helping and we just didn't know it. At least that's what Aunt Ellen and Daddy said. They never interfered with our life. Some people have said years later that maybe we didn't ask the angels for help or didn't ask in faith. Aunt Ellen told us to ask Jesus Christ Father only and when an angel showed up we were to ask them if they came from Jesus Christ and if they said no or didn't answer for us to tell them to go away in Jesus Christ. We asked but mostly to protect us while Daddy was gone. And protect him and bring him home safe. We were never afraid to stay by ourselves. Our home and Aunt Ellen's home was always filled with peace so there wasn't anything to fear. Aunt Ellen said that was our proof that God was with us. I asked the angels to teach us about Jesus one time and Aunt Ellen thumped my head so hard I knew to change that prayer quickly. The thump helped me to remember not to ask anyone for anything but God our Father in Jesus Christ and Holy Spirit. She said Jesus gave us the Holy Spirit. He was our real teacher and he lived inside. If we wanted to know anything about God or Jesus or Holy Spirit or even angels to ask Jesus Father only, he was the only one with the right answers. She always felt the Holy Spirit was our Mother God because only mothers knew how to really comfort us. But she could be wrong and just feel that way because she lost her mother so young like we had, she added. So we always had help and could ask the Holy Spirit to explain anything we didn't understand. But we had to sit quietly and listen to hear or feel the answer and in your case, Cowtail, see the answer also as she tickled me. I often wondered if maybe that was the reason we didn't miss our mother. Sometimes I asked them to explain the Sunday school lesson. I asked one day why there was three gods? She said only one God Creator but He came in three parts to explain to us about our spirit, soul and body. She said we were three parts yet one person.

If we had to give credit to just one human being for teaching us the Bible and about the heavens, it would have to be Aunt Ellen. She told us about two kingdoms. One was God's kingdom and one was Satan's. One was light and the other was darkness. One was good and the other was evil. We had to choose daily which one we wanted to live in. We had to check our motive out as to why we wanted something or someone. That only the pure in heart would see God. For if Satan got an inch of our mind he would steal a mile and make the biggest mess. She said Jesus kingdom was the good one and we needed to work hard every day to live out of that kingdom. We asked her how to work out of that Kingdom. She said we were to study and meditate His Living words daily and apply them. Applying them was the key like any subject we took in school. Knowledge without applying was dead knowledge. We were to examine ourselves daily and look for the motive behind it. Was it for selfish reasons or for the good of others? When angry replace it with forgiveness. It was alright to get angry but find out what it was that actually made us feel that and then surrender it to God. Don't hold onto anger it will lead to bitterness and destroy your joy. If we couldn't forgive then we were to surrender to God and asked Jesus to replace that anger with forgiveness. That un-forgiveness keeps more people out of heaven and church than any other spirit she said. Unforgiveness was just another word for fear, fear that someone will take something from you or fear that they did and may come back and take more. When you get to the root of fear it usually is from selfishness.

She and Daddy both said Satan was a wannabe and people who followed him were wannabes. Jesus did things right the first time. Satan and his crowd wanted to be God and that's what prevents them from getting it right. Jesus teaches us how to do stuff right where that other bunch didn't teach you anything but how to get in trouble like Cowtail fighting boys, jumping out of windows and such. It was her anger that kept her in trouble. She was angry at God, her Mama and Daddy. I came back at her with I did it right. I won the fight, didn't break any bones when I jumped out of that window on that boy. She rubbed my head like she was rubbing some wisdom into it and laughed then back to her cooking.

Daddy said God had little birds that reported to him and God. When we chose to do wrong or even think wrong thoughts they saw and told. That alone kept us conscious of a very involved God all around us. It certainly made us consciously aware of our thoughts as well as our actions. Growing up in rural Virginia conscious of God in us and all around us made my mind wonder as to why some people were evil at all. Weren't they afraid of God? Aunt Ellen said being afraid of God was the beginning of wisdom.

Daddy didn't like hypocrites at all and owning a grocery store he came in contact with many. He would tell us to be aware of the masked people when we went off with church people. He said they were human like everyone else and made mistakes but there were some that looked for the opportunity to be mean, abusive and cruel. Many hypocrites hid out in churches deceiving people into believing they were good people but at home it was a different tale. How you treat your family? How you talk to them tells the true story? We watched *The Lone Ranger* every Saturday morning and that lesson stayed conscious in our minds. Every time we saw the lone ranger and his friend in their mask we associated it with what Daddy said. He called them *Church going wannabes.* According to Daddy they were the people who wore a mask on Sundays and in public but were different people behind closed doors. He said they were of Cain's family and go around deceiving people. At church and in public they appeared and talked like saints but at home and at work they were liars, used ugly words and thieves. They would steal from their own mamas. He said they were selfish people, just plain old selfish people that had to have their way. Their every motive was for selfish gain. They didn't care who they hurt or what they had to say or do as long as they got their own way. Cowards they were because they didn't have the courage to do right. They were just ignorant people for they were to prideful to ask God for courage so they could do better. Then he would add, some preachers stand behind pulpits with one motive, money, and deceive the people every Sunday, from tithing to going to heaven. He would close with, Ellen will tell you to pray for them but I tell you to stay away from them. I use to hate those speeches. Now I feel so blessed to have lived long enough to know truth and know Daddy was right more than he was wrong. Daddy was so far from being perfect himself but his kindness and joyful attitude made you want to do more and be more around him. All he could see was the best in God and felt so unworthy in God's presence. He wanted his children to be the best at whatever we decided to do. People have asked us if we thought our daddy wanted us perfect. I don't think so because he would say we learn our lessons from mistakes and life was full of them. Our job was to be a little better today than yesterday.

Daddy said a home was a safe haven full of peace and always welcoming anyone who stopped by when filled with God. If you are not welcomed in a home there were secrets somewhere or evil brewing. If they came with peace in their hearts they would leave with greater peace and return to visit another day. He said if they came with strife and worked to turn one family member against another, or started arguments, or judged, then know, they weren't our friends. He said they were wolves in sheep clothing and some wolves were in the family bloodline. Beware, he said for us to not ask them to come again but stay away from them even if they were family members. They would bring much pain and suffering on themselves and all around them. He said you can't help them. They must decide to be right and do right and then they would bring peace. He said, we would know them for they would make excuses, find fault with others and never take responsibility for their words or actions. They were always blaming someone else for their own mess. Just plain old cowards he would add. They pretend they like good people just so they can get something for themselves. They are the poorest people of all. Always thinking about themselves, their small little world and what they can get next. Daddy said you want to get takers out of your life just stop giving and see if the attitude stay the same. If their attitude changes and they are too busy to visit or help you, there's your takers, he would laugh and say. He said they were the most miscible people in the world and wanted everyone else miscible because they lived in constant fear of being found out. They don't hang around good people very long periods because their mask gets heavy and they are afraid they will slip and show you their true selves before they get what they want out of you. Beware, he would say, for hiding behind that smile stands a monster. Even Jesus said we can't trust doubled minded people. When I asked what double minded meant? He took an ink pen and drew a line down the middle of my forehead and said, *one side acts like God and the other side acts like Satan. Surrender both sides to Jesus Christ and just be one. Then you can be trusted.*

Daddy would use someone we knew and would say, now take so and so, he will do a good deed today and tomorrow he will turn and shit on that good deed and leave the mess for someone else to clean up. Do you know why Mrs. So and So raises those grandbabies? I'll tell you why. Some old sorry boy showed up one day and hung around being so good, helping with chores, and work. Like an old snake in the grass just waiting for an opening. When he found that opening he jumped on it and got that little girl pregnant. Then he high tails it back up north leaving that little girl with a baby to raise. Well that girl needs an education so that means her mama has the baby to raise. Do you see what I'm saying? A good boy wouldn't touch that girl until after he married her. A good boy would come in and be a blessing to that family, proving he was good enough for that girl. A good boy would wait until that girl finished school and got her parents blessing. A good boy would have a job and a place to live and support his wife before getting her pregnant. He's not a snake in the grass but a good boy.

Daddy like Aunt Ellen would say, some people were just plain ignorant and those were the ones we were to teach a better way of life too. He said some parents didn't love themselves or their children enough to send them to church and teach them about Jesus or the kingdom of God. And some parents did send their children to church but they were to ignorant to pay attention and just stayed dirty minded and ignorant and kept on living out of their selfish selves instead of God. And some people had Jesus in their heart and just too ignorant to know that they already had the good life and the kingdom living inside and all they had to do was bring it out. He said it wasn't a sin to be ignorant but only a fool stayed ignorant and that was sin.

Aunt Ellen added. Then there were the snobs. Those people counted wealth by dollars, land they owned and houses they built. Some ever so blind they think they are rich because a lot of people hang around them that they call their friends. But you let sickness or disaster come and those snobs will see those so called friends scatter like flies when you pick up a fly swap. Guess what? She would say. Old Satan would keep them ignorant so he can keep using them until he destroyed their home, children, and wealth and make their precious life a dying hell. Then he will make them think no one loves them not even God. Don't put so much store in these physical things, they said. Daddy would add, *when I step out of my old physical body I'll be finished with it. You take it and throw it in a ditch and cover it up. It'll go back to dust. You look for me up there in the heavens. That's where you'll find me, up there with Jesus, my Mama and Daddy and your Uncle Jesse. Do you understand what I'm saying kids? You need to understand this, for it is truth.*

Sometimes I really didn't want to hear them tell those stories. When they got real serious, telling some stories I did become afraid like they thought they were gonna die any day. For the most part we just sat and listened as they poured their wisdom into us.

Meal time was also three times a day we all enjoyed. It was family togetherness time. We always had a meat, one or two veggies, gravy, potatoes or mac-n-cheese and a desert with coffee, milk, tea, water or Kool-Aid and homemade biscuits with buttermilk, sometimes, but always homemade even if made with milk or water. We liked the water biscuits when tomatoes were ripe. They would hold a big slice without crumbling. Aunt Ellen said we serve meals the same way Jesus served the word. Like a baby starts off with its mother's milk and worked up to a little water and veggie. Just one veggie at a time to make sure it didn't upset the stomach. Then as the baby grows you add a fruit to his meal. Then later add a meat. Before long that baby is a boy or girl and can eat all of it at once like we do. Well God's word was the same way, she said. Jesus always starts off with milk and adds to it each day as we eat the word. The meat being the most expensive and hardest to digest was always last. She said the meat of the word was more expensive because it came with signs and wonders and sometimes with much pain and suffering. If we grew and ate right each day we could handle the meat and the price that came with it and grow up strong. Develop in wisdom, knowledge and understanding that would carry us in any storm. But most people wanted just to get from God like eating the desert first and wonder why the body, bones and teeth rot out. When I asked what the meat of the word was. She would laugh and say, I knew you would go to the end of the road and work backwards Cowtail. Uncle Press would jump in with, well El what do you expect from a girl that was born backwards to start with? She has been backwards all her life and you can't change her. You and Henry are always teaching her but she always goes to the end of the road and work backwards. O a big huge laugh would roar from everyone and we all would dig in to eat while the food was still hot.

Breakfast was just as big and important as lunch and supper. We would laugh when we told them that some people ate dinner instead of supper. One of the four, Johnny, Uncle Press, Aunt Ellen or Daddy would say they were our rich family members that ate dinner. But around here we eat supper and you better sop up all you can eat because you won't come back to snack later. Roars of laugher would start and meals were eaten with much joy. Since we raised our meats, vegetables, fruits and food there was always plenty for us and anyone who stopped in at meal time. If they showed up before we sat down Aunt Ellen would asked them to stay and would throw another potato in the pot, she called it. But if we had already sat down then the children were to get up with their plates and make room for the guests. One guest meant the youngest child got up and up the line. Then they had to eat whatever we had which was always good enough for a king the guests would say.

Mealtimes are where we discussed the plans of the day, made plans, shared family, neighborhood, and church business. Money business was discussed after the kids went out to play. We always hoped they talked money business at lunch and supper because it was a break from work and chores and play time for us. Extra play time we called it.

Work was the important topic for all since we raised tobacco, wheat, corn, gardens, hogs, chickens, cows, orchards and whatever else that could grow and be sold. Farming was a big business and a family business where we shared it all. The household had to be ran and organized like a large corporation or there would have been total confusion. Aunt Ellen said confusion belonged to the devil and she wouldn't allow it in her home. Work was hard but also very joyous. Everyone would have spring fever they called it. They would be so happy we made it through the cold winter and could start planting. Every tree, plant and flower was smiling at us Aunt Ellen said. They were so happy to see the warm sun and our happy faces. What a God we serve Johnny would yell to the sky, to give us all our health to work another year together. To be alive and strong enough to drive a tractor Uncle Press would add. I use to watch and laugh my butt off at Johnny as he shouted to the sky talking to God as if God was deaf. He looked like some Indian Chief calling down rain. Daddy saying they were all crazy and he was going to the store. He got it and got in on the laughter like the rest of us but he just didn't like hard work, where they all thrived off of hard work. They would get so excited just to see a new plant come up on its own, like someone in the family just had a baby or something. It was shear madness for about a month around there and oh so much joy and laughter. So many long distance family members visited. Uncle Willie was always the first to arrive right before the sun came up with those beautiful daughters Aunt Ellen called them. Coming for spring just to see, enjoy, visit and be in on the preparation planning. Those that didn't show up the first week of spring we knew we would be going to check on them and see if we could help them get crops started.

That's another memory I love so much, visiting family, our family got together every month sometimes twice a month. Visiting family when they were sick were the greatest as we watched the family together caring for one another. Family came first and that meant all of the family, if one part hurt then all parts hurt they said. I can remember when Uncle Jesse took sick just one example of many. Every family member from Maryland to Florida packed up their automobiles and went to help. When each one got there it was as if they were at home and knew what they had to do. Here we would be standing off out of the way since we were the three last babies born in the Smith family. If we got in the way we were told by the nearest relative next to us to go and play. We knew when one spoke it meant all agreed and so we would obey quickly. One aunt would go in and get the clothes and start washing, while another would go in the cabinets and start making a list, asking Aunt Annie if she had such and such spice and so on. After the list was made it was assigned to one of the uncles to go get what was needed. Another aunt would start pulling down blankets, pillows, moving furniture around making room for cots and pallets for all the guests. One would be cleaning, another chopping wood and another getting it in. They moved like worker ants each knowing exactly what to do, laughing and talking all the while. The men and boys would be seeing about the crops and livestock. It was always a glorious time to watch our family helping each other. They never said 'call us if you need us.' My family was smart enough to know if one was sick there was work to be done and went to be a blessing. No one had to ask them or beg them. They loved with such a depth and knew God's word well enough to know when one part of the body hurt or was in lack all the other parts hurt and was in lack. To be a blessing was the greatest gift of all, they said. Aunt Ellen said if we didn't help those we could see, then God wasn't in us, especially your own family and community. I guess maybe that is one reason Shirley, Tommy or me never felt like we weren't as good as they were after Mama left. It just meant Henry needed his family a little longer I remember Aunt Annie telling us. And they helped with such grace and honor it made you feel like a king or queen to have been born into the Smith family or carry that name. Surely we watched the Bible applied every day. Not saying that all went perfect or no one lost their tempers or had bad days, they did like everyone else. They just didn't seem bad because so many people in the family helped to get right again.

I remember one time at Uncle Jesse's I wanted to hang out with Johnny and James. They were at the barn feeding the cattle and I could hear them laughing all the way to the house. I was told to watch Shirley and Tommy. I didn't want to watch Shirley and Tommy and keep them out of everyone's way. Aunt Ellen always said if you didn't keep Cowtail busy she would think up something to get into. Well she was right. I decided to watch Uncle Jesse sleep. I went around and leaned on Uncle Jesse's bed like I did Uncle Press's. Buttttttttt when that tall skinny man rose up with his eyes wide opened I got so scared I went running out the back door screaming. I can still see Aunt Virginia running after me and can still hear Aunt Annie yelling at Uncle Jesse, "What did you do to that baby, Jesse?"

I still laugh when I think about that day. He looked like a skeleton with big frog eyes, all snow faced white. But it also makes me sad because he went to the hospital a few months after that and died. He was so tall Uncle Press said they had to cut his legs off to fit him in the casket. He got chewed out for telling that big tale and upsetting me by all his sisters.

I never forgot Uncle Jesse. When I think of him now I still see my little small six year old to eight year old self walking beside that big tall man, looking up as he ever so gently held my hand going in the church or the Woodman of the World building. I can feel his strong hands wrapped around my waist as he picked me up and sat me on the church pew. "This is my Brother Henry's daughter. Tell the nice man hello, Carolyn Ann," all in one breathe, as he unwrinkled my dress. His smile was so big it reached from big ear to big ear. "Isn't she beautiful" he would ask the nice man.

Yep, she's a beauty alright, the nice man would say. Her daddy will have to beat the boys with a stick to keep them away. But Uncle Jesse would quickly jump in and say, no man better ever touch this baby or I will go to my grave a murderer. Some say he would have hurt somebody if he ever heard of a little girl being abused. Others said he looked just like Great-Granddad Alexander with his black hair and tall build. I never met my great-granddad Alexander because he died on September 25, 1881 from typhoid fever like daddy's oldest sister Leslie and her twins and his baby brother Roy. My Great granddad Alexander was only twenty-eight years old and was buried on one of the family farms at Ingham Virginia. He was married to Caroline Moore Smith. They had two sons my granddaddy Lawrence and Uncle Edward, whom I never met either. That was just a little of the family history my Aunt Ellen had taught me. She said looking at my Uncle Jesse was like looking at my great granddad. I knew my Uncle Jesse was a big man. When I visited Salem Christian Church to this very day all I have are very good memories of Uncle Jesse taking me with him to that church. That memory is imprinted in my mind with his loving touch. Uncle Jesse's youngest son James kept up the tradition by asking me to come and go with him to the same church. He seemed just as proud of me being there as his daddy ever was. He called me Ugly since his daddy called me his Pretty Little Girl.

Joy was one of the greatest gifts I guess you could say the Smith family had for they seem to always have a good attitude. They could find good in everything and look for good even in the worst people. Daddy would say, El, he's rotten to the core. Why don't you just give up on him? Trying to get Aunt Ellen to stop helping whoever it was at that time. But she would smile at him and say, now Henry, you know we found good in you, and just laugh and laugh. Daddy would shake his head, take a sip of coffee, and then laugh with her. I felt Aunt Ellen was mama to Daddy just as much as she was to us. He was only thirteen when his daddy and mama passed. As the story went they said Daddy lived with Uncle Jesse awhile and while there he and my cousin Jesse Jr. became the best of friends. I think they were closer the same age and daddy would take him with him most of the time. Jesse Jr. even now tells us stories about Daddy and we sit and listen for every detail. He told Daddy one day if he gave up that casual beer and camel cigarettes he would be a perfect man. Daddy would reply there's only one perfect man the rest of us would have to die and go to heaven to get that perfection. They would laugh and laugh as they went down memory lane of the things they did together. Then Daddy would move to Uncle Press and Aunt Ellen's where he and Johnny became the best of friends and played and went out together. One story when he lived with Aunt Mae and Uncle Sam who owned a funeral home business and they lived in the apartment over the funeral home, they said to keep Daddy from going downstairs at night, knowing he had a curiosity spirit Uncle Sam would tell him to stay away because the dead would be up and walking around. They said Daddy went down one night and being afraid to turn a light on he went in the one room that had a small lamp burning. The next thing they were awakened by his screams. They jumped up and ran down stairs and there Daddy stood frozen in his tracks right in front of a dead body on a slant. They said they laughed so hard tears ran like pouring rain off a tin roof. He swore to them that body was alive because he sat up and then fell back down and his arms fell off the bed. He didn't do it. Uncle Sam said he never told Henry it was reflexes and Henry never went back down stairs again. But they learned later he had written Virginia to come and get him from those dead people. Then he moved with Aunt Virginia in Maryland awhile where he enjoyed the city life until he joined the army at age seventeen, lying about his age. The army wasn't checking birth certificates at that time because they needed as many men as they could get to fight World War II. The story was told when he stopped getting his way at one place he moved on to another place they said. With Daddy being the baby in the family I'm sure he was spoiled and loved ever so dearly. Many of the family members said Daddy was never one to complain but happy all the time. Uncle Jesse said Henry was lazy just like Jesse Jr. They didn't like farming or getting dirty so God had to give them a brain or they would have staved to death. Daddy never admitted it or denied it but just laughed until he cried along with them. Daddy was the baby that we knew for sure and was spoiled by the whole family. He was more Jesse Jr's and Johnny's age than he was to his brothers and sisters. All the cousins loved their Uncle Henry and they have so many stories they share at every reunion of Daddy's young years. Daddy just sat and let them talk and laughed right along with them. . All of them knew better than to tell something bad about him or they would have to battle with Aunt Virginia. Like one time, they said, Daddy got drunk and Aunt Virginia jumped in and said he wasn't drunk, he had high blood pressure. Everyone laughed and when we asked which it was, they said the way Aunt Virginia remembered it. All of my generation said Daddy was a good boy and man there really wasn't any bad stories to tell. Even to this day they brag on Daddy and it makes us so proud to be his children. Daddy saw life like a big adventure and thought there was a good lesson in everything, a hint to learn how to live better. He didn't believe we made mistakes unless we just didn't learn the lessons from it. Then the mistake was not learning the lesson and having to keep climbing that fools mountain over and over.

Another trait I loved about the Smith's. They honored their elders. They would never tell an elder to shut up or sit and allow one to stand. They took that Bible commandment serious, "Honor your father and mother that you be blessed." You could feel that honor too. Now a days when I hear or see a young person tell an elder to shut up it makes my skin crawl. If they only knew how ignorant and foolish they sound and look they would stop all that disrespect. Daddy said they were cheating themselves of blessings by not respecting their elders. Children especially that didn't help their parents or grandparents, aunts and uncles were only cheating themselves of wisdom and Godly blessings. He believed one of the worst sins a person could do was talk back, be disrespectful of their parents or talk bad about them. I have one memory of telling Daddy to shut up. I thought I had lost my teeth after he slapped me in it. It hurt my feelings just as bad and I ran down the road to run away. He sent Tommy to catch me and stop me. I ran faster because I thought Daddy was going to beat me to death. Something he never did but I hadn't made him that mad before either. But all he wanted to do was to explain why he slapped me. Rest assured I never forgot that lesson. Just to be slapped by him and then see him cry afterwards as he explained why it was so disrespectful, bad habit that never needed to take root in me, he said as he wiped his tears away.

Whatever you do, do it with a cheerful heart, was one rule the entire Smith family lived by. If they got mad, they didn't stay mad, they confronted the person they were mad at, not talk bad about them. They firmly believed no one was perfect and all were to be forgiven. If Jesus could hang on a cross after he was beaten and nails driven in his hands and feet and say, *"Father, forgive them for they know not what they do,"* then we certainly could forgive others. Sometimes when all gathered after they had voted in their state at the home house to watch the election, fellowship and fussing, as to whom the next president would be, you would think a bad fight would break out any moment. They would be up in each others faces screaming and turning red one minute and getting coffee and cake the next. But you never felt anything but loving energy in the room, that told us they weren't mad but having fun together. They made us go to bed around ten but they stayed up until the race was called. Then they would get in that kitchen and fix a celebration feasts. They found joy in everything from sweeping the yard to killing hogs.

Killing hogs, boy that was an experience of joy and work combined. It was always like homecoming around there with family and neighbors. Standing on the sidelines again and taking it all in from a child's viewpoint, there is nothing to compare those days too. I would run in the house behind the men carrying the meat and watch them give it to the women. Then stand around and watch the women cut it up and listen to them talk. Aunt Ellen told them that I was so curious I kept up with everyone in the family. She said I was the walking information book. She believed I would grow up and be a news reporter or lawyer one. She had never seen a child so hungry for knowledge and every subject excited me, she would say. I wouldn't stand and listen to them talk about me long. I didn't like them talking about me. I would run back out to the fence with Tommy and Shirley.

This one particular day I ran out right behind Johnny to meet the men coming to help kill hogs. Johnny said, "Carolyn Ann, go in the house with Mama. I replied no. I'm watching them kill those pigs today. He looked at me so mean and said, ok come on big stuff, and let's kill hogs and we kept walking. Any other time when I told him no, he would have picked me up like a sack of potatoes and threw me over his shoulders and carried me in the house and told

Aunt Ellen to keep me inside. But not today, he was gonna let me be one of the boys today.

Sitting on that fence with Tommy and Clarence I can hear Aunt Ellen yelling from the back door, "COWTAIL, come to the house." But I yelled back, "No! Johnny said I could stay and watch them kill the hogs." She went back in the house slowly like she didn't like that answer. I didn't know what that meant from the look on her face. A few minutes later I saw her coming out of the door and headed over to Uncle Press. They spoke and she turned and went back in the house. I breathed then a sign of relief and knew I would get to watch. I turned back around to watch the men tag the hogs feeling real good about myself. I asked Clarence why they did that. He said to know which hogs to kill. If they killed the wrong hogs Mr. Smith would probably kill them, talking about Uncle Press.

Talking kid talk and whispering while we waited on the fence for we knew if we got to loud or got in the way at all we would be sent in the house to stay. A few minutes later I saw Shirley coming down the hill. I yelled, go back in the house. You are too small to see this. She gave me a mean look and said shut up. You ain't my boss. Aunt Ellen said I could watch if you could watch, as she climbed up on the fence, I can watch. Reaching to help her and saying you better not fall. If you fall and I get a whipping I will beat you up. Shut up she said again as she reached to hold onto Clarence's arm. She knew I had to keep Tommy from falling off and reached to push him so I would get a whipping. I pushed her back and she yelled. I said shut up before we all have to go in the house. I hate you. You have to do everything I do. Why can't you stay in the house? But she just sat there laughing and saying I have a secret. We all wanted to know what the secret was but the men were coming and we had to be very quiet.

We watched in silence as Johnny and the rest of the men came with chains ready to hang up the hogs. When they stepped inside the hog pen Johnny asked them if they were ready. Ready one said. Uncle Press said, aim, fire. The guns went off as I held my ears. I saw Shirley and Tommy out of the corner of my eye laughing and didn't even have their ears covered up. Some of the men were shooting the hogs and others were reaching for them before they hit the ground. They couldn't touch the ground they would get dirty. I heard that hog squeal once before the man caught him and cut his throat. The blood poured and that's all I remembered. The next thing I saw was me lying in Aunt Ellen's lap and she had a big smile on her face as she fanned me. Shirley was laughing because I fell off of the fence as she told me what happened. Tommy laughing and said I looked like I had seen a ghost. Clarence right in my face looking at me saying, you al right, as he started tickling me so I would laugh.

I pushed them back and got up. Shirley said she is al right. She's still mean. Aunt Ellen was laughing right along with them asking if I had learned my lesson. They said when that blood poured from that hog I turned snow white and fell off the fence. I landed right on my back and Shirley Mae went to screaming. Then they said Johnny ran up the hill, picked me up in his arms and ran with me in the house screaming for Mama. They said Johnny's face was white too and Uncle Press went to fussing at him when he got back. He said, Johnny you knew better than to tell that baby she could watch. Now you have put us behind. But George the old black man, said, that's all right Mr. Smith. We'll stay as long as its takes and not charge you any more. Just glad that little girl is alright. Then they went back to talking and laughing and killed the rest of them hogs, Clarence said.

I said, "Is Johnny mad at me?" Clarence said he didn't know but Tommy said he didn't think so. But maybe I had better stay out of sight for awhile. Well I didn't want to be in the house where the women were cutting up the meat because my belly felt shaky and sick. I didn't want to ever see blood again. I just went to the formal living room and sat and looked at picture albums alone. I just wanted to hide and I wanted that funny feeling in my stomach to go away. I knew I would never hear the end of that. Besides if Johnny was mad at me it meant I couldn't go with him that night or to Henry's Mill after church on Sunday one or the other or both. Johnny could hold a grudge for days when you made him really mad. I was afraid I scared him since they said he was white as a ghost and that was worst than making him mad. I stayed in there hating myself for fainting and scaring everyone.

I guess an hour went by when Aunt Ellen walked through the door. She sat down and asked me what I was looking at. When I showed her she began telling me a story about the picture. She said this man right here is a very good friend of hers. He was in love with her and wanted to marry her a long time ago. They met in college. He was very wealthy and lived in a huge house down on 360 like we go to Uncle Jesse's. She said one day I'll show you. But for now you need to keep my secret and come and wash up. I started putting the book away and added, they are gonna tease me, aren't they? Why did I black out Aunt El? She smiled as she placed her arm around my shoulder and we walked towards the door. Because Carolyn Ann, she said, you are sensitive to all living creatures. That's because you see spirits as much as you do their bodies. You should know those hog's spirits went to a better place and gave us their physical bodies to eat and enjoy. You are so smart, strong and brave most of the time. You look after Shirley Mae and Tommy and help us with work and do it cheerfully. You do real good in school and sometimes people get jealous when they see that God has given so many gifts to just one little girl. They have all those gifts inside also but just don't use them. They don't mean anything by it. It's just their way of showing you they love you. Come on now lets stop crying and feeling sorry for ourselves and let's show them how brave you really are. You take their teasing with a cheerful heart okay. Show them how brave and strong you really are. By the time we were out in the hall and almost at the hall door leading into the den I stopped and looked up, "Aunt El is Johnny mad at me?" She laughed and said, "No, he's not mad at you. He came in a few minutes after you ran out and hid just to see about you. You know he is just a big teddy bear. You will have him wrapped around your little finger before the sun goes down.

We walked through the door and everyone sat at the table, waiting for us so we could eat. Johnny was the first one that spoke, "Here comes that big tomboy Cowtail, who can't stand blood. Now your name is Baby tomboy Cowtail."

I came back at him, "I can so. You're just jealous because I'm smarter than you. Johnny said, "Well come on up here smarty pants and let's eat," helping me in my chair beside him. I knew then he wasn't mad. They all knew Aunt Ellen had given me a pep talk and that's why they didn't argue with me or disagree. They acted like they were glad I was alright. And that subject was closed and they moved on to how much meat they had for winter and how much they had to sell.

It was a year or so later when I thought I had matured enough to hang with the boys again and watch them skin a deer. I saw the hunters flying down the road as the red dust was roaring through the air. One truck behind another flying meant a big kill. Aunt Ellen was taking her apron off as she headed for the back door with all smiles and me already ahead of her. She got just as excited as the hunters did about a kill. It was like Christmas morning around there with everyone getting their favorite gift. She hung in there with those men as they told their hunting tales and laughed right along. One question would start each story and the part each one played in it. Spirits were soaring high. The air filled with so much joy and excitement it was electric. Before we left the barn we knew who killed what. How many shots were fired? Where they were and where all the rest of the hunters were. We knew what was said on the radios and down to who missed their shot and lost their shirt. After about an hour of glory and praise time it was time to prepare the meat and feed up or look for dogs that hadn't made it back to the house by then. Aunt Ellen knew exactly when to say let us ladies go to the house and get these hungry men something to eat. All the ladies that hung around and disobeyed well the men knew exactly what to do. They would start cussing. If they didn't leave well we knew the men saw them as no lady because we heard about that later after all the hunters had left. Smith men liked their men time where they could talk freely and didn't care for women who hung around to be one of the boys.

This hunting day there was only one deer left to clean and Johnny and Uncle Press hanging around. They had already gutted and divided the other deer and the other hunters had left when a hunter rolled in late with a last minute kill. I asked if I could stay. I was around thirteen at the time and Johnny asked if I thought I could handle it. I replied I wanted to try so they let me. Johnny had the knife in his hand as he looked back, you ready Cowtail, he said. I said, ready. He cut and the blood poured out and I hit the ground. I heard him say, damn it, as he ran to catch me. Needless to say that was the very last time I ever stood around to watch them kill or clean or do anything with blood again. Aunt Ellen was right. I was too sensitive to watch anything killed or abused.

Surrounded by love, we were surrounded by so much goodness and plenty we didn't notice the dirt on the floor we had tracked in. We never noticed the dirty clothes piled up in the hall waiting for Aunt Ellen to catch a minute to wash. We never heard anyone fussing about dirty clothes or who was going to clean house today. Sure the house and all that was important we all pitched in and helped. When guests were coming, or an illness or whatever, we all pitched in to help more but never any fussing. The house was always filled with love and joy. Always time to stop and read the Bible when troubled in soul. We have talked about it over the years and at every family reunion how we were always the important thing in that house. Family each person was important and had a job to do. Not the house or the stuff.

How Aunt Ellen found time for it all we still ask ourselves. She certainly was a super woman. Not too many women could keep up with her even in today's times. Most women loved her or were jealous of her. Some that did complain about the dirt on the floors we tracked in or other kids had tracked in found out why it was there. She thought consoling a wounded soul or fixing a broken heart or repairing a sick body was far more important than a clean floor. If she had time she swept the floor but if it meant time away from a lost or hurting soul well it just had to wait. She believed in joy, peace and love and lived by that motto. Her quiet gentle spirit as she hummed her prayers and songs lingered in the air. She was more than just a wife. She was more than just a mama. She was more than just an aunt or in-law or friend. We keep her with us with every story we share about her. There's not one thing I can do in my own home or with my own children that she wasn't the one who took the time to teach me and taught with such patience. If I sew a button on or make a dress I have every happy memory of us sitting at her old Singer sewing machine, she the teacher and me the student. If I cook a meal she is there smiling.

I remember the times when we would spend all day cleaning and putting down new tile in that old kitchen. By the end of the day Clarence and Tommy or someone had come in with a sting of big fish all bloody and just slapped them down on her new tablecloth with the blood dripping off on her new tile floor. She never said a word. When I did say something, she corrected me by saying, "Cowtail, be thankful. God has blessed us with a nice catch of fish for supper and plenty left over for another day if company doesn't drop in for supper." I would get mad at her and tell her she needed to stand up to those men and just tell them off. But she never listened to me. She just smiled and went on in her humble self. Love never offends she would say as she cleaned the catch and wiped up the blood.

I didn't understand that kind of love. At times I thought she just allowed everyone to walk all over her and show her no respect. But as time and years passed I learned she was living in living patience. The soul of a person was far more important to her than who got credit or who was right or how clean a floor was. Her soul had peace with God many years ago and she bathed in living patience every day. In all my years with Aunt Ellen I never saw her mad or even raise her voice in anger to anyone. I saw her cry and it always made me cry. I never heard her complain about anything. She would say, 'let's count our blessings and see if we have anything to complain to God about.' She had found the secret place in God and that's where she lived every day. She said she wasn't always that way. With much practice and waiting on God to get her in the right attitude or the right frame of mind she learned all really is well with God. That God would take care of anything or anyone we surrendered to him. She said reading the Bible daily is like going out to the stable every day and picking up a baby calf. You don't notice the calf is growing a little each day. It's just as easy to pick him up at a hundred pounds as it was at ten pounds. One day someone says that cow weights six hundred pounds and you pick him up like he weights ten pounds. Then you realize how strong you've become just by practicing every day. She added, it takes more strength and courage to be nice when someone is rude than it does to allow ego to blow up and say ugly things that hurts a soul for a lifetime. You can catch more flies with honey than with vinegar. Always remember God is listening, seeing and feeling. Every second of every waking day we have a choice to make to allow good to reign or evil.

The Cousin - Brothers Picture

Johnny, James Virgil Smith on Aunt Ellen's Porch.
Not Pictured is Jesse Jr.
They made themselves her Big brothers and protectors.

Chapter 6:

The Secret Room

The Secret Power
Psalms 91

The only room in Aunt Ellen's house that we weren't allowed was the formal living room. I can still see us running in that front door, down that long hall and out of the back door as we brushed by Aunt Ellen smiling. She loved the laughter of children. I hear the doors slamming. See the dirt flying as we dashed off that back porch to see who could make it back around to that big front porch where so many children had played. I can see Aunt Ellen in that kitchen either cooking a meal or baking a desert for the next meal. Sometimes making a special desert for someone coming to visit, she loved making people feel special when they dropped by. A special desert meant that person's favorite and if she knew in advance that person was coming they got their favorite every time.

Even now at every reunion we can feel her spirit all through that house. I can feel her smiling when the little kids are running through those halls and my mind floods with happy days gone by. A certain dish warming in the oven or someone brushing by me I think it's her. Peggy one of our cousins can feel her also and we share memories every year. We look forward to the reunions every year just to see whose spirit we will feel. As the years pasted the reunions have become more special for us who have gotten older because of it. It's a good thing most of the time to have the gift of discerning spirits. Whenever the house is full of peace we know Aunt Ellen is there. So many wonderful secrets and joys in our family. In today's generation it seems to be a lost art.

Aunt Ellen touched so many hearts and was mama to so many children in her life time it sounds almost like a fairy tale to tell her story. I still miss her every day and can only share small portions of her life in each book that I write.

But this secret room was our place. A place we could pour our hearts out and talk about God's secrets from the Bible. She loved talking about God, and I believe her deep love for God is what she transmitted into me. I loved listening to her tell me Bible stories and read from her big Bible. Maybe that's why we connected with such intimacy. Maybe that's why I discipline myself each day hoping to do better and bring God more glory than the day before. Inch upon inch, day upon day she was consistent in her love and faithfulness to God and family. Some days I feel I disappoint her so bad I just want to run and hide. Some days I wish she was still in that big house where we could go in the secret room and talk with God together. Some days I feel so rotten and such a failure just to hear her say, it's okay. We'll try again tomorrow. It may have been a secret place for all the kids that lived there one time or another for all I know. If so, she kept it a secret. It has so many wonderful warm loving feelings in it that I don't really care if there were. Her formal living room was the first room to the left as you walked in her front door. The door was always shut and we all knew it was off limits. Johnny use to tease her and say, Mama saves that room for her rich family, salesmen, snobs and rich friends. Aunt Ellen would laugh at him but didn't deny it. It was her sacred holy ground. I always felt she could feel her ancestors and God in that room. She never said yea or nay.

One day while running through the house I decided to hide in the secret room. I knew they would never find me because they were too afraid to enter in. Johnny had told us all that the last time a dirty little kid went in there they couldn't walk for a week. When his Mama finished tanning his behind it was red hot like the burners on her stove. That boy said his behind burned for a week and he never went in there again. Of course Johnny could make us all afraid with his big muscular self, acting out all the roars and screams. . Well I guess you have figured it out by now that I was the curious kid. I had to test every story and everything to see if it was truth or not. Aunt Ellen knew quite well what she was dealing with when she taught me. I guess she had already figured me out too when she heard me screaming from her bedroom one day. Their bedroom was another room that was off limits to kids. She came running in one day as the dresser was tilting over on top of me and caught it just in time. After she got it sat up and checked me out she asked what I was doing. I told her I was going through her drawers to see what I could find. She laughed and asked me if I understood that her bedroom was off limits to everyone but her and Press. I answered I did but I wanted to see what was in the top drawer, like that was more important than obeying her. She went and got a chair and sat it right in front of the old dresser. Then she told me to stand on it as she pulled opened the drawer. She said now Cowtail look all you want while I fold these clothes. She sat down on the side of the bed and folded clothes quietly and calmly while I rambled through her stuff asking questions. What that was and who gave her that. What do you call that and why did you keep that? I guess we were in there an hour or so. When I finished rambling and had satisfied my curiosity she said it was time for me to get paid for my rambling. She said that every disobedient act carried a consequence like every obedient act carried a reward. God had set the rules up that way before he created male and female. She led me out into the hall where she had pulled out all the dirty clothes and had separated them. She said now Cowtail for rambling through Aunt El's drawers you now have the pleasure of rambling through these clothes and washing them, hanging them out, and getting them in. I just said okay and went to work. It was worth it to look in her dresser and be in her bedroom. I had a secret the other kids didn't have. I don't think she thought I would react that way by the surprised look on her face. But I felt it was worth it and felt good to step out in courage as she put it. Aunt Ellen said I was a born leader and it was her job to teach me how to lead properly.

Well back to the formal living room after Clarence and them had went and told Aunt Ellen they couldn't find me she told them to go play and let her look awhile. At least that's what they told me. I was busy looking in an old book when she quietly opened the door and stood there. When she spoke I almost jumped out of my skin. Yeap I knew I was caught. She smiled and asked me what I was looking at. Just an old book I replied. Then she asked if I would like to know something about that old book. I got excited for I knew story time was coming and answered yes. She walked over and sat down and began explaining each picture in the book and then pointed to a picture on the wall and told me something about that person. That history lesson lasted about an hour before she asked if I would like to help her fix supper. I looked up and asked, "Aunt Ellen, are you going to whip my behind red hot or make me work?

She smiled and said no. We will keep this our little secret. If you don't tell where you were and don't tell anyone that you didn't get a red hot whipping on that behind, I will forget about it. I agreed.

Every week after that, we would sneak off and go into the secret room. Our special time together as she taught that we were on earth to develop God's character and nature and Jesus was our example to follow. She taught a family history lesson also. If we had any bad people in our blood line she never mentioned them. By the time I had moved from her home I knew every piece of furniture, which made it and what type of wood it was. I learned during the depression some people were so poor they lost all their valuables and land. That to own one sewing needle you were considered rich. My Great-grandmother Caroline owned several gold sewing needles and many other types that were used for quilting and such. That every quilt we slept under one of my grandmothers had made it and she kept them all for us. I knew about every picture on the wall and who they were and who had painted them. She had one piece of furniture in there that I loved. It was an oak chair table with a soft piece of black leather for your behind. One way you folded it, it became a chair and when you folded it another way it became a table with a place to hold books. It was so big Aunt Ellen and I could sit in it with plenty of room left over. It looked like a throne chair to me. One day after asking her about that neat chair she pulled out a real old book, brushed the dust off of it and said, come and sit with me. She opened it very slowly and carefully wiped off each page with a cheese cloth she had in her apron pocket. I could tell by the way she handled it that it and that chair was special to her. I just had to find out why. What were the secrets hidden in that old book and chair? With every page she pointed to a picture and told me a story. Then she would close the book and say it was time to fix supper or lunch or go work the garden or whatever, like she had a built in clock that just told her when the hour was up. I would beg her to tell me more but she would say I would have to wait until another day and keep our secret place a secret. The contents had to remain a secret as well. A room of mysteries is what it was to a curious minded little girl. Aunt Ellen said by practicing each day to keep our secrets was building trust in us.

One day while in our secret place she decided to tell her most intimate secret. She told me about the book and the chair and why it meant so much to her. I could see her voice was sad. She didn't have the smile from her heart that usually boiled over into me but more of a deep soul hurt. Her heart was heavy and burdened as she shared with me that day. Feelings poured out of her that I hadn't seen before. Like her well was overflowing and she needed someone to catch her before she fell. She shared many secrets about herself when she was a young girl. She told me just how wealthy and powerful her family really was. She said she was giving me deep secrets because she felt she could trust me with them and respect them. When I asked her what did she mean by respect them, she answered by not adding to them nor taking away from them.

She shared her history with Gov Bill Tuck and how he fit into her life. Then she told me about a very gentle caring man Senator Howard P. Anderson. She said he was one of the finest men she had ever known. He and his wife were some fine people. She said they were making a difference in this life because they chose to follow Christ's character and nature. That she was sharing stories about them to show me good people to look up too and follow. Being good to people makes you feel like you are in heaven. Anytime we need to feel heaven all we had to do was think of a good thought and do something for someone else.

In tears she continued that day and said she felt some people thought she had wasted her education. She said she knew some people looked at her and figured she was a failure. That she wasted all her wealth and just enjoyed life and maybe they were right. She began to cry deeper and added that she had no regrets. Maybe one of those little children she took in and trained would be president or win more souls to God than a thousand she would've taught in school. When I asked her why the Smith's were so important to her that she would give up her wealthy family for us? She hugged me very tight and said it was the magic in the whole family. She said I wish you all had known your grandparents. Cowtail they had so much love it poured out into everyone that came in their presence. She said they welcomed her in the family and treated her better than she had ever been treated. She added that they made her feel special and loved. That some people only cared about money and how much more money they could make. And there wasn't anything wrong with money or having abundance. That money was only an earthly tool to be used for good to help yourself and others. Of course the more money you have the more you can bless. That Jesus became poor so we could be rich. That prosperity was inside all of us and we were to draw it out and use it. Just don't allow money to become your god and make you greedy. Careers and money were all some people loved. Big houses and as many acres of land they could buy. It was never enough, never enough when gotten in greed and selfishness. She dried her eyes and said Mr. and Mrs. Smith were two of the most generous people she had ever known.

She said she wanted me to see that there was more to life than just a farm, or money or stuff. She took me to meet some fine business men and their families who had a love for God, family and country. Then she said there were many businessmen who were as honest as the day is long. She wanted me to pattern my life after such a pattern. To chase after money is a waste of God's time. She said real wealth is in the heart.

She told me about Uncle Press being in WWII like my daddy and how hard it was for everyone. She shared the lost of her baby girl. How she had rented out the upstairs to women that needed a place to live during the war and that was why the upstairs was built like apartments. She said big houses should be full of people working together. She said she was in that big house all alone when Johnny was a baby and she got lonely. Helping people filled her days and nights until Press came home. Some people had turned their nose up at her for doing that. She said Mrs. Smith, your grandmother, said I was learning the secret of real wealth.

Before we knew it an hour had passed but I could tell Aunt Ellen was in no hurry that day. She continued sharing about her past. That day my Aunt Ellen shared a lot and all of it made me sad. She said maybe one day she would have a grandchild as curious about God and history as I was and how we could predict the future just by knowing history.

She said she could come in this room and tell God anything. If those walls could talk they would reveal many years of secrets, some good and then she laughed and some not so good. She asked me if I knew that my grandmother had slept in that room as well as my great-grandmother. Some days there would be wall to wall people in this big old house. Children running all through it and yelling, men making plans and even some war plans have been decided between these walls. She said she was only thirteen when she took over the construction of that old house and had it finished. You should have known my daddy, Carolyn Ann. He was one fine builder and businessman. He built most of this house. But then he died and I had to live with two aunts. They loved me and were very good but strict. That's when I lived over at that other huge house, the one you call a haunted mansion. I lived in that house when I met your Uncle Press and his family who lived over here on this farm. We had everything. I even had someone to bathe, dress and fix my hair as a child. Maids did all the house work. Workers did all the farm work. Yardmen's did the gardens and yards. Cooks cooked the meals. We had it all, all but love. I couldn't feel any love in that house even though I know they all loved me. That house didn't feel warm like your grandmother's. Just no love at all as her voice lowered to an almost silence as she thought out loud. When I came over here to this house, to Mrs. Smith's, there it was. It was always everywhere. Love bounced off of these walls. And laughter, there was so much laughter it felt like these old walls shook love out.

When I went to school we had to wear uniforms she said. I hated those uniforms and all the strict rules. The stricter they were on me the more I rebelled. I guess that's why I understand you so well, as she laughed and patted my knee. Then I asked the magical question. Aunt Ellen is that why I feel like I am in the presence of royalty when I am with you? She laughed so hard, then got up and said, "Girl, let's go fix some supper." As she closed the old book and gently pushed me to get up.

At the door she turned and looked back and asked if I was ready to leave all our secrets here in this room safe with God, and our ancestors to keep safe until we returned. Are you ready, she said? Then she would open the door and the questions stopped unless we were alone in the house. Some days I felt I was the little girl she longed for in her heart.

In our secret room Aunt Ellen shared many happy memories as we walked together down memory lane with our ancestors and friends. She said Mrs. Smith held the key to all the riches in the world and I was like her in so many ways. Which Mrs. Smith she was talking about I don't know. Both Mrs. Alexander Smith (Caroline) and Mrs. Lawrence Smith (Leila) lived in that house at one time or another. Aunt Ellen never bragged about her wealthy family or family ties. As far as I know she never used them for favors either. I learned she and my Daddy were more alike than they even realized when it came to family values and truth. I learned titles didn't mean anything unless they were given by God and used for God's work. Money and assets meant nothing unless they were used to further and better the lives of the whole family, community and country. Daddy and Aunt Ellen had many friendships and connections with some powerful people but they were to never be used in name or deed to further anyone's selfish desires alone. Have you figured out the secret in that room that carried her and Daddy all their life with such joy yet?

Years later, some of those secrets and secret friends helped me from time to time. I remember trips to the court house researching deeds and working on a pet project of my own. One project some young people with an old fashion dream turned on some of the wisest and most powerful minds in Halifax County. I enjoyed seeing Aunt Ellen's friends get excited about our generation. None of them wanted any credit. They just got fired up to see a group of young people wanting to hold onto roots and work together like the good old days. *Where two or more are gathered together in peace there I am in the midst of them.* Many trips to that old historic court house were met with important people who would slip a note into my hand. The trips to the lake houses and cookouts that gave me so many leads, showing me how to get around a block in the road by some wannabes, they would laugh and say, with me remembering that word so well used in our family and its meaning. Sometimes just a quiet walk at Stanton River State park was all I needed or a late night phone call at my place of employment to pass an important code or something right before the morning meeting that would have shot it down without that little bit of info.

I have so many memories of some very important people in our great state, all because of my Aunt Ellen and My Daddy. Every time I visit a certain eating place in our little Halifax town I can't help but look up on the wall and smile at a certain picture. Just seeing that picture brings the memories that cause the smile that warms my heart and soul. When I visit the South Boston Museum and see our history there's so many memories that Aunt Ellen and Daddy can take credit for but never would. Just knowing Smile, you might enter the Most High Secret Place before you lie down to sleep tonight.

One day after Aunt Ellen had been long gone to heaven, I was at the court house researching a deed when an old friend walked up and rubbed shoulders with me. That day I felt if I was ever going to ask why they all wanted to remain a secret I had better ask now. Neither of us were getting any younger I laughed and told him. Knowing that would cause his face to fill up with a big soft smile and turn red because he never knew what I might ask him. His answer burned in my heart even to this day. He said, "*Carolyn Ann, every good deed, every good friend, and every good decision made from love is an eternal one. Not one to be shared because there is no one worthy enough to have the credit. Those are the true riches, the real titles, and the most important decisions. Your Dad and Aunt El knew that. That's the true difference we make in this world if given a chance. Those we take with us forever.*" Then he placed his right arm around my waist with his reassuring hug to stop my tears as he leaned in close and kissed my left cheek. Then he said I saw you when you walked in the court house by accident. Here's a little note to remember me by. Then he placed a tiny piece of paper in my left hand. I was surprised for I had not asked for anything but he held my hand close as he whispered in my ear, "*the help you gave those young people on that farm will go down in Virginia history. I am proud of you young lady and I bet El and Henry are too. Follow your dreams and visions for God has many secrets for those who will seek them out and believe strong enough to carry them out. And the greatest secret of all is that most people won't get it. You did it all out of love, not for profit and it confused the hell out of those selfish bastards.*" With a strong laugh he walked away as slowly and quietly as he had entered and never looked back. I carefully looked at his note close to me so no one could see it. There scribbled on a tiny corner of what looked like a note pad, *I love you. I am proud of you too.*" It wasn't long after that he went home to heaven.

Those that knew him will have their own special secrets, words of wisdom, and golden nuggets. Who it was wasn't important. But who he honored was most important. With every step, every decision his motive was to bring glory to his God and make this country a better place for future generations. He did that by honoring his God, his family, his friends and his country.

That famous Virginia man loved selfish people too. He would say something like this, *I love selfish people because all they talk about is self. They honor only self and love only self. They do very little to help anyone unless there are strings attached. They are very impatient people which make it easy to get them to wheel and deal. They are the first to tell an elder full of wisdom to shut up, so they can have the glory light, and the last to get the greatest secret of all time, if they ever do. Don't try to fit in. You were born to stand out. Follow your dreams and visions and tell the world some day what a blessing they missed out on if they didn't take the time to know you, he said.*

There was one thing Daddy and Aunt Ellen didn't always agree upon, work. Daddy was a business man. He owned and operated country stores. He tried his hand at a small hotdog stand restaurant, a car wash and a few other adventures but his love was a store. Aunt Ellen ran a large farm, house, and family. Johnny said she had a children's business and they ran the farm. But I saw who they came after when they were interested in any type of investments. Daddy said Aunt Ellen had the most important job and that was keeping every one straight. They both believed work was a gift from God and should be appreciated. Both said work without joy was hell on earth. Daddy would add a fool couldn't find joy if it was under his nose. When we ask what hell was? Daddy said its working without joy and with someone without love and doesn't know the meaning of peace. Aunt Ellen would say, "Henry, shut your mouth before you confuse those kids." To late we were already confused.

Daddy fixed that by handing us a persimmon and a peach and told us to take a bite. Tommy and Shirley were too chicken so I bit into the persimmon and it turned my mouth inside out. It was awful. I spit and spit. I ate two sweet peaches and it was still awful. Daddy, Aunt Ellen, Shirley and Tommy were crying from laughing and I was crying from my mouth being turned inside out and tasting awful. Shirley and Tommy were dancing around and around, laughing so hard, and clapping their hands, while I fussed and cried. I got madder and madder. I bet fifteen minutes went by and my mouth was still turned inside out from that thing. The more they laughed the madder I got until I pouted and stomped off, screaming at them. I could still hear them laughing and I heard Aunt Ellen tell daddy that was cruel, Henry. You should be ashamed of yourself. But I knew he wasn't.

Aunt Ellen came out on the porch and sat in the swing beside me and tried to cheer me up. "Cowtail, what have I told you about that curiosity spirit? But I have to admit, it was a good lesson for you. One you won't ever forget. And your Daddy is right. Hell is full of bitterness, hate, turmoil and strife just like that persimmon made you feel and taste. See, some people are persimmons and some are like those peaches. They look pretty and sweet on the outside but when you bite into them they are full of bitterness and hate. Once you got it in your mouth, you couldn't get rid of that bitterness to easy, could you? It took a whole lot of sweetness to get that awful taste out of your mouth. In time you will forget the taste but not the experience. But look at the peach. If you had taken the time to examine the peach, you would have discovered its fury coat, its sweet smell and soft heart. But you chose the first thing that was offered to you. It just happened to be the bitterness.

I asked how do you bite a person and get away with it. She said, a person comes along, acts and looks so sweet on the outside. After much investigation you find what looked good and smelled good on the outside turned out to be a persimmon on the inside. Those persimmons are only having one motive, what you can do for them.

To this day I remember the lesson on heaven and hell every time I see a peach or persimmon. I remember it when I meet a person out in public acting so sweet and nice yet at home they act like the devil in the flesh. As I grew and developed in life, every lesson became clearer. All the cute little sayings began to make sense as I saw how people lived and made decisions and examined myself. I realized my life had been greatly enriched by their wisdom they so freely gave. They didn't see a child but a soul, a gift from God. As I began to understand just how much they truly loved me, how they had used their precious time to teach and transform a young soul that had crossed their path I became more appreciative of my childhood. As we move forward to the years of marriage and our own family we understand the sacrifices good parents make for their children.

I look at the present generation and see many Godly and family values dishonored. I wonder what good did we do giving our children a better education? So many take that education and waste it by choosing to live in the sinful nature. As I see the local news and all the problems we face today after Bible was taken out of our schools and discipline taken from parents. I witness young men in churches telling someone his mother's age to shut up or hear a teen telling a parent what to do. When I see our youth on welfare with no desire to better themselves or this country I wonder how long God will allow it to continue. I have visited many churches that deny the power of the resurrection and losing their youth to drugs. Churches that don't even believe or teach the gifts of the Holy Spirit yet taking the money and building bigger buildings and getting richer and richer off of their people and have no shame. They witness their seniors struggling to buy food or medicine. They justify it with smooth words. Like one Christian man said, if you are ignorant enough to give me your money with no return investment I am wise enough to take it. While seniors' need their homes cleaned, grass mowed, and a way to get to the doctor and grocery store but the church people are busy supporting themselves, their pastors dreams of a big ministry and no time left over to help the needy or old. Where did the good deeds in ministry go? Girls having babies so they can stay on welfare. Where is honor and respect for God, self, family and country? The non-caring attitudes of some children yet if you confronted them they would deny it. Saved from what? It appears they are saved from work, respect, honor, courage, faith, and love. What are they saved from? Our churches have become a place to collect and beg for money while our youth continue to move further and further away from God's principles. Preachers throw temper tantrums and admit they are control freaks and youth watch and listen yet no change in sight of doing better.

I hope you will love, honor and show your loved ones more respect than you did before you read this book. I hope you can see the joy in everything or at least look for it more now. I hope you tell your parents how much you love and appreciate them in deeds and words before you have to stand at their grave. Show them how valuable they are to you. Remember it is YOU that is the gift.

Chapter 7:

The Marriage Code

Daddy did allow me to date at age fourteen but B.C. wasn't my first or second date even after the dream. Daddy said I should play the field awhile and be sure the boy in my dream was this B.C. So I doubled dated a boy I had met through a friend. We went to Lynchburg to a Wrestling match. The date was ok and he was a nice fellow, good looking and all but on the way home with two people in the front seat he wouldn't stop putting his hands where they didn't belong. He didn't understand what no meant and getting home became my favorite goal and best event of the night. When I got home daddy was up and waiting. After I told him what the boy did his face turned blood red and he said well now you know dating is not all the fun you dreamed it would be. But I came back with my answer, no dating was great. It was the price tag he put on the date and what he wanted me to do that I didn't agree with. Treating me that way made me feel dirty. It felt like he had spent his time and money on me the first part of the night and expected me to pay him with sex the second part of the night. But he got fooled.

Daddy smiled and said he just hadn't met a Smith until tonight.

My second date a few weeks later wasn't much better. Ray was from Roxboro N.C. whom I had met through another friend. He was a real gentleman and showed me the utmost respect. I respected him a great deal for the kindness and respect he showed me the few months we actually dated. But there just wasn't any vibration between us. I hoped he wouldn't feel like a dead person after a few dates but that feeling didn't change. Even his good night kisses were cold and did nothing for my heart. It was physical. The time we dated did give me experience and time to size him up. His niceness made me hope he would have some life inside. I often wondered because of the dream that I didn't give him a fair shake. In my heart I knew who I was supposed to be with and Daddy needed to accept that soon.

Daddy didn't think I was ready emotionally or mentally to date. We disagreed on that because I just couldn't see beyond the chores and responsibility I had. "What is it about thirteen or fourteen that teens think they know more than parents?" Daddy said. Daddy and Aunt Ellen both were trying to teach me the Bible kind of love but I was always in a hurry to grow up and wouldn't listen. I felt they had made me grow up to fast and now because dating was something I really wanted to do they were trying to slow my growth process down. It only confused me as to what they expected from me. They certainly didn't treat Shirley that way when she wanted to date. Their biggest fear was my curiosity spirit and I knew that.

Who do you honor was the question I heard a lot? Is it God? If it's God then why aren't you about his business instead of this dating business? Is it self? If self then why aren't you interested in school and career? Is it family? Can you hear the sound of honor? Then tell us who you honor? The code of honor is a lifetime seed. What do you consider worth honoring? Think child and when you can give me the answer then maybe we will consider this dream boy you have on your mind. What is your motive? When you can answer these simply questions we will discuss dating.

Daddy said words were seeds that sowed to feelings which could not be trusted. Any seed will produce a harvest whether good or bad. The question should be what type of harvest do we want? The mind needs pictures therefore the imagination produces dreams and visions to give the mind what it wants. How do you know the man in the dream is the right one or not? By his character and the character of his family Daddy said that's how you know. What do they believe in?

Of course my answer was how do you expect me to find out when you won't even allow me to see or date him? Just calling him every day at lunch time with people standing around listening to every word won't tell me. What are you afraid of Daddy? Let me date B.C. and find out these answers. He may be like the Roxboro boy cold and lifeless or like the first date all hands and no respect. I was arguing my case and used facts to do it. Daddy didn't like that even though he respected me. Again he asked what is it that teens think they know more than parents.

He said he was afraid I put to much focus on these dreams and visions, the unseen world and not enough on the physical world around me. Most people put to much attention on worldly stuff, money, cars, clothes, and homes and such and very little attention on the unseen. Carolyn Ann you are just so different than most kids. You keep your attention on dreams, visions, angels, the Bible and don't care anything about the physical world. Has it ever occurred to you that God put you in a physical world to learn and put your attention on physical stuff? An unbalanced life was just as dangerous as the devil himself. You need to get your head out of the clouds. Can you put a price on the person who taught you about the savior of the soul or the soul itself? The mind is a dangerous field when not cultivated in good deeds. What you focus on you honor regardless of what your mouth is saying. Your words and actions should be the same thing. You need to learn balance.

The more my Daddy talked the more afraid I became because he wasn't speaking of the conscious mind but had gone into the subconscious himself. Why did that frighten me so? He had never said if he could see angels or if he ever had. The times when I asked him he ignored me. I really wanted to change the subject but I could tell this day that wasn't going to happen. I had put to much attention on this dream husband of mind. After seeing him washing that windshield in the physical realm and then getting behind my bus and going as far as noticing me to ask for my phone number and name, daddy was right he and the dream was all I could think about. I was focusing too much on him and the dream. I hadn't asked God what he wanted at all. Thinking I would trip daddy up I asked him what code of honor does the Smith's live by? If he would allow me to date him I would find out if B. C. and his family lived by a code of honor or not.

As soon as I heard, "*well young lady,* since you asked I will tell you. I knew I had opened a can of worms as they say or I had bit off more than I could chew at one time. Very sternly he said, you think you know so much. Let's just see how much you do know. Get a piece of paper and write what I tell you down and you get the answers from your dream wonder boy. I will bet you he doesn't have one and will refuse to live by ours. You just watch and see young lady."

Oh, what did I do? I thought. But the can of worms was opened and I knew I couldn't stop him then. Our morning talks usually were just small talk but lately they sounded almost like life or death or a broken record. I couldn't use ignorance as an excuse for they had been taught to us daily since we were born. Now he is brave enough to give them to me and have me write them down. He must be really serious. And his lists went like this: A Smith owns property and only rents long enough to get on his feet. A Smith is a giver and a receiver of gifts, not just a receiver, sometimes you have to give more than you receive but you do it without complaining. If your turn comes to give and you don't give back after receiving then you took after your mama's side, you definitely no Smith. You show a Smith always taking and not giving back he may go by the Smith name but he isn't a real Smith. A Smith doesn't settle for anything but the best, the best he can do. As long as you do your best it is accepted but it has to be your best. A real Smith honors God by living his laws every day not just on Sunday. He honors self by being truthful. Who is he really lying too, no one but himself. A liar can't remember his lie tomorrow but the truth will stand forever remembered. A real man honors his good name and protects that good name by not shaming it with shameful deeds. You don't hang your dirty underwear out on the clothes line for the entire world to see. You wash them first. And he honors his family and work. Good honest work. It's a shame and disgrace not to support your own family and have a little to help others with also. A Smith wears good quality shoes, there's nothing better than a solid foundation. A Smith is proud of who they are and where they came from and work hard to leave a good name and a good reputation to his heirs. A Smith honors their ancestors in deeds as well as words. That's why we have the family reunion every year and why it is important to be there and raise your children to honor and respect it. None of us is perfect but talking about the bad won't make the good look any better. The more you stir cow manure the worst it stinks. Can you put a price on the parent who taught you right from wrong or anyone for that matter? Then why do you argue with someone wiser than yourself? Honor your mother and father and be blessed all your days. They aren't perfect just human like you. Don't go to bed with anger and unforgiveness in your heart. Forgive people and yourself before you close your eyes. You might wake up staring God in the face. Then what will you say about that unforgiveness. He won't listen to your judgments or excuses so why have any.

Daddy, what about Mama? She didn't do most of them things you are asking me to live by.

We aren't talking about your mama. She will answer to God for her deeds, as well as you and I will. Don't you concern yourself with other folks? They aren't your business. You have one business on this earth you will answer for and that is you. Your past, present and future depends on you and what you put right there between those big blue eyes. Right there as he pushed his forefinger deep into my forehead and pushing me backwards in the chair. I'm falling backwards screaming, Daddy, Daddy, reaching for him to catch my hand before I hit the hard floor. He laughs and says see how fast you can fall off your high horse. Get me a coke he added as he continued to laugh to break the ice.

Cowtail, do you know why I don't talk about the war and those metals and purple hearts? Because good men died for this country, good families lost husbands, sons and fathers. It is our duty to live and make as much money as we possibly can, do our very best to help mankind and make this great planet a better place for the future generations. Better than we received it when we were born. That's what they died for. Would it be fair to live any less? You are young and need an education, a career before you even think about boys or marriage. I saw him choke up as he reached for that old red handkerchief to blow his nose. Tears filled my face as my body filled up with cold chills because I felt the pain behind his words. I knew for the first time what honor meant to my Daddy. He didn't live it to better himself but he lived it to give honor to all those World War II solders that died and show God appreciation for coming home to his.

He blew his nose and wiped his eyes and looked at me and asked, do you have any idea what it's like to be in a foxhole for days covered in mud? You see your friends and fellow solders shot off one by one and think you will be next. And all you have are these three little books to keep you from going insane.

What three little books Daddy? He stood up and walked into his bedroom and opened a green footlocker. He had told us a long time ago it was his army box and we were to never go in it without his permission. I watched as he carefully laid aside metals, ribbons, purple hearts, coins, papers, and picked up three little green books. Of all the pretty stuff and valuables those three little books were his most valuable treasure in that box. These books as he shook them at me. This is what kept your daddy from going insane many times in a foxhole filled with his dead friends, or laying somewhere in a German hospital. He opened the tiny little pages very carefully as he just thumbed through the worn sheets eyes full of tears. I could see he was remembering some painful events as he flipped page after page. You have no idea what its like to be in a foxhole with dead bodies and don't know if you will ever see your family again. You don't have a clue what its like to wake up in a hospital and not know what country you are in. Surrounded by wounded soldiers with legs shot off or arms or half their face, hearing the screams all around you and not a soul will tell you anything. After seeing what we saw overseas fighting for the freedom of the Jews and this country it's an honor to live in this country and work. Knowing if we didn't beat them they would come over here in the United States and do to our families what they were doing to the Jews.

You learn not to let too many things upset you anymore. You learn not to listen to complaints or excuses. You are just so grateful to be alive in these United States nothing else seems to matter. You just so thankful to wake up every morning in a peaceful country with family, you just can't wait to get out of bed and start your day. You see, I want you three kids to have the education they fought and died for. I want you three to have more money, a better home, drive a better automobile and wear better clothes than any of and all of your family did before you. I want you all to do more and have more than I did. Then I feel I have done my best in raising you. Is that too much to ask for? I know I didn't do right when I left you with Press and Ellen those two years while I went to Canada. I thought I needed to get away and get myself together but I missed you three so much I couldn't enjoy anything. All I could think about was my kids. I was so glad when my contract was up and I could come back to my family.

No daddy it isn't and it wasn't fair. After Mama left and then you left us we had to learn how to survive without you. I had to learn how to be a mama to Shirley and Tommy. I held them when they cried for you and Mama. I had to change the bed when Shirley wet it and washed her clothes. I had to play with Tommy to keep him from crying. I had to learn how to clean house and cook so when you came home I could help you keep house and watch after Shirley and Tommy. While you were in Canada and Mama gone too you don't know what we went through either. You don't know how we felt because you never asked. You and Mama claimed you loved us but both of you abandoned us. So if B. C. abandons me I figure I would survive because when I was six years old I survived so I know I will survive at fourteen or forty years old. I learned how to survive and how to care for Shirley and Tommy at six years old so if we had a baby or babies and he left I know I will survive. Why wouldn't I feel confident about dating or getting married now? I had to grow up at six when other kids my age were playing. I don't want to disrespect you, Daddy, but I know if this dream isn't of God it will come to nothing. But if it is and I disobey God then where will that leave me? I don't know if the dream is from God or not but in my heart I feel it is and it won't go away. No matter how hard I try to focus on Jesus, the Bible or work all I can feel is this drawing inside of me. It feels like a magnet stronger than anything I have ever felt. I have no peace inside and it's like my soul area is spinning in a tidal wave. I might not even like B.C. but at least have enough faith in me to let me find out.

Daddy's silence told me he understood what I had said or I had touched a painful spot one. After a few minutes he said you are right. I see what you are saying. Daddy had touched my heart no doubt about that and I hoped B.C. or whoever did have a code of honor they lived by. To hurt my Daddy by dating just anyone just wasn't going to happen and Daddy should have known that. He realized he had hurt me by not trusting me.

Later in the week as we went to Aunt Ellen's and we were alone I shared with her all Daddy had told me. She just looked at me with a serious look and said Henry is right. That was a terrible war and many people were killed, wounded and came home to families who had abandoned them. Israel became a nation the same year Shirley Mae was born and it's a healing time. A time to grow, learn and be thankful each day for what we have and who we have. God spared your daddy and he feels guilty sometimes when he waste his time knowing there are others who wished they had the opportunity and family he has. Now we are facing this Vietnam War and people don't know how that's going to affect our country. He sets up at his store and hears reports about that war and pictures what he went through and get all upset over the lazy boys back here to lazy to go to school or get a decent job. He just wants you to see all around you and do your best that's all.

You see this little butterbean seed I hold in my hand? It's like you, all wrapped with expectation and only time and choices you make will reveal what's actually inside of you. Only you can investigate yourself and draw out of you what has already been planted within you. Only you can determine if you have valued, the you, in you. For you to see how important it is for you two walk in agreement with God and man there is peace and prosperity, the true riches of life. The butterbean and the earth must work together before it can produce any fruit of value. Marriage is all that wrapped up in one person and when that one person ask you to marry him, he is actually asking, will you marry my beliefs and family, will you marry my God? Will you marry his beliefs, family and God? That is what a marriage proposal really is. Do you both agree and believe in the same God, same values? These are the things your daddy wants you to understand. Marriage is a big step and you shouldn't be dating anyone unless he is worthy to be your husband. No dream can tell you what is inside of a person, only time will do that. He may be the one God wants you to date and marry but did God tell you in that dream when to date him or marry him? You see Cowtail, God has given you Henry to support and protect you, to help you make wise decisions, to teach you how to do all those things. That dream has confused him also and all he wants is for you to have the best out of life. The Smith men are like those eagles you see flying about watching over their little eaglelets. The Bible is full of honoring your elders and the eagles represent those elders in the family. Will he honor you; respect you and your family? At first I just sat in silence and allowed her words to sink into my soul for awhile for I could feel what she had said even though I didn't have words to explain it.

Before we finished our talk session I asked Aunt Ellen if she knew what the three little green books were that kept Daddy sane. She said she didn't.

Then she added, a wedding is not a small thing but a universal one. Do you know that Jesus life and death and resurrection were like a wedding to us? There's planning, preparation and investment, the last supper Jesus attended was preparation supper before the marriage. Jesus knew he was a single man with choices, where each party is still an individual, and he knew he had time to say no. He knew Judas also had time to say no to Satan and be saved. Then there's the wedding agreement where you stand before witnesses agreeing to come together and blend as one soul. It's like the dying of oneself and blending into the likes of another. Jesus knew him dying on that cross was him giving his own life up for a life of suffering just to pay the price for all of our sins. He knew once he stepped on that cross his life would never be the same again. He was agreeing to marry us with all our ignorance and short comings. He was agreeing to love us no matter what and forgive us of all our past, present and future sins and wrongs. Well that's what each individual standing at that alter is doing when they make those wedding vows. God also said it was better to never vow than to vow and not keep them. So you see God takes those vows very seriously and that man and woman need to also.

The harvests are the babies you bring into the world to support, care and love for. With this harvest comes the responsibility of feeding the spirit of that little creature, feeding the mind with positive thoughts which is the word of the living God for those babies to have a healthy emotion and body. Each one is spirit. Each one has a soul that must decide for itself life or death. Each one lives in a body that needs physical attention, food, clothes and much more. The better the education the better the job to support those physical needs. The better the education the better you study God's word for yourself and not be deceived by greedy or needy preachers. Then you can teach your children spiritual things. It's an awesome responsibility to marry and be a parent. Remember Jesus asked his disciples, have you any meat? All the while he had walked with them in his flesh body he fed them baby food. He provided the needs of his disciplines like a husband and father would do. Now he was asking them if they had any meat. The time had come to feed them the meat of the word for he knew they were maturing and needed substance. Growth is very important since we all are growing daily in one direction or another. The person whom you want to spend your life with must be willing to grow on the same road as yourself in order to keep from becoming separated. He must be willing to feed his mind with God's living words also. Will he be able and willing to honor God's will and honor the eagles, which are the elders of both families? Will each of you honor, protect, provide, serve and care for each other above all and cling only to each other no matter what you may have to face together. Always putting the relationship first and in order to do that means putting God's relationship first in all things in your daily walk? And last are you worthy to enter this family and will the partner you have chosen be worthy of your family? This is the code your grandparents and great-grandparents lived by and pasted down from generation to generation. This is the secret I saw in them and hungered for it. I had all the material wealth a girl could ever dream about but it didn't satisfy my hungry soul. Will you teach them to your children at meal time, upon rising and before laying your head down at night? That means live them daily before your children and speak of them at every meal. Will God and church be number one? Then you will be a blessing to his family and his family a blessing unto yours. This is what you are to ponder over before thinking about dating or marriage regardless of any dreams. This is what your daddy is trying to get across to you.

When you told your Daddy you wanted to have sex with this dream boy you may as well spit in his face. Allow me to read you something from the NIV Bible, II Corinthians 12: "The Apostle Paul is speaking here, the one who saw the resurrected Christ on the road to Damascus and Christ asked him, 'Saul, Saul, why doesn't thou persecute me? When you persecute these you are persecuting me.' Here the Apostle Paul is speaking to the Corinthians, "I will go on to visions and revelations from the LORD."

Carolyn Ann, you have had dreams from the Lord since you were six. Your first miracle was your own resurrection from death at your birth. Not many but more than most Christians have had a lifetime. Your next step will be visions. You will go on to visions where you will see things from the Lord, some call it day dreaming. From there you will move up to the third step where you will go on to revelations from the Lord, Himself. Can you see your future here? Can you see where you are right now? You are in a place with the Lord right now that most preachers and teachers aren't at. You will teach them, those wise enough to listen. They read this Bible and tell you what they read or explain to you what some human teacher has taught them. But you see it from the Lord and understand it when the Lord teaches you and you are still a child. You have been caught up to paradise. You have heard inexpressible things that you are not permitted to tell. Let me read further down and I believe you will understand why your Daddy is so upset about all of this. Paul continues, 'to keep me from becoming conceited because of these dreams, visions, and revelations, there was given me a thorn in my flesh, a Messenger of Satan, to torment me.' Down a little further it says, the Lord speaking to Paul, "My grace is sufficient for you, for my power is made perfect (means Mature) in weakness." Then Paul says he will boast all the more about his weaknesses, so that Christ's power may rest on him. That is why Paul said he delights in weaknesses, insults, in hardships, in persecution, in difficulties. For when I am weak, then, I am strong. Reading further down Aunt Ellen said, "I fear that there may be quarrellings, jealousy, outbursts of anger, factions, slander, gossip, arrogance and disorder. I am afraid that when I come again my God will humble me before you, and I will be grieved over many who have sinned earlier and have not repented of their impurity, sexual sin, and debauchery in which they have indulged. I already gave you a warning when I was with you the second time. I now repeat it while absent for on my return I will not spare those who sinned earlier or any of the others, since you are demanding proof that Christ is speaking through me. Christ is not weak in dealing with you, but he is powerful among you."

Carolyn Ann, all I just read to you go on among the evildoers as we speak. All evildoers are not so noticeable, some hide under their mask of kindness until they get what they want. Then they are quarrelling, jealousy, outbursts of anger, factions, slander, gossip, arrogance and disorder as well as impurity, sexual sin, and debauchery in which they have indulged and have not repented of. Do you know who your thorn in the side is? Suppose it is this B.C.? You would live a painful life and all your Daddy wants to do is protect you. You have plenty of time to leave home and be on your own.

Let's say for argument sake you have married this dream boy or another boy and you find out after the marriage that he lives like that, that he has those Satan spirits inside of him. Do you realize that you become part of that? That those spirits which are not from the Lord are transmitted over to you through sex and being in his company? That is what your Daddy is trying to get across to you. He could be a Messenger of Satan who has come in a kind, helpful, caring, loving manner to build you up and tell you how beautiful you are and cause you to become conceited. The time will come when he will ask or someone in his family will ask you to prove that Christ is speaking through you if he comes from Cain's family. Why? Because Cain's family don't know Christ for themselves, if they knew Christ they wouldn't need to ask you to prove it. They would know for themselves it is Christ speaking through you. Can you see the danger and why your Daddy is so worried about this dating business? Henry and I have kept your secret and kept you safe as best we could all these years but we can't protect you if you marry or surrender to another regardless of who he or his family is. You must be very sure of what you are doing and who you are associating with. Examine yourself daily and see whether you are in the faith. Test yourself so God won't have to come and examine you. King David said, Lord search me and cleanse me. Let there be nothing in me that is not of You Lord.

By the time I had turned fifteen I had heard these codes every day sometimes twice or three times per day. Daddy and Aunt Ellen both had given their blessing for me to date B.C. April 1964 with one catch I had to take Shirley with us on the dates until Daddy was confident that I could be trusted.

August 1, 1965, Shirley had married Dennis and Daddy was very pleased with her choice. He bragged on what he spent on her, bragged on how nice he was. He even bragged on Dennis's Mama and Daddy, and how they worked at a decent job and how he could afford Shirley. He had so much respect for his parents and what they stood for he gleaned with excitement about her marriage. You would have thought Dennis was one of Jesus' favorite apostles listening to Daddy go on and on. Aunt Ellen smiled a lot but never commented about Dennis other than he seems to be an all right fellow that came from an upstanding family.

September 30, 1965, B. C. gave me a diamond and asked me to marry him. Daddy didn't like the engagement, said it was too short and the diamond was too small, more like a diamond dust rather than a diamond. He made me feel so ashamed and yet more determined to prove him wrong. Daddy tried so hard to run BC off. He did and said many things in hopes BC would run. He would tell family members who came to visit that hadn't seen my diamond, "go get your magnifying glass and look at that big diamond Carolyn is wearing." Then he would laugh until he cried, making everyone else do the same. With each test that BC endured and stayed and laughed with them, them being Aunt Ellen, Uncle Press and Johnny he won more and more ground with Daddy. I had warned him on our first date that he would be the grandest thing since peanut butter if they liked him or he would be the joke of the day if they didn't. It would all depend on his attitude whether he won this family over or not. Being the baby girl in the Smith family wasn't always a happy place to be. But whatever you do please don't put on a front or kiss up to try to win them over. If you do that they will never accept you and crush you under their feet like a bug. If you can't stand up to them and take it please just stop seeing me. I would understand and you wouldn't be the first boy they ran off or got thrown over a car for putting hands where they didn't belong.

Many dates rather than going on an actual date we went to Aunt Ellen's for her and Johnny to give him tips on how to win my

Daddy over. Johnny laughed and laughed each time and would tell BC to win Uncle Henry over and get his blessing to marry Carolyn you had better be Jesus in the flesh. Johnny knowing no man, woman or child could ever fill that bill but it made for many family jokes. Sometimes I wished Daddy wasn't so straight forward and outspoken but he knew people. He could read them like a book on the first encounter. He would say, I am nothing but even so I am not inferior to the preachers, teachers, lawyers or bankers, they put their pants on every morning just like I do. The things that mark a true apostle are signs, wonders, and miracles done daily among you with great perseverance. He meant the way you lived, talked, dressed and worked daily at home and place of employment. He would add it's not your possessions I want but you. When I see the real you then I will be satisfied. Daddy sized up people from inside out. He didn't care whether they were rich in materials or not only what was inside of them.

I remember the day of Thanksgiving 1965 when BC asked Daddy for my hand in marriage. Daddy stopped eating and looked at him and asked, "Should parents save up for their children or spend all they make and leave no inheritance or live to be a burden to their children? The whole room fell silent as we each waited for BC's answer. I was so embarrassed and could feel my face burning from shame. All I could think about was how could he expect anyone to be perfect when he himself made so many mistakes? BC spoke; I believe parents should save for their children. Daddy came back with; do you believe in spending your money on your wife and children or spend it on your wants? BC answered, I believe a good man will work to pay bills, save some, give us away, and spend it on his wife and children and spend some on himself. Daddy looked straight at Johnny and said, that boy isn't as dumb as he looks and everyone started laughing. I felt the whole room relax for everyone knew that was the closest yes we would get from Daddy.

Aunt Ellen jumped up covered in all smiles, clapping her hands and dancing around in the kitchen that told me she liked BC but had kept silent waiting on Daddy's approval. She said well we have a wedding to plan. Aunt Grovine can make the wedding dress. Johnny said him and Frances would buy the corsages and whatever else Mama needed them to buy. Then as he was getting up from his chair, looked at BC and said, "BC, you can buy what you want Cowtail to wear on her wedding night." With that statement and laughter all the hunters got up to go back hunting even BC. Daddy left for the store, leaving the women to plan a wedding down to the last detail. Since it would be a Christmas wedding the entire Smith family would be there anyway and it would be Christmas flowers and colors. Aunt Ellen got the church to supply the flowers and Frances and Johnny got the candle opera. Mrs. Sam Church made the wedding cake and believe it or not BC took Johnny serious and purchased the nightgown with respect, knowing a few Smith's would see and approve. You wouldn't believe how quick and beautiful my wedding was and how all the Smith's worked together in harmony. Aunt Ellen said God had blessed and put us together. That was one of the happiest memories of my Aunt Ellen I have because of her joy and excitement in planning my wedding and carrying it out. Like a happy Mother feels when she helps her daughter plan a wedding and want every detail perfect. I realized and believe Daddy realized for the first time how much his children had actually become the children of the entire Smith family. We truly were the Smith babies.

I only shared that so you could see how well our family worked in peace no matter what the project was. Daddy knew I wouldn't do well with anyone that fussed and carried on like heathens he called them. Families were to love, honor and respect each other and that was my family.

Only a few little problems, Daddy said he wouldn't give me away if I had a church wedding. Why? We don't know and never found out. But the location was changed to Aunt Ellen's living room which worked out better any way.

The second problem was; Daddy cried for two weeks right before the wedding and from Thanksgiving until December 23rd he still tried to talk me out of that wedding. Daddy couldn't shake his feelings that BC was a coward underneath all that niceness and believed when times got tough he would run away. He believed he was a skirt chaser underneath that entire pleasing attitude. Daddy feared I would give one hundred per cent to him and his family only to be hurt in the end. He believed BC was like the cowards at Jesus cross and I was like the three Mary's who stayed no matter how painful it was. He feared what would happen when BC found out about my insight or gift of discernment as some called it. Daddy said I lived in the fifty days after the resurrection called the honeymoon where Jesus taught, cuddled, courted and romanced his people like a strong father. But feared after Jesus ascended and like the Apostles who had to get down to some serious work, teaching and suffering he would abandon me. He said marriage was like the cross, resurrection and ascension. After the honeymoon was over BC would go off doing his own thing instead of staying on course. I had seen Daddy cry in the past and it always tore me up inside. He was so soft hearted and kind and didn't show his emotions in tears very often. Not like all his brothers and sisters who presented a tough exterior with strict rules to live by. When they hurt and you saw their tears you knew you had better walk softly and quietly until they got it together. But Daddy was just so tender and cared so deeply it touched the core of your soul when he cried. I really didn't know what to do so I continued on with the wedding plans. It took boldness and confidence to live with Daddy those last weeks.

We believed it was the way the Smith's raised us that gave us so much boldness and confidence to move forward no matter what. Quitting was the only way we could lose. We grew up witnessing time after time how they picked up a family member who had fallen below or down on their luck. Not judging just helping. Like one of my favorite uncles, Uncle Willie. He had a drinking problem and from time to time he fell off the wagon and Daddy or Aunt Ellen one or both would be there to pick him up and get him started on the right track again. They never gave up on him even after his divorce and wasn't a part of the Smith family legally. I still see Daddy and Aunt Ellen's snooty look when someone made a comment about it not being our legal problem. Aunt Ellen would say, well tell me how to get this love for Willie out of my heart and we will stop helping him. No one ever did because there was no answer. You don't stop loving a person just because they fall down or not part of the family legally. You love them back up when they are ready to get up and walk again. You waited until they returned and then threw a party and helped them on their feet again. That's real love or at least the way I saw it. It gave me courage to try, if I fell down, they would be there to pick me up and help me again. Don't let anyone judge you is what Daddy would say. Go look in their closet. You will find they are gossiping about themselves and judging you to cover up their own filth. You just remember that Immanuel means God with us. He sees, hears, and feels all. You can't hide anything from him. That's what you need to remember before you go pointing your finger at someone else.

I waited my time during those two weeks to hear that judging statement and threw it up in Daddy's face the night before my wedding. He blew his nose and went in his bedroom. Feeling a little afraid I stayed in the living room and sat in silence. He returned with those three little worn green books and said, "Here, you will need these more than I do." I took them and they were the book of Proverbs, called the book of wisdom. The book of Psalms, called the praise book of the Bible and the book of John, which is known as the book of love. He said those three little books are what kept him sane when he was in those foxholes, hospitals and when Geneva left. I was the one crying then and Daddy sat in silence. I thumbed through them one at a time and felt the heat in my hands like they were burning them but I didn't understand at the time what were in them or how important they really were. I didn't even understand what the heat in my hands meant. I knew they were important to Daddy and carried great value for him. I knew the time would come I would sit and read them to see if they gave me the comfort and strength they had given my Daddy but not now. I had a wedding to attend and I was the bride.

After a short while I looked up and told Daddy I couldn't take his little books. He needed to keep them for himself. I had them in my Bible and would read them. He took them from me and stood up and said good night and left for his bedroom.

That night I didn't sleep at all. I spent my night praying. Asking God to speak to me, to lead me, and show if this wedding was right or wrong. A little late to be asking since in a few hours I would be a bride. I asked God to touch Daddy's heart and heal him. I believed he was grieving for Mama more than he wanted to admit and had been remembering his heart so full of joy when they married. Yet he was remembering the ache in his heart when she left him for another man and didn't want me to experience that kind of pain. I felt he thought he was losing me and that was the reason he was against the wedding and BC. I believed the biggest battle we faced was the sin nature within our own body wrestling with the Christ nature within. That came from a dream I had right before my birthday where in that dream I was fighting with Jesus. It appeared like I was inside a bubble with Jesus wrestling. I heard what I thought was God the Father who said, "You are fighting with yourself." I didn't know that night adding a husband to my life was more than I ever could dream but like anything else I had encountered I was willing to step forward and find out. I didn't know I lacked understanding but Daddy knew all this.

I asked God to bless my wedding, the day and every person that helped and save their soul forever. When the sun came up I got up and started packing my stuff for Aunt Ellen's and couldn't get there fast enough. Daddy got up and helped with breakfast as usual but in silence. He drove me to Aunt Ellen's in silence. When 4 pm came I told Aunt Ellen and Frances that I was afraid Daddy wouldn't show up. The wedding was to begin at 4 pm. They assured me he would. That he wouldn't let me down. My heart was so grieved and troubled over his silence I couldn't smile or even enjoy getting dressed. Frances, Shirley and Aunt Ellen tried to cheer me up and told me it was my wedding day I was suppose to be happy. I could feel the fear in the pit of my stomach and would go to the door and look to see if he was there. I felt anger rise up after awhile for I felt Daddy was trying to ruin my day.

Finally Johnny came up and said Uncle Henry is here. He doesn't look to good but he's here. Daddy showed up I replied with a sign of relief. I peeked out the door to see for myself. He was standing at the bottom of the steps. I heard the wedding music and opened the door and was ready to get it over with. I wanted to be married more than anything else in my life as I felt my heart relax seeing Daddy waiting for me to walk down those steps, with his arm out to lead me into the living room that held so many secrets of the Smith and Tune family. Seeing Daddy standing there with swollen eyes from crying and all dressed up waiting, put a smile on my face so big, for that was just as important as being a bride to me. I'm sure my guest thought it was for BC but it was two-fold.

The wedding was beautiful and plenty of food afterwards to feed an army. We soon left for a short honeymoon trip. That dream had come to pass with the young man I had seen in my dream. The secret room could now hold all my inner secrets and joys along with all the others.

The Wedding Dress

Carolyn in the wedding dress her Aunt Grovine made standing
in the secret room where she married Bernard Lee Creasy;
her journey began with the human heart verses the spiritual
heart and her emotional battle verses her spiritual emotions
with herself, In the secret room where she married she also
learned how to surrender all to God!

The Man I Dreamed I Would Marry

BERNARD CREASY

**I also dreamed his last seven years on earth:
his stroke, his death, the day, week, month and year.**

Chapter 8:

The Human Heart

My journey as a wife had begun. A whole life of new experiences than what I had experienced before. All the teaching had been planted and a life time to bring them to a prosperous harvest. Having a partner to walk with me side by side was a wonderful thought. I felt we were soul mates the way we had been drawed together like a magnet. Now the blending of two souls was beginning. A life that included intimacy and sex added to what I thought was normal.

The human heart is full of questions which proved there was still understanding to come. In the meantime it was learning to walk in faith like we had done since Mama left and we began that new journey. Grace bears it all and answers them all I was told. Jahveh means I was, I am, and I shall always continue to be, I am whatever you need me to be, is the meaning of I AM THAT I AM or so I had been told. Faith holds the hand which says, certainly I will be with you forever even to the ends of the earth. God answers the big questions and the small ones. So ask what comes up and out of your heart. You are not offending God. He is your father and mother. Seek understanding and stick to his word. In some Bibles it says, Zion is a daughter which is a female form, which is emotion. It says the Holy Spirit is a comforter and teacher. How many men do you know that can comfort you every time? Grace and mercy are feminine names and wisdom is called a she so I had been told. I didn't know anything for sure but what God had showed me and taught me. Little did I know then that I would come to know these things for myself? Know that I know with no doubts or questions but a process in life.

Maybe because I was raised in a family where men were so powerful I grew up believing God was even more powerful. But the only role model I had to teach me how to be a wife or mother had been Aunt Ellen. Would she be enough now knowing I could never be like her? Maybe because Daddy put so much value on us I was able to understand a little better the value God placed on us when he sent his only son to suffer and die for us. Receiving God's promises was our job and enjoying the fruit of them. I didn't know how to love like that but I believed if he would give us his only begotten son he would give us anything we wanted. Being married to the man I saw in my dream proved that one in my heart. Up to that point God had given me a dream for every major decision in life. He promised he wouldn't leave us in darkness but raise us up into light or life. I knew because Mama had left us, there was always that chance that BC would leave me too. Just the thought brought fear but I didn't understand how deep that fear had been planted. I didn't understand the depth of pain that was buried inside of me for what Mama did. I didn't understand seeking after God was my way of looking for someone I could trust that wouldn't leave or abuse. I wanted BC to be just like my Daddy, kind, caring, and understanding and supportive. I wanted him to make me the apple of his eye like Daddy had done for us. I wanted him to work and have goals and dreams of our own home and provide all the material things that we had and didn't have. I was full of hope and dreams and only time would reveal if they came to pass or not.

I had such a close intimate relationship with Christ it was a little scary to think I shared him with someone else as intimate as a husband.

I believed God wanted us to have the best and be smart because Daddy believed it. He said God hated ignorance and sent us to earth to grow up out of ignorance. Daddy said ignorance was just another word for darkness. Daddy believed like attracted like which meant whatever you focused upon you became no matter what it was. He wanted us to focus upon the good, upon prosperity. Daddy believed an idle mind was the devil's workshop and made us think, decide, and accept the results without complaints or blame. I didn't realize on my wedding day how he and Aunt Ellen had molded and shaped me or the depth of their teaching.

He and Aunt Ellen believed "follow me" meant living a selfless life, giving our wants, will and self to God daily. Surrender and submit as long as it is what is right because you are not surrendering and submitting to a man but to God and His Principles. Don't walk in the middle of the road or jump from side to side they said. Stand firm for what you believe as long as it lines up with what God believes or you would fall for anything. Pain, suffering, hardships and such was the flesh body screaming as the darkness leaves us and God pruning us. Just a way of life, helping us to grow up in Christ and finish his work within us. He sent us here to surrender and know His power and learn to do our work with a cheerful heart. We would never understand how much darkness we had or how deep it was when Christ entered our hearts. He entered a sewage pit. He decided to enter that sewage pit for one reason to clean us out and make us beautiful inside. He decided to enter us full of darkness and begin his work in us. They believed God would show us where to go and who to associate with based on the story of God telling Abraham to go where he showed him. They believed every human being was God's true children some just didn't want to be used. They loved the world and the darkness within and we were being separated, set apart for God's own purpose and God used such as he saw fit. Daddy said there are always two roads to anywhere we wanted to go. One was darkness and had many potholes and the other was light and had potholes also. It was the joy and peace within that kept us on the road of light or right. They also believed there were many quitters who wouldn't finish God's race. Cowards they called them, spineless people who compromised, lied, and always blamed others for their problems, never taking any responsibility for any weaknesses they had. Daddy said if you couldn't see your own weaknesses and admit to them and learn to laugh at yourself, then you were blind as a bat and too ignorant to know it. Canada had been a trip for daddy to come in tune with himself as he put it. He never really told us what kind of work he did over there or even talked about it. When he shared his little nuggets we would assume because Aunt Ellen said Henry had some growing up to do, that's why he had to go to Canada. I say all that to share a dream I had right after BC and I was married. All of this I had pondered over in the night after BC had gone to sleep.

The Army had drafted BC and his orders were to leave January 28th 1966, which meant we were married only one month and four days before he left. I learned in that short period of time that I wasn't ready to be married yet I was. I learned what I had imagined we would do together in that short month and few days were different than what BC seemed to be interested in. While he spent his days with Jimmy, friends and other family members during the day I sat at his daddy's home waiting for him to return. Some days he would come home early and get me just to leave me with family members as he ran around with the boys. His excuse he or they could die in the army and he wanted to spend as much time with them as possible before leaving. I felt he should have spent that time with me but Daddy said if his heart wasn't in it he would be miserable with me. So I gave him the freedom to do as he wished except for nighttime. I soon learned that I had some demons in me as Daddy called them. Jealous and confused very quickly rose up shortly after that wedding day because we had married to be together before he left is what we said. But it wasn't feeling like that after the marriage. I was doing what I did at Daddy's except the sex had been added to this picture, which I discovered was not one of my strong desires.

After awhile I realized how young I really was and how spoiled and protected I had been. I remembered when Daddy told BC that I loved center attention and wouldn't take a back seat for anyone. That you don't want to make her mad or cross her because her wrath was just as powerful as her love was. I could feel that wrath rising up in me. I kept telling myself he would be leaving soon just hold your temper. You better not ask her to do something that she believes is against that Bible or you will never forget her wrath. I remembered Aunt Ellen telling BC that Henry was trying to scare him off and BC answering he was doing a good job at it. He told her he loved me with all of his heart and would die for me. That he was willing to learn how to make me happy and keep me happy. Right there I talked myself out of sharing my feelings with BC and laid the blame on myself. Right there is where I realized what made me happy wasn't what made him happy. Right there I decided I was too strict and too Christian. Right there is where I started making excuses for him.

Here I was married less than a month and feeling my anger rising up, feeling my jealousy, and feeling like I was on the back seat to his family and afraid I would hear 'I told you so' from the two people I had leaned on all of my life for the right advice and wisdom. The two people I had convinced I was so mature and so ready for marriage. I really felt alone in my feelings even though I was surrounded by people and loved BC. I wondered if love really was enough like Daddy had asked. Every night his smooth words, kisses and love making just pushed my feelings on the backside rather than addressing them, acknowledging or even saying, I understand how you feel or I am sorry I made you feel that way and will change right away because you are the most important person in my life. I allowed my feelings to be pushed aside and that made me feel less of a person inside. Less important didn't set well with me but I held it all inside. I felt like I was throwing in the towel rather than having a confrontation before he left for the Army. Where was my praise, my compliments, my good feeling I had received before marriage? I remembered what Daddy said, Satan comes immediately to steal your joy. When two people have sex they are transferring energy to one another Aunt Ellen had said. It's part of the blending process. I hadn't read any books on marriage and didn't know if Daddy knew what he was talking about or not. There's more going on than just physical contact or making babies. I became a little more afraid as their words came up out of me. I tried real hard not to line him up with the Bible and preach to him or point a finger as to how God says he was suppose to be as a man and husband. I tried not to blame BC or even be jealous but with each passing day and him leaving became closer, every minute of time with him became more valuable to me. Even that thought reminded me of a saying Daddy or Aunt Ellen one had said. When you marry it wasn't about *'the me'* anymore. The *'me'* had to die so you could give yourself to your husband. But the anger inside said he isn't giving his me to me. He was spreading himself around. Voices inside of me speaking I hadn't heard before. Maybe because I had been so focused on being the perfect child for Daddy and Aunt Ellen to be proud of me I never allowed *the me* to speak before.

By the time he had left I was ready to return home and just be the child again. Let my Daddy make all the decisions and let me just follow. I knew how to please Daddy and even though I didn't always agree I obeyed out of respect most of the time. Once the tears of him leaving and all the emotions settled down I was ready to be me but because I saw a need in his family I decided to stay with his daddy and help with his two younger sisters. Six weeks later the me inside of me was craving attention, joy and wisdom and wanted out. I knew I needed to go home. I couldn't handle all the flesh in that house and told his daddy and brother I didn't like the way they lived or the decisions they made. I didn't think I was better than they were but I wasn't raised that way. Being happy and around family to me meant surrounded with work and family that cared and shared. A peaceful life without confusion and I was moving to my Daddy's. His daddy understood at least he said he did and helped me put my things in Daddy's car.

Daddy had seen all along I wasn't ready for a long time before I dreamed that dream. His tears and arguments made sense a little more with every day I stayed in that house with people who had different values than what I was use too. I hadn't had a dream for months and hadn't heard God's voice either since I had married. I had lost my desire for reading the Bible and meditating. I had no place to go and enter my secret place in God. I prayed very little and had stopped church and when I did pray I could feel my words bouncing off the walls and back at me. It seemed every Sunday BC had plans that didn't include God or church and being his wife I felt I had to submit. They put the flesh body and its desires first and it didn't set well in my soul is the only way I know how to explain it. After I moved back home with Daddy the first thing Aunt Ellen said the voices came because you put self and a physical relationship before God. That's how easy and quickly the dark side of us can sneak in. Putting God back in first place in my life brought back my peace and joy. Living a routine daily with organization and planning, having responsibilities and doing for others in the neighborhood again brought back calmness within me. I had two years to mature and stand up for what was right regardless of what BC did after he returned from the army. I knew I had better make the best of those two years and get myself ready, strong and respect myself and beliefs. I fell in that trap as quickly as I had almost fallen out of that chair when Daddy pushed me backwards.

Another surprise showed up. Soon I learned I was pregnant and that gave me a whole new vision and focus. With another human being to care for my education became important again as well. I wanted to be prepared to work whether I had to or not. I wanted my child as proud of me as I was of Daddy and Aunt Ellen. They said the dreams had stopped because I was living out the last dream. That if God had anything to show me he would. Keep going to church, keep reading the Bible and keep talking to God and keep going into the secret place with God. Take one day at a time and plan your time wisely. Try to live each day a little better than the day before. Let that be your prayer.

Daddy was just as excited as I was when he learned he would be a grandfather. He was planning and buying like it was his baby. He bought me a sewing machine because I wanted to make my maternity clothes instead of buying them. He had the baby bed and all its trimmings about two months before the baby was due. I wanted BC there but Daddy made sure neither the baby nor I went without. In those two years while BC was serving his country I was home working on the farm earning and saving. I had purchased a car and it was paid for. Had money in the bank for our own furniture and plans to own our own home as soon as he returned. Without any dreams during that time I felt I was right where God wanted me to be once my inner peace returned. Shirley had married and Tommy was in high school and riding the roads with friends. Daddy and I had a lot of time to share together. We both cooked breakfast and sat down at the table together and talked about anything that came up. That close intimate relationship had changed from what it was before I married. He treated me like an adult and asked me what I needed or wanted instead of telling me. He allowed me to make decisions and carry out plans. It was years before I realized what daddy was really doing those two years. I had returned home like a baby but he knew I was married and if luck had it that husband would come home to me and a baby. He prepared himself for my leaving as well as taught me how to stand up for myself and make decisions rather than being told what to do. He said submitting and surrender was great when doing it for the right reasons but very hurtful when done for all the wrong reasons. If I truly had BC's heart I would have his time and money willingly. If not, then no one but God could change a heart. He believed the army would make a better man out of him or a more selfish human being, either way the lectures were over and the cultivating had begun he said.

Have you figured out the family secret yet? Have you figured out that we learn understanding by experiencing life and knowing for ourselves? What did Aunt Ellen see in my Grandparents that she desired more than riches or wealth? What was the big secret in the secret room that wasn't shared with non-believers?

The secret was Aunt Ellen realized that my grandparents had something she knew nothing about but was willing to sell the whole farm to obtain it. The gift of love so ingrained in a being that they can hear God, see God and have dreams and visions that came to pass like the old Bible days. She desired to hear God for herself and thought doing good deeds was the way to obtain it yet she trained a child who had no good deeds and yet could see and hear God and angels. The secret in the secret room was her holy ground where she went to mediate and seek God's face. It was her own secret place where God opened the written word up to her so she could understand the Scriptures better. She learned to rely on the inspired feeling she received within and walk out that peace and calmness rather than her college education. She learned knowledge was a great gift and we all needed it but wisdom and understanding, insight was a far more valuable gift. Even though the Smith family wasn't as materially rich as her family she considered the Smith family far wealthier and longed for that wealth. She had learned from my grandmother how to feel God and know when God was present instead of the enemy like she was teaching me. What my Aunt Ruby had she was afraid of at first and too ashamed to admit it to anyone. Yet she knew it had been inherited by the very ones she admired and loved so much. With her education and background she said it was hard to accept that God had prophets and seers on earth with less wealth and education than her family. Over the years it humbled her in such a way she refused to judge another doctrine, or belief, or anything she didn't understand. She said she learned to carry it in that living room and place it on the mantle until understanding came. If it didn't come it was there for the next generation or whatever generation God chose to bring it forth out of.

I already had the secret and the wealth inside of me for my generation like Ruby had it in her for her generation. God was using it in her presents and she knew that meant God hadn't forsaken my generation but blessed it greater with increase. It wasn't about the doom and gloom but about God's glory being revealed in every generation. She knew I had to discover the value of the riches for myself. I would have to walk with God, talk with God, fall down from time to time so he could help me up and turn me loose to practice walking once more. When the habit of walking with God was so ingrained in me there wouldn't be any devil or demon, no man, or amount of money that could pluck me out of God's hand.

I guess now is a good time to explain what a seer is. What is a seer? That is the question we need to address before we move onto sharing further dreams and visions since I have told you the family secret. Why share with the world our secret? Because the world is ready to receive truth about seers, visions and dreams. What we behold we become. A true seer is someone inspired so deeply that the main goal in life amplifies the nature and character of Jesus Christ. But first you must learn and understand what the nature and character of Jesus Christ is. *Jesus said, "When you see me, really see me, you see the heavenly Father that sent me."*

It's not about doing but being. Just be, that's what God said. Just be. God told Daniel to seal up the book for the time hadn't come. Jesus came over 2000 years ago and plainly said he opened the books and the book of life. Who are the books he opened? Who was worthy to open the books? Revelation says Jesus Christ the Lamb of God was worthy to open the books. We are the books? Every one of us is a walking living book or a walking dead book. If we are alive we vibrate life. If we are asleep or dead then we vibrate death. Only Jesus, who is the living word and the Holy Spirit in Him can open us up and draw us to God. God would not allow even us to open up our spiritual hearts for he knew we needed purity. There wasn't anything pure in us. If we had opened ourselves up it would have been contaminated in one second or less. He told the angel in the Garden of Eden to go and drive them out before they ate from the tree of life and remain in that death state forever. People come and read our book when we invite them in. People come to read and enjoy or be part of each chapter when we invite them in. Every chapter is another step on the ladder of life moving upward and higher in God or moving downward further away from God.

Paul teaches visions, dreams, revelation and all the rest teach healings, abundance and faith. Well what is faith? It is substance and evidence. That's why all we need is a mustard seed faith- because that's all it takes to believe and receive. The bigger the ego the bigger the answer and more confused it becomes. Egos love to make things seem complimented. But once God reveals it to you, you can bathe in God's simple truths and smile at them. Some preachers say they want knowledge. I want God who is so simple when you run him down he is only energy or vibration. The Holy Spirit moved and hovered over the waters. How simple is that? Energy moved and vibrated. Take the tithe for an example. Now where did Jesus pay tithe to a church building fund or anything else. Peter put him in a position to pay taxes one time when he opened his big mouth. So not to offend anyone Jesus sent Peter to catch a fish and get the huge piece of gold out and go and pay taxes. Do you think Peter got a lesson on when to keep his mouth shut after that?

Why don't we tithe since Jesus came? God doesn't need your little ten per cent. He wants all of you. It's all or nothing. Nothing is what we all give God. There's no such thing as paying a tithe since Jesus came. God owns the earth (you) and the fullness there of (you and all the sewage you own in there), so what do we own that we can give or pay? Nothing! Yet what is God's is ours! Jesus was constantly giving of himself, his time, his knowledge, his provision, his everything. What was he giving us? God, he said I am nothing. What you see is my Father. It is my heavenly Father giving these things to you. Constantly giving and gave with a cheerful heart and they beat him and hung him on a tree and killed him. Did they kill God in him? No they killed the self person. When he resurrected it was Father God who resurrected. The poor widow woman gave all she had because she gave from the heart. She didn't have anything to give but her soul. What is the magic word? Soul! In reality God said not to fear the one who can destroy the body but fear the one who can destroy soul and body. Do we really own our soul? No. We have a choice to decide. So if we want a soul we had better give it to God real fast to keep it for us. You spread love, peace, joy, kindness like Jesus and they will hang you on a tree and kill your butt. The self rule will burn or be hung on a tree but if you keep it you will surely die for there's no life in you. God is life in you flowing through every vein, in every nerve, cell and organ when you have life. No man took Jesus life or self. He gave his self rule up freely. We must do the same. Then we pick up God who is life and live a free life. Everything God gives back to us we are to receive with a cheerful heart and give out to others with a cheerful heart. What are you giving out when you pick up life? God himself. So if you got to die anyway why not give all you own away with a cheerful heart and have no load to carry? What we give with a cheerful heart is blessed back to us a thousand fold. When the prodigal son came to his senses he decided to go home to the father. He had to come to his spiritual senses in order to make a wise decision to get and go to his father. What senses did he come back too? Wasn't he smelling, seeing and feeling how wonderful immoral sex and drugs were? Sure he was with his physical senses. But those senses were temporary for a temporary physical body. So what senses did he come to? His real spiritual sense then he was sane to make wise decisions. He got up and shook off the mud, sinful nature or foolish man and went home to humble himself and beg for forgiveness. He didn't take his drug habit or immoral sex acts home with him to give to his family or for his family to accept. He did exactly what each of us has to do if we want a better life or life at all.

David said in Psalm 17:3, "Though you probe my heart and examine me at night, though you test me, you will find nothing; I have resolved that my mouth will not sin." Then Solomon told us in Proverbs 6:2, "if you have been trapped by what you said, ensnared by the words of your mouth, then do this, my son, to free yourself, since you have fallen into your neighbor's hands (your foolish self): Go and humble yourself; press your plea with your neighbor (your wise self)!" Then in the New Testament Jesus says, what comes out of man's mouth makes him unclean. And in Luke 6:45 Jesus says the good man brings good things out of the good stored up in his heart, and the evil man brings evil things out of the evil stored up in his heart. For out of the overflow of his heart his mouth speaks. Who was Jesus speaking of? He was talking about everyone of us for in each person is the wise man and the foolish man or spiritual senses and physical senses. We must choose which nature we will bow too every day. When the spiritual senses are awakened then the physical senses are asleep. How simply is that? When we invite Jesus, who is the living vibrating energy word of God or God Himself, Creator of all in all, in our heart then and only then can the senses be washed whiter than snow. We need the spiritual ears to hear what the Holy Spirit power is saying, (some call it the sixth sense). We need the spiritual eyes and spiritual mind to see beyond the natural physical present or even obey Jesus who said, *'keep your mind fixed on things above, pure and beautiful thoughts.'* We need the will of God and God's sense awakened, the spirit of God and soul of God awakened within us. We need emotions, sex and the consciousness of our Creator then we can be as Jesus was, is and always will be. When our entire physical sense family is asleep and we surrendered to God for Jesus to awaken our spiritual senses then we truly understand what God breathed in each of us at our physical birth when he gave life to our soul and body and we cried. Then and only then will we be totally transformed or transparent. Then and only then we will live in the realm of ascension as Jesus lives. That's every true Christian's goal and that's what most of my childhood dreams and visions meant. Different forms and symbols in each but the spiritual meaning was the same.

In our grandparents generations which hasn't been that long for those of us born after World War II when we were called witches and were hung or burned alive. That's why they had to go in hiding and keep their gifts a secret. That's why God has many children of light all around the world like sleeping cells waiting to be awakened, waiting patiently for the call, and here the words "come up here". It hasn't been that long ago people, in our grandparents generation. Think about it. The way some religions are today they would still like to hang us or burn us. A seer is a person with the gift of discerning the spirits or seeing in the spirit world. Today in this generation God has restored us to life and making us aware of spiritual insight by many channels from books to television to movies. Rest assured no religion will stop the flow of the Holy Spirit power. Like a butterbean planted in the dark ground waiting while the earth does its work before it will come forth out of the earth so are the children or sons of God. In the years of 1947-1958 there was such a move of the Holy Spirit that supernatural healings and miracles came forth and people heard about them all over the world. How much greater in our generation will be the hovering of the Holy Spirit or its shifting? Tent revivals sprung up everywhere and eyes were opened, ears opened to hear God, many miracles, me being one of them. I grew up in this era when God was real and is real and is right here with us. What happened to people in such a few short years? What made man take God, Bible and anything concerning Jesus as well as prayer out of our schools? Look at the results for the past 30 years? Look at our children around the world and see where they are? It used to be, when I was a child, that if you were lazy, or considered bad you stuck out like a sore thumb. Now, 30 years later, if you are righteous you stick out like a sore thumb and are not popular among the preachers and religions at all. We're not talking about a thousand years ago or even five hundred but less than a hundred. Our parents and grandparents generation look at our schools then and now, look at the crime rate then and now, look at the drugs now. There weren't drugs and few youths getting in trouble. Families were centered on church-God, family and families prayed together, worked together and played together. That is one major key I hope everyone that reads this book will get ingrained into their hearts and minds. Families took care of their parents, grandparents, aunts, uncles, and each other's children and their animals, if necessary. There weren't any welfare programs or food stamps. It was church family and family that helped one another. Now a days we have sons that don't even call their parents much less mow their grass or take them somewhere. We have grown children still living off of their parents instead of making their parents golden years a blessing. It's not in a few families people it is in all families now. They have no respect or honor for their parents or anyone else and they actually think God is not watching. As Jesus said, fools. Wake up; arise and shine for the glory of God is come. Is it upon you? I suggest you get somewhere and start repenting if it isn't for we are living in the end times. Man's nature is about to destroy mankind with all their knowledge and technology. Doctors taking credit like they are the smart people not acknowledging that they are only servants of God. Scientists so full of pride and ego that they actually believe they invented something or a cure when in truth God allowed them to discover what He wanted them to discover in His own timing. God is in control whether you believe it or not.

Today in 2010 there's a shift birthed, which began October 2009 and waves like the world has never seen are coming upon us even as I sit and write these words, waves of the Holy Spirit power of Almighty God. Healing waves are covering the earth touching every person who believes for it. Manifestations of God's power again in simplicity, purity and God's prophetic ministries will be on the streets and highways again like Bible days. It won't be the preachers and religious leaders but the everyday people all around us and if luck has it we as well will be who God is using now. A shift of power began in 2007 the conception of the shift, when God started reaching his youth, his people who have sat on pews and studied His word for years and kept silent. People that have listened to preachers preach falsehood yet they themselves know truth. God started opening their minds and hearts to know and experience His Truth regardless of what the religious preachers taught. When he started pulling down preachers, the world was made known of it. Most of them don't even recognize the prophets or seers in their own churches and don't respect and honor their elders. God never intended for any man to be over his church. Yet church after church has leaders whom the people make their god, shower with gifts, and follow his words as faithfully as the children of Light, not even realizing they have made a man their god. Now the youth, little children will carry God's message in all simplicity and purity. Youth ministries will spring up all over the world with supernatural power. People are tired of the fate religions. I believe God made us tired of it. But new energy is upon us now. Multitudes of people all over the world are experiencing their spiritual senses opened. There are many books and movies made to education the intelligent people now, intelligent meaning those willing to listen to

God and obey. The ego minded is the hardest to humble and believe but egos will be crushed. Many ego minded people stick their head up in the air like a banner rooster streaking around the yard, saying, you shut up. I am the educated one. I am the one in charge of the church, do as I say and keep quiet. Just give me your money for any little project I dream up. They may not be literally saying it but their own countenance vibrates it loud and clear. Listen to me, the day has come that God is exposing all and bringing to the light all that and all who have deceived his people with lies. Their hidden motives are being exposed all over the world even as I write. The churches in this country alone are folding in this generation because they have taught God's word is dead, from the past and not the same yesterday, today and forever. God is shouting I AM the SAME. I change not. Are you listening? If so, start applying the real Jesus, not the sun god but the real Jesus to your soul and body. Don't be like the people standing outside of Noah's boat. Don't be like the people in Sodom when the angel of the Lord came to burn down the entire city and all the people who didn't hear God and help build the boat for their safety.

The Bible is our guided image, it creates within us inspiration, and thought, blessed we are to have the living words of God spoken to us and in us. The words leave an imprint upon us that is eternal. God's words are the only eternal living, vibrating energy we have to plant in ourselves and our children. It's not about saving souls or changing people to think like us. It's about planting the life words and allowing God to awaken or save souls for His kingdom. The same tools we used in darkness we now use in the light for the glory of God. That's what I learned from my Daddy, Aunt Ellen, dreams and visions.

How blessed I was to be born into a family that believed in the spiritual gifts of God and watched for those who had the gift awakened, and taught and cultivated the gifts with the words of God for the glory of God. I could have just as easily been in a family that hung and burned at the stake people like us. I believe God chose my family and the time I was born on earth for He said He knew me before I was conceived in my mama's belly. Before He formed me and shaped me and brought me forth He knew me and knew what His plan and purpose for me was and implanted within me all I would need for Him to finish His work in me on this earth to work out of me my own salvation which He planted in me before the worlds were created. He knew you too. He knew exactly what you would do with your gifts, waste them or cultivate them. He knew what mistakes you would make to learn the lessons He intended for you to learn. He knew what family to put you in to finish the work He wanted to complete. That sounds hard to believe when you think of the evil men and women who do such evil and cruel acts. But as simply as drinking water or drinking wine they had the choice to make, to eat and drink from the tree of life within them or eat and drink from the tree of good and evil within them. It's every person's choice to accept or reject their true nature. This I also learned from the dreams and visions.

I felt a strong need for you to understand the gift of discerning spirits in order to understand why we are all different yet the same. You first needed to understand you have the gift. You have the same God as I do. You might call him by a different title but the same God. You might believe some of His words and disbelieve others but He is the same God. He is God all in all. He is intimacy. You want intimacy seek the kingdom of God you will find it. You want joy and peace. Seek the kingdom of God and you will experience it. *II Corinthians 4:18 says, seek for the unseen and you will find.* Insight is one spiritual gift from God, there are many. Who I am, God says. He is one Creator God regardless of what you call him He is the living God.

In the last chapter in this book, I will share a few dreams that have already come to pass. The last dream I will share with you is the most amazing and most powerful of all. The word *replace* will be better understood by understanding how intimate our Creator God really is. Every dream, vision, visitation, enlightened words in the Bible, spoken word whether from God or through another person, all of it just proves God is love, an intimate loving God who still wants His family to honor and respect Him as Father, as Mother. Honor thy father and mother so that you be blessed.

PaPa Smith and Tadpole

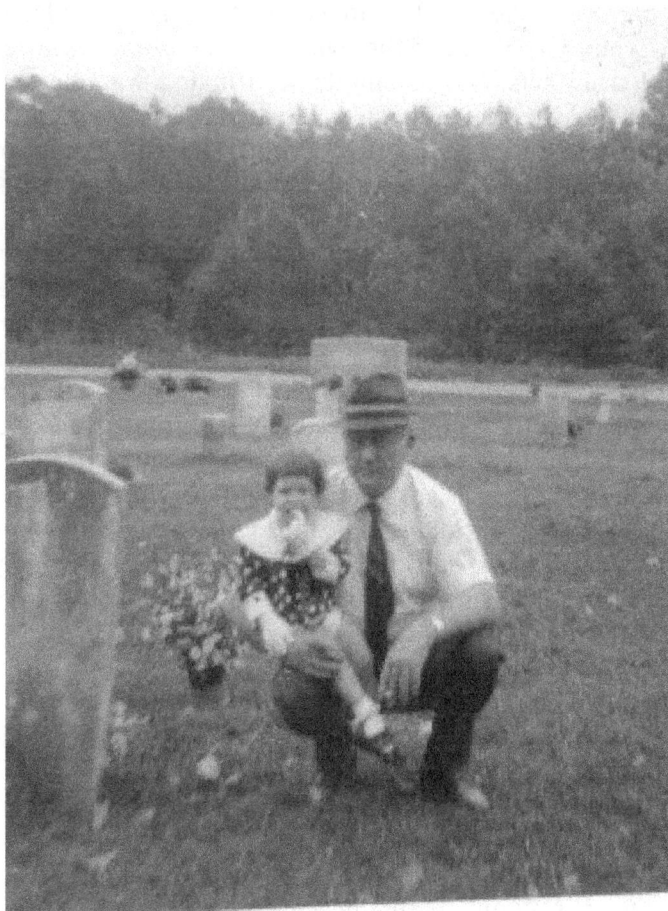

June 1968:
My Daddy with his first grandchild, Tammy (Tadpole).
A proud Papa kneeling at his mother's grave
while attending the family reunion; Dreams change things.

Chapter 9:

Dreams Change Lives

"**I** will go on to visions and revelations from the Lord," the Apostle Paul said in II Corinthians 12:1. "I, Carolyn will go on to visions and revelations from the Lord," and have.

BC came home from the army and seemed more appreciative to have a family than he did two years back. Maybe the army had matured him. Within the first year we were renting our own place and using the furniture bought with money I had saved those two years while living with Daddy. It was there at that home that I had a scary dream about a flood. It was June of 1969 when I saw a flood coming to Riverdale. I saw it covering his brother's trailer and the whole trailer park. I saw BC with many rescue workers and policemen going in on our small boat to get them out and their belongings. I saw pictures ruined and everything just a mess, all muddy. To my knowledge South Boston Virginia had never had a flood before. Seeing this in a dream really scared me because all the businesses in Riverdale were flooded and people were in a panic.

Telling BC and his brother was a waste of time and energy the next morning. They laughed so hard and called me crazy for days. I had been called many things but crazy wasn't one of them. I begged them to listen to the warning God had given. I got in my car and went to tell Brenda and her mom who lived in Riverdale along with a few business people I knew. They listened and questioned but didn't believe it because none made any attempts to move out or protect their belongings. None that I told believed me and that hurt deep. What did I do? What I had always done. I ran to Daddy to tell him and then to Aunt Ellen. Both said I had warned them and none listened so for me to keep quiet and pray inwardly for peace and calmness. Aunt Ellen prayed that the flood wouldn't take any lives. I prayed with her for God to change it since no one was listening.

But on August 20, 1969, the flood came and it was just as I had seen it in the dream. BC had to go in on his boat and rescue what he could but only a few photos were saved from the flood just like the dream showed. The entire trailer park where they lived and the whole Riverdale area were under water. Below is the natural report from the National Weather Service and Barbara McNaught Watson's report as I found it on Google search.

Copied from the National Weather Service written By Barbara McNaught Watson South Boston Virginia was # 8th on the list:

Historic River Floods	Flood Stage	Sep. '96	Jan. '96	Nov. '85	Jun. '72	Aug. '69	Aug. '55	Oct. '42	Aug. '40	Apr. '37	Mar. '36
South Boston (Dan River)	25ft.	33.2 *	---	---	33.4 **	---	---	---	31.8 *	---	---

Key: * Major Flooding; ** Record Flood Stage

Top Ten Floods determined by looking at river stage records for 15 gauges across Virginia on 12 Rivers. For each gauge's top ten floods, 1 through 10 points were assigned with worst flood receiving 10 points and the tenth flood receiving 1 point. Extra points were given as follows: 5 points for a record flood, 3 points for major flooding, 1 point for moderate flooding. Points were totaled for all of the floods and the top ten floods were ranked according to the highest point totals.

* Camille was Virginia's worst flash flood and its worst disaster of the 20th century in terms of loss of life. August 20-22, 1969.

Do you think they believed me after the flood? Yes to a degree they did but to late like so many in today's generation who don't see the warnings or don't believe them and like it will be when Christ returns. BC was in such awe he took many pictures. The dream warning them and them not listening didn't change the dream at all but it did change them. (*Jesus said the end time would be like Noah's flood, Matthew 24: 39 and Genesis 9:28). Isaiah says in Isaiah 59:19, "From the west, men will fear the <u>name</u> of the LORD, and from the east, they will show honor and devotion to His glory, for He will come like a pent-up flood that the breath of the LORD drives along. The Redeemer will come to Zion, to those in Jacob who repent of their sins. In Daniel 9:26 he says, the end will come like a flood, like an irresistible flood. He will invade many countries and sweep through them like a flood. In Luke 6:38 Luke tells us when a flood* *came, the rushing stream struck that house that hears Jesus' words and put them into practice but could not shake it, because it was well built on a solid foundation.*

The next dream: I had become pregnant with my second child in 1969 and my due date was March 1970 just like the dream I had had after the flood but when I told BC he didn't believe. All during my pregnancy he denied it was a boy and accused me of getting pregnant on purpose since he didn't want any more children. Since I didn't have any dreams during my first pregnancy I was surprised when the flood dream came and then this one. Actually that was the first dream I had had since the marriage dream. God wasn't surprised that I was surprised. He had taught me humans couldn't put Him in a box. The Lord spoke Galatians 4:19-31, *"My dear children, for whom I am again in the pains of childbirth until Christ is formed in you, how I wish I could be with you now and change my tone, because I am perplexed about you! Tell me, you who want to be under the law, are you not aware of what the law says? For it is written that Abraham had two sons, one by the slave woman and the other by the free woman. My dear children, for whom I am again in the pains of childbirth until Christ is formed in you, His son by the slave woman was born in the ordinary way; but his son by the free woman was born as <u>the result of a promise</u>. The women represent two covenants. One covenant is from Mount Sinai and bears children who are to be slaves: This is Hagar. Now Hagar stands for Mount Sinai in Arabia and corresponds to the present city of Jerusalem, because she is in slavery with her children. But the Jerusalem that is above is free, and she is our mother. At that time the son born in the ordinary way persecuted the son born by the power of the Spirit. It is the same now. The son born in the ordinary way represents the flesh natural human where the son born by the power of the Spirit is the spiritual self. The Jerusalem we seek is above and our mother. But what does the Scripture say? "Get rid of the slave woman and her son, for the slave woman's son will never share in the inheritance with the free woman's son." Therefore brothers, we are not children of the slave woman, but of the free woman. We have been born by the power of the Spirit. It is for freedom that Christ has set us free. Stand firm after you have been set free, and do not let yourselves be burdened again by a yoke of slavery. Let Christ be of value to you. The only thing with value is faith expressing itself through love.*

It was only after the birth of my son that I realized some of the meaning of that dream. What stood out after BC found out I was pregnant again and after his rudeness and mistrust by accusing me of tricking him by not taking my birth control. He used that as his excuse to drink more, stay out all night, and not keep his word and finally committing adultery. He refused to believe that God had revealed the pregnancy in a dream, and I had gotten pregnant while on birth control. I saw the weakness in him that Daddy had seen, cried and begged me not to marry him because of. It was only after the birth of Jay, our son, that he believed, repented, and asked forgiveness. Then the words that stood out in the dream suddenly made sense. God was forming Christ in BC, and I was in the pains of childbirth like Christ was when He formed Christ in me, *"My dear children, for whom I am again in the pains of childbirth until Christ is formed in you, how I wish I could be with you now and change my tone, because I am perplexed about you! Jay had been born as the result of a promise. I had prayed since Tammy was born if I found favor in His eyes then allow me to give BC a son.* BC's disbelief meant he was still enslaved to his flesh nature but God was revealing Himself to him through me. I can't say I enjoyed the pain and suffering but I sure did enjoy the gift of joy and gift of revelation. Also the part of the power of the Spirit being our mother struck a chord in me and set my curiosity on fire to know our mother the power of the Spirit.

The next dream came as a vision and came six months after my son Jay was born. It was September and we had actually moved back in with Daddy. I had had a difficult labor and delivery on March 31, 1970, then discovered the baby stayed sick more than well, which was really a heavy load on my energy level. I had started having black outs again, which I hadn't had for a few years and felt with all that I was going through, I needed someone to help me that believed in me. I had lost trust in BC and didn't want to discuss anything with him much less my intimate feelings. I was still struggling with forgiveness and was trying to work and stay up all night with Jay. He wasn't satisfied with anyone but me and slept on my chest when he did fall asleep. I really needed some stability in my life at that point and someone who believed in me. It's a hard pill to swallow when a mate is unfaithful at any time in a marriage but when he is unfaithful while you're carrying his baby is just a little too much, at least for me. Daddy never said I told you so not once. All he said was I needed to forgive and make the marriage work. I felt I was in a war zone within myself seeing his flesh nature and having to battle with it. Whether I was suppose to battle with it or not I did while juggling all the other tasks of wife, mother, employee and daughter.

That certain Sunday in September 1970 Jay began with a fever and trouble breathing that sent us to the ER the first time. He was examined, given some medicine and sent home. Within two hours we made our second trip to the ER. His fever was increasing instead of decreasing and he was as limber as a dish rag. Again he was examined, given medicine and sent home. By 7 pm that evening we were rushing him back to the ER for the third time. This time the nurse asked if I would agree to see a Dr. Judy who was there on call from the Clarksville Virginia area. We agreed and he immediately ordered Jay to be put in an oxygen tent packed in ice. He administered drugs and said all we could do was wait. He was being admitted. Sometime during the night they moved him to a private room upstairs where we stayed with him.

By Thursday, he was in a comma and doctors were saying they didn't know what was wrong with him. His kidneys were shutting down, and the fever had gone so high they were afraid he would have brain damage if he lived at that point. They suggested we call the family in. After they left, BC and I both stood in total shook and were completely speechless, how long I don't know. One thing went through my mind, was losing our son the price or consequence for BC's affair earlier in the year that caused me to move back with Daddy in the first place? When I was able to speak I asked him if he thought God was allowing this to show us we couldn't get away with sin. Did he think his sexual affair had anything to do with this situation we were facing? Had he truly repented of it? It may have sounded judgmental but knowing man brings on himself the consequences as a result of sin. God never puts evil upon us. It is always brought on by our foolish choices or least that's what I believed at the time from the teachings of Daddy and Aunt Ellen. BC didn't answer my question but said he was going to call Marion. That was his sister whom he looked up to after his mother's death. I tried to get him to stay but to no avail. He stood up and walked out of Jay's room. I watched him leave, not looking back nor saying bye, just like Mama had done years earlier. Walking away from problems and not taking responsibility for his actions was a side I hadn't gotten use to since he had returned from the army. One I battled with daily which caused a barrier between us. My heart rose up in my throat, as my being filled up with the most alone feeling I had ever felt. I ran to the bathroom like I had ran in the house to Daddy at six years old to seek some answers and get this alone feeling out of me. Quickly I closed the door thinking I would throw up any second from the hurt I felt inside. The bathroom was dark with no windows and I didn't bother turning on the light. I cried out to God in the darkness. I asked God not to take my son for the price of BC's sexual sin. I asked God to search me and see if there was anything in me that I hadn't repented of and remove it. There in the silence I began to feel calmness, just a little calmness within me. I sat on the commode and waited in the calmness for an answer from the Holy Spirit. In a few moments I felt led to stand up, almost like a push from behind me. I even looked back to see who pushed me. My mouth opened and words flowed from it. With a mind and heart full of fear I cried out loud, *"LORD God in Jesus Christ Name, you gave me this child. You and only you have the power to heal him or take him from the earth. I ask that you give me strength to live with your decision."* Then I sat down and waited for His answer.

No sooner than I felt the commode on my butt I saw a most magnificent light fill the bathroom. It was a pure white light with every rainbow color weaved into it. Then like a huge television screen I saw this old man dressed in what appeared to be was an Indian blanket or desert robe and desert sanders on his feet. I could smell the desert dust from his clothing and see his hairy arms as he lifted a baby boy naked wrapped in the same type of blanket material up toward the sky in an offering unto God. His arms looked like the arms of a rugged hard working outdoorsman. I could see the colors in the blanket, lines of dark blue, light blue. Some were tan and green while others were red and yellow. Then there were the deep purple and the white lines all weaved in a perfect line throughout the blanket. Why did the colors catch my mind's eye? What was he doing with the baby boy? What did it mean for the baby to be naked? Why couldn't I hear what he was saying to God? As I watched the old man offering the baby boy up to God I wondered if this was God's answer. Had he decided to take Jay home with himself? My mind wouldn't stop wondering long enough to hear the vision. In the silence all I could hear was my own mind asking questions. I thought shut up mind so I can hear God. In a few more moments I began to feel stronger and the tears were all gone. I felt lighter within but not one answer was given, only the vision before me. Was the vision the answer I wondered? What seemed like an hour was only seconds. Then as I watched the old man hold the baby boy up to God a beam of radiant light shown down on him. The beam of light looked like a huge tube moving in a circular motion as it shone onto the baby. Was this the glory of God I wondered within myself? It appeared to be aimed at one focal point that baby and went miles up in the sky as far as the eye could see. Once that appeared I couldn't take my eyes off of it. I could feel the energy and vibrational wave of warmth in the beam as it flowed directly onto the baby and lite up the entire bathroom. Like a magnet it was holding my attention bypassing my thoughts. Its powerful force was drawing me upward causing me to feel like I was rising up off the floor and entering the light. After a few seconds it disappeared.

My first thought was God had decided to come and take Jay to heaven. Thinking this I wanted to say bye so I rushed to the door so nervous I didn't think that knob would ever turn. Once I got it to turn I immediately opened it and rushed to my son. Feeling the familiar warmth in the room that I had felt in the bathroom I looked up and noticed the whole room was filled with radiant light. The same powerful beam of light that had shown in the little bathroom filling it up with its radiance was shining through the hospital window directly on Jay. I stood in awe as the radiance shone on my baby. Within a second I saw Jay's eyes open and he was using his arms to push himself up. He turned his head and looked at me and smiled as he continued to sit up in that oxygen tent. I reached inside those holes on the side of the tent to touch him. He reached for my hand and pulled himself to me, smiling the most beautiful smile, almost heavenly. Once he reached me he kept on coming until I had both arms in the holes and holding him to the railings to keep him from falling backwards. I was witnessing the glory of God at the same time I was seeing what was happening in the physical realm as a result of that glory. How I knew it was the glory of God only God knows. It was like God had transmitted to me what I was witnessing as I witnessed it. Suddenly the machines went off and nurses came running.

"What are you doing? Are you trying to kill him?" one nurse said in almost panic. I could see the fear all over her face as she realized he was still in the tent standing up between my arms holding on. He wasn't old enough to be standing up and she knew it.

Jay smiled directly at her while he squeezed my arms pinching the skin, holding on for dear life as he said, "Ma Ma." He was only six months old and before the beam of light he wasn't pulling up, standing up or talking. As shocked and surprised as I was so was the nurse. She quickly ran out of the room to get the doctor. I began pulling Jay to my chest with only the tent between us. I tried to get him through the two holes that were there for the doctors and nurses to administer drugs, change IV's and change his diaper or whatever else he needed but they were too small.

Ma Ma was the sweetest words I had ever heard coming from my son's lips as he held onto me with all the strength he had. Soon the room was wall to wall with doctors and nurses. Each asking questions as to what had happened. I told them I came out of the bathroom and there was a beam of light shining through the window directly onto Jay. Immediately he woke up and began pushing himself up to sit up. Once he sat up he crawled over to the edge of the tent where I was standing and started pulling himself up. Before I knew it he was standing up holding onto the bed rail and I reached inside to hold onto him when the nurses came in. I could tell from their expressions they didn't believe me but didn't have a medical reason either as to what had happened. They were having difficulty believing their own eyes as I was. After a few minutes thinking and trying to believe their own eyes Dr. Judy wanted to examine Jay. Once he had finished the examination he didn't understand what had happened but, he seems to be fine, he said. He asked the staff to walk with him outside as he left orders with one of the nurses to get Jay out of that tent and give him to his mama. As they all walked out in the hall one of the nurses un-zippered the tent and handed Jay to me.

I can't tell you what it felt like to hold my son alive in his physical body again or to see the glory of God manifested all around me. I don't remember any thoughts going through my head at that point just the overwhelming feeling of joy. The image in my head was the beam of light and the old man holding the naked baby up to God. Believing it was Abraham holding Isaac up as a love offering. Knowing I had done the same with Jay when I prayed and said, *"Lord, you gave me this child. You and only you have the power to heal him or take him back home with you. I ask that you give me strength to live with your decision. Amen."*

His daddy had missed such a glorious manifestation of God at work but I wasn't about to leave my son to find him. I was so pleased with my Daddy God that day I don't think anything could have upset me at that moment. After all the tests were run and results came back, all they found was a black spot on his lung. That was the only evidence that Jay had had a near death experience, naked until God clothed him in his glory. They did believe that it was caused by me being on birth control for the first three months of my pregnancy but they weren't even sure of that. Jay's smile was as warm and sweet as if God Himself was smiling through him. After we brought him home from the hospital he slept all night. He had changed from a sickly crying baby to a happy healthy one. Like the naked baby boy had been clothed with the glory of God. I prayed and thanked God for such glory and for his life and peace. I also surrendered Jay back to God that day and asked God to use him and his earthly life according to His will. Not knowing what that meant but I knew Jay was God's child and should have a desire to seek God. Whether he did was between him and God as time passed.

The little red brick house and what it meant. The next dream I had in January 1971. I woke up as usual with BC on one side, Jay on the other with Tammy in the middle. Thank God we had a king size bed at that time. Trying to get out of the bed to fix Daddy's breakfast and not wake up anyone was a job I had practiced every morning since Jay had come home from the hospital. Since his near death experience I wanted both children near my side all the time until my own security returned before allowing them to sleep in their room down the hall. I knew it was my own fear that caused me to be so protective but it was the only way I could sleep. Slipping out of bed took longer than cooking breakfast, only to hear little feet just before we sat to a quiet morning at the window enjoying the beautiful warm sun. Daddy and I both loved to watch the sun come up and sit in its light while eating. Just as soon as we sat down Daddy smiled and said I believe I better get my knee ready because I hear Tadpole's feet coming. Daddy had nicknamed Tammy the day he brought us home from the hospital. After laying her in her beautiful oak baby bed he had bought her with all the trimmings, he said she wasn't as big as a tadpole. After that day she was Papa's Tadpole.

After Tammy got in her Papa's lap for him to feed her out of his plate I began telling Daddy about my dream. As always he listened with great intensity. In the dream I saw a little red brick house. The yard was green with fresh cut grass with a tree off to the left with two colors of flowers growing from it, white and pink. I thought how odd to see a tree with two colors. I saw BC and myself walk up the little gravel driveway to the back yard. There I saw a white out-building with a cement floor. Then the lady showing us the house asked if we would like to see the inside. Quickly I replied, we don't need too, I know this is my house by the front and back yard and the tree with the two colors of flowers pink and white. BC said quickly, yes we do want to see the inside. Then as we walked towards the front yard to the front door, he whispered to me suppose the inside is a mess that needs a lot of repairs. I whispered back we will fix them. Then we walked up the few little steps and as the lady put the key in and went to open the door I woke up.

Daddy said, "Well I guess you'll be looking at want ads today."

I answered, "Yeap and if I find it can you let BC go with me. Is there anything you need to go to town for? Daddy had talked BC into working at the store with him and gave him a sofa to sleep on after we had separated because of his adultery. That was his way of getting us back together. I guess Daddy knew I would never forgive him and live at home where it was safe forever if he allowed it. I loved all of my family and knew I had a home with anyone of my aunts and Johnny or at least I felt I did. I had too much pride to live with a man that committed adultery. Smith's knew they weren't perfect but had a hard time forgiving anyone but a Smith. Just one of our weaknesses we worked to overcome. BC had lived like that since March. I only allowed him in the house after Jay went to the hospital, which was September. Jay being raised from the dead had softened my heart quite a bit. It made me very appreciative for everyone and everything except for that woman who had slept with him.

The lady I caught him with had come to my door knocking and begging my forgiveness but I slammed the door in her face each time. She didn't give up. She came back every Sunday for a month. The day I opened the door and accepted her forgiveness was a beautiful sunny day. This day she did something different other than just knock. This time she yelled, "Carolyn, I'm not leaving until you forgive me. I will keep coming until you open this door and tell me you forgive me. I have accepted Jesus in my heart and been baptized in the Holy Spirit. You are my sister in Christ and I did you wrong. The Lord said I had to get your forgiveness for Him to forgive me. Please open the door and tell me you will forgive me.

Those words melted my heart and I opened the door with my eyes full of tears. Her words had burned in my heart like a torch. She stood with her husband waiting for me to invite them in. I stepped out onto the porch and listened to what she had to say. She shared when, how and where she had repented and accepted Jesus in her heart to be Lord. She said after hearing about Jay's hospital stay her heart troubled her so deep she hadn't been able to sleep. One night, while praying for forgiveness, she swore she heard a voice that said, *"I can't forgive you until Carolyn forgives you. Go and ask her to forgive you. If she does then so will I."*

I knew in my heart she was telling the truth and invited them in. The confession burned inside of me and humbled me into silence. All the ugly words I wanted to say and had practiced in my mind for months vanished when I heard the Holy Spirit say within me, *"Those you forgive I will forgive."* Before they left that day she had my forgiveness.

Now back to the house dream. I searched the classifieds and found one house, it had all we needed but didn't say if it was brick or not. When I called and set the appointment I asked if it was brick. The realtor said she thought so and would show it at 2 p.m. I went to the store and told BC what time we had to meet the lady. I dressed Tammy and Jay and took them over to the babysitter. We met the real estate lady but it wasn't the house. It was down highway 501 with no brick houses next door and it wasn't even brick. I didn't want to go in. What was the use of me wasting my time I thought? But the realtor insisted we go in. She made a very strong sales pitch but I wasn't interested at all. When she tried to get us to make an offer I flat refused rather rudely. No, this is not the house I saw in my dream. Let's go BC. I started walking toward the car and BC followed. Upon leaving BC asked why I needed to be so rude to her. She was just doing her job. I defended myself by saying I wasn't rude just to the point. She was wasting God's valuable time showing us a house not red brick in the first place. Then try to talk me into a house I didn't want. She better be glad I was in a good mood or she would have gotten more than a straight forward answer. BC shook his head as he drove us back home. He had a hard time dealing with my forwardness and boldness at times and we traveled in silence the remainder of the ride. I didn't care. I used that silence to thank God for showing me my little red brick house with the tree in the front yard with pink and white flowers next time. You could like me for who I am or get out of my presence was my attitude most of the time, especially when I knew I was right. I hadn't survived by being a coward and bowing to people and wasn't about to start.

Once we arrived back at the house I looked again in the classified but this time I prayed and ask God to forgive us for wasting his time and show me the house if it was in the paper. Immediately I saw like bold print the ad and called the number. I set the appointment for 9 a.m. the next day since it was almost time for me to go to work. We got up early the next morning and rode down to look at the house. As soon as we pulled up in the driveway I knew it was the house God had said he would give us. After looking over the outside the lady showed us the inside. BC didn't like it. He said the floors needed tile, the hardwood floors needed buffering and inch by inch he picked it apart. I tuned him out after awhile and asked the lady for the owner's name and phone number. Once we returned home I called Mr. Nester and set an appointment for the next morning. He asked us one question if BC was an honorable veteran. Once he heard he was he agreed to meet us at the bank. He told us before we entered the bank that he would accept whatever offer the bank would lend. Once the meeting was over and we were back outside I asked what he would charge for us to rent it until the closing. He thought for a moment and said it was costing him $33 a month to keep the electric on for the furnace. That's what he would charge and I looked at BC to give him the money. All we had on us was $33 and he wrote us a receipt. That weekend we cleaned the house and put up curtains and started moving in. They had our lights transferred by Monday and the phone installed so we officially moved in the following week which was in March 1971. To this day I own that house and have called it God's house ever since.

The next dream from God didn't come until 1977 while we were in Tennessee. In the dream, I saw BC's daddy lying flat on his back in his bed and couldn't get up. The next morning I told BC he had to call his daddy. After he spoke with him, he said we had to return to Virginia. His daddy's legs and feet were swollen so bad he couldn't walk. While BC went to the job site and told his boss we had an emergency at home I packed our things and was ready to pull out when he returned. Once we arrived home and went over and saw how bad his daddy was we tried to get him to go to the hospital but he refused. He said he would go to his doctor on Monday morning. We had him in Dr. Brown's office at 8 a.m., after speaking with the doctor we called his other children. He had cancer. After that he moved in with us and remained there until his death in 1978.

No sooner than we had gotten over the lost of Mr. Creasy I had another dream about Uncle Press being in the hospital dying. Upon him entering the Veterans hospital I stayed with Aunt Ellen and Johnny two weeks until he passed April 7, 1979.

November of the same year I dreamed Daddy was admitted in Richmond hospital but it didn't show why or the outcome. Just that he was in the hospital. I chalked it up to my fears since the dream had little detail. A few months later to my surprise Daddy told us about a minor surgery to remove skin cancer from his face. I felt very uneasy about that surgery even though during Thanksgiving and Christmas he reassured me it was nothing. We had already lost two very close members of our family and I certainly wasn't ready emotionally for this surgery or anything else pertaining to Daddy. I wouldn't allow my mind to even wonder in that direction. I knew Daddy and Aunt Ellen were my pillars, and I didn't ever want to lose them. I depended on them for my wisdom and strength. Just the thought of losing one of them made me sick to my stomach and set off my black outs, which caused everyone to worry about me. I hated that I was so weak emotionally and got physically sick, but it was like I had no control over it if I worried. Daddy had the surgery as an outpatient and did well, very well, which made me feel even more stupid and insecure. His spirits were very high, and he was very confident that they removed it all, but I kept asking, "Are you sure?"

In the February of 1980, Daddy, Aunt Virginia, and Shirley went to Richmond for doctors to remove stitches in his face. They had stayed at Uncle Thornton's and Aunt Mamie's the night before so they could be at the doctor's office when it opened. Daddy wouldn't allow me to go; he said I needed to be home with my children. There was nothing to worry about. I called early February 13, and Uncle Thornton said they had a country breakfast and had left for the doctor. I asked him if Daddy seemed alright. He said he did. I also asked if Daddy remembered they were to come to my house for his birthday supper the same day. He assured me they were coming and said if I called they were supposed to tell me he would be there around 3 p.m. or so. Well 3 p.m. came and went and they hadn't arrived, so I called Uncle Thornton's again. Again, I was reassured he was fine when he left the doctor's office and spoke to Virginia by phone. They were going to stop at his favorite 360 restaurant to eat lunch, but Shirley had also mentioned doing a little shopping, also. I still felt uneasy about all of it and couldn't sit at the house any longer. I called my office and told Cathy if anyone needed me I was going up to the 360 house we called it to appraise it. Knowing the people very well, I just took Penny with me to play with their kids while I measured and got all details for the appraisal. I hadn't been there fifteen minutes when one of the agents from the office drove up and asked if I needed any help. Strange, I thought, he didn't know how to appraise a house but I thanked him and politely said no. A few minutes longer he hung around and I thought that was strange also since he acted so nervous, so I asked him to hold the measuring tape. He took it but never moved just said, "Oh, by the way, someone called the office and said your daddy was over at the hospital and wanted you to come over." He said it so non-caringly I replied I bet he picked at that spot on his face and Aunt Virginia panicked and made him go by and check it out. I apologized to the people as I gathered my things and that time I had a very joyous and peaceful feeling about it. I thought it was because Daddy was in town and alright. I sang the happy birthday song to Penny all the way to the house. I had told the agent as he returned to my office if they received any further calls just tell them I was taking the baby by the house first. Tammy and Jay would be home in a few minutes from school.

Upon arriving at the hospital I noticed all of Daddy's brothers and sisters were there. I thought, what the hell? I know Daddy is the baby but that's a little overboard. Shirley jumped up and ran to me saying, "He's gone. He's gone, Carolyn. Daddy is gone."

I answered what do you mean, gone where? She in all her hysteria and screaming I figured it out and walked up to the desk and asked to see my Daddy. She knew who I was talking about and said I couldn't do that. I answered her very cold and stern, "Well you better find someone in this hospital who can tell me where my Daddy is because I'm not leaving from this spot until you do." About that time Mrs. Regan stepped up and asked, what's going on Carolyn? I replied, "They say my Daddy is back there and I want to see him." She looked at me with such compassion I almost lost my coldness. She said follow me. As I followed her all of the family jumped up and followed. I walked in that room with every intention to speak him back to life like Jesus did Lazarus. I stepped in that cold room and saw Daddy lying on that flat bed a purple blue. The Holy Spirit within me said, "Let him go."

I pushed the tears back as I reached over and kissed his forehead and said, "I love you Daddy. I will see you in heaven." I turned and looked straight at Johnny while still standing over Daddy's body and asked where my Daddy's car was. But before he could answer me Shirley jumped in, "he's my Daddy too Carolyn." I couldn't hug her or touch her or anyone at that moment because every fiber of my being felt like fine crystal cracking into a million pieces. I wanted to scream, hit someone, disobey God and call for the entire God in me to raise him up off that table, but instead of doing that I walked out of that cold room as cold and hard as Daddy was lying there on that flat. Upon stepping out I told Mrs. Regan to call Powell's Funeral Home, they were family they would take care of the rest. Then I turned again and again asked Johnny where Daddy's car was. This time he answered me. Up on 58 at the garage on the right where he pulled over to leave this world. I asked him and Clarence to go get it and bring it to my house. Once you get it there park it in the back yard, lock it and don't allow anyone to touch it. Knowing how much Johnny loved and respected his Uncle Henry I hated that he had to sit in the same spot Daddy had left his body but someone had to get it. I knew Daddy would want Johnny to pick it up also. Aunt Virginia gave them the car keys and went to hand me his bill-folder, other keys, check book, and stuff he had in his pockets but I said no. Keep it until I need them. Shirley again spoke up and said he was her daddy too and she was the oldest and she wanted them. Aunt Virginia said, "No. Henry's last words were to give my bill-fold and keys to Carolyn Ann. She would know what to do and tell her not to go in the lockbox until all three were together."

I noticed her bottom lip quivering and reached and hugged her and told her to keep them then. I turned and said I was going home if anyone wanted to come by they were welcomed. I needed to call BC and Tommy and tell my children.

In my car all I could think about was fifty-nine years old today and my Daddy was dead. I was so mad at God at that point I couldn't cry or even feel my emotions. I had not one feeling that should have been there only anger. I kept saying, "How do I tell my children? They have lost their Papa Creasy and now this." If I ever was going to turn my back on God it would have been that day.

At the house, I went in to make coffee and someone said let them do that so I did. I told everyone to make themselves at home while I called BC and Tommy in the bedroom. I also asked them when Tammy came back with Jay not to say a word to them. I would tell them myself. But I guess Shirley saw her opportunity to get back at me and told them in her hysterical way. She was like that when she didn't get her way. I heard them running down the hall screaming and entered Tammy's room as I stepped out of my door. I ran in to them but I couldn't say a word. I couldn't hug them or show any emotions towards them at all. I couldn't speak so we three just sat on the bed and cried until we couldn't cry any longer. Then I told them to stay in the bedroom as long as they needed too I had to call their daddy and Uncle Tommy. When I stepped out of Tammy's room Aunt Virginia and Shirley were waiting for me. I looked at her and asked are you satisfied. Now they are as hysterical as you are. Are you satisfied as I opened my bedroom door to enter? Shirley tried to follow me but I told her she would be safer if they just left me alone. She replied I needed to break down and cry. I stared at her and said and be like you. I have phone calls to make, a funeral to plan, a house full of guess that need to eat something, two hysterical children, a baby and you're telling me to get hysterical like you. Someone has to keep a clear head around here in a hurtful and angry voice. I shut the door as I finished my sentence. Shirley ended hers by saying, "I love you Carolyn." That was her way of saying she was sorry.

BC and Tommy came in late that night and all had left but the kids and me. I shared what had been told to me as too the day's events that lead up to Daddy's death and what decisions I had made. The next morning Aunt Virginia had returned with the lockbox and keys. Shirley, Tommy and I went in the bedroom and opened it. Lying right on top was a white envelope addressed to the three of us. We opened it and there were funeral arrangements, his birth certificate, and army papers, everything we needed including money. Daddy had requested that we not spend more than what he had saved in the envelope on his funeral. Around 11 am we went to Powell's with the envelope and did as he had asked.

Family night I felt like Daddy was on display. I vowed I wouldn't have one at my funeral but family said it was needed for so many that couldn't make it to the funeral. About half way through it my chest began to hurt and I became very dizzy. BC noticed I was fixing to pass out and helped me to a chair where I sat the rest of the evening. Aunt Ellen and Johnny became very worried about me knowing I had a heart condition and told everyone they were taking me home. BC helped them get me in the car and I went home and went to my bedroom. Quiet time with God was what I craved. Just sitting in the silence with a blank mind and allowing

God to fill me with His strength to get through all this. At that point I just wanted it over.

The morning of the funeral I asked if the family would stay at the house and allow Shirley, Tommy, and me to go over and sit with Daddy's body a few minutes. They all agreed and so we did. Once there I asked Mr. Powell not to allow anyone in the room or knock until we came out. For some odd reason, I felt Daddy or God was going to say or do something that morning with the three of us. We were willing to stay and wait on the Lord until time to move him to the Halifax Baptist Church if need be. As we sat we told Daddy what a great father he had been to us and how much we appreciated all he taught us by example. We each promised to pass down his wisdom to our children and keep his memory alive forever. Then as each one finished talking to Daddy we sat in the silence. Suddenly all of us had an unction to get up and circle him hand in hand and we did. Daddy opened his eyes and sat right up in that casket looking at us. We couldn't believe it and thought God is raising him up like Lazarus but when he laid back down and closed his eyes our hope fell. We starred at each other in total awe as to what we had witnessed. Tommy noticed the amazing peace that surrounded us. I said, "Daddy, you're still watching us even from the grave" as we laughed. We bathed in this amazing peace and just knew we weren't alone. We took it to be the Prince of Peace and soaked up as much as we could before Mr. Powell knocked and said it was almost time to carry his body to the church. When we shared with him what had happened he explained it away by saying it was his muscles relaxing. It happens all the time. We didn't buy it because he couldn't explain away the glory in that room or the amazing peace.

In the car back to the house I shared I felt if the three of us went over God would do or say something but not wanting any doubt in the room I kept it to myself. We shared our memories especially the one every time we went some where without daddy. "Remember to be good and remember God and Daddy will be watching. Don't do anything in the dark you don't want the light to expose."

We all agreed it was a sign from God that He was with us and would help us get through this just like He did when Daddy went to Canada.

Back at the house everyone was surprised we were laughing and at peace but when we shared the funeral home experience they looked shocked and the room went into total silence. Aunt Ellen broke the silence by saying, "See, your daddy is still watching you and he will be around to help you." Some believed and some didn't but all got up to finish getting dressed to attend the funeral. I went in the bedroom with BC and we prayed the 23rd Psalms and asked for strength. The family cars arrived with Kenneth Powell driving which gave me relief since he had been so close to us over the years. At the church we saw Les Powell and knew with all the Powell family there all would go well. My only thought was Jesus raising Lazarus on the 4th day from the dead even after he stunk. Maybe just maybe He would raise Daddy on the 4th day.

The family car pulled up in the church yard and I couldn't believe all the people standing outside at least five hundred. Kenneth said the church was running over was why they were outside. As we stepped out of the family cars I could feel the honor and respect they had for Daddy and his family. I thought about what Uncle Press use to tell Daddy. Henry if you don't start attending some funerals and church again you won't have enough people at your funeral to carry your casket. I looked up towards the sky and silently said under my breath, Uncle Press you were wrong. Look at the people here. I know you are watching Uncle Press, as I smiled up. The people outside had formed a line on both sides for us to walk on the red carpet that entered inside of the church. We walked through with hanging heads and shaking legs. I saw every one of Daddy's best friends, the Honorable Senator, the dedicates, the judges, attorneys, and business men all huddled together in a straight line and bowed in honor as we passed through. I saw their pain in losing a dear friend as I made eye contact acknowledging them. We entered the church and sat as we looked up to see Daddy's body one last time. I had requested his casket remain opened until after the funeral. Something about closing it made it so final and I still hoped God would raise him up. I don't remember too much after that. I couldn't tell you what the preacher said, or even what they sung.

But when they closed the casket before dismissing the family first as I had requested, I screamed, "No! It's not supposed to be this way!" BC grabbed me on one side as Tommy grabbed the other arm to hold me in my seat. If I could've gotten out of that pew I would have went up there and demanded God to raise him up like Lazarus. They knew it, too. I fought as hard as I could but they wouldn't let go. I watched as the casket went by us and the flowers followed. At that moment, I felt Daddy had taken my place. I remembered my own death and funeral in my dream at that very moment and screamed again, "No, it's not supposed to be this way."

Tommy and BC held onto me as we walked to the gravesite. I could feel my legs giving way and just knew I wouldn't make it. Picking my legs up that felt like stone pillars as they pushed my back to move one more step. Once we arrived and we sat under that tent, I couldn't bring myself to look at that closed casket. I don't remember what was said or sung there either; just BC and Tommy leading me back to the family car.

Once in the family car, I let out a deafened scream and the tears flooded. I was probably heard a mile away but all that I had held inside for four days flowed out of me. The hope of God raising him up from the dead left me as I collapsed on the seat. I couldn't be strong any longer. I couldn't hold back the pain or the fear one more minute. Uncle Press, Mr. Creasy, and now my Daddy all gone from my sight in a year's time, I cried out to heaven, why? Why take my Daddy too? It was suppose to be me, not my Daddy, my friend, my anchor, I heard myself screaming. Tears flooded down onto my dress until it was as if someone had poured water on me. The pain in my heart felt like it had engulfed me. I forgot about the people standing outside and hadn't realized that BC, Shirley, and Tommy were sitting in the car with me in their own pain and tears. Just as I was able to pull myself together, Shirley reminded me we weren't the only ones there suffering. Suddenly like a flash, I saw our cousin Virgil, Uncle Press, Mr. Creasy and remembered their families and knew she was right. Jesse and James had buried their brother Virgil after he had been murdered. Aunt Ellen, Johnny, JP, and Wanda had buried Uncle Press. And poor BC was still grieving over his daddy. Remembering those and all the others standing outside that car grieving for their loved ones and now another one just dried my tears right up and I welcomed the crowd that had waited so patiently to speak to us. .

No sooner than I allowed the crowd to hug me or touch my hand the tears flowed again until Willie Mason stuck her head in that car and said, "Carolyn Ann, dry up those tears and let me see those heavenly stars in your big blue eyes that you were born with. You know your daddy wouldn't want you to carry on like this." Immediately I realized she was right and forced out a smile for her and thanked her. She was Daddy's cousin on the Moore side. Her words and smile were like seeing Daddy face to face. It gave me hope right there that I would see Daddy again. I remembered what he had said to us all of our life. "When I step out of this body, take it and throw it in a ditch and let it return to dust. I won't need it any longer because I'll be up there smiling down on you." Willie's smile was transmitting that memory to me and I could feel it.

As the family one by one lined up to speak to us, hug us and give their love I made eye contact with them to let them know I appreciated them being there. There's no greater feeling in this world than to be surrounded by love, family and friends at a time when all you want to do is fall apart. Fighting the emotions you're feeling inside that feels like a crumbed up cracker and the only thing it's waiting for is a breeze of wind to blow you away. I knew I was drawing strength from each one there that day and well needed to face to the days ahead. Daddy always said when the crying was over you are left alone the day after and every day after that to deal with business, emotions and choices for your own future. The last four days had been days where most of the family had taken over and made the decisions but I knew after the funeral the remainder of the decisions were lying on my shoulders to carry out as Daddy had written. Seeing his business friends there I knew I wasn't alone in the business realm. Seeing his family there also told me I wasn't alone in the emotional realm so why did I feel so alone?

After the funeral and as Kenneth drove us back to the house I asked him how he could do that day in and day out and not go crazy. He said, "I don't. It bothers me every day, especially when I have it to do for my family and friends like your daddy. But I tell myself they are in a better place and some one has to do it. So I feel it's an honor to be part of the final plans. A child I don't handle well at all. After all these years it still touches my heart very deeply and shows me we still have so much to learn about God's plans. Most of the time I try to get out of those funerals unless the family requested me." I heard him clear his throat like Daddy use to do when he wanted to hold back his feelings and tears. I saw Kenneth take out his handkerchief and wiped his eyes and blew his nose like Daddy also and then he continued. "Your daddy was a good man. A well respected business man and friend. You can hold your heads up in this county and country and be proud of your daddy. He left you a good name and reputation to follow that will help you throughout the remainder of your journey on this earth. It was an honor to know him. You should be proud," as he looked at us through the rearview mirror. In unity we said thank you, thank you for saying that. We were proud to be Henry Smith's children and be ever so loved by him.

Back at the house the family cared for the guests while I walked around like a zombie. As usual each family member took charge of the house, food, kids, and clean-up and went to the store for anything we needed. Even after the funeral it felt like I was in one of my dreams. Soon bellies were full and people were leaving as I felt with every good bye hug a little lonelier and lonelier. Our promise and desire was to keep Daddy and our family proud of us and the legacy each had left us. Daddy's death had come so suddenly and left us all with a question who would be next. Each of us knew God had answered Daddy's prayer. With every trip to Richmond to see Uncle Jesse and Uncle Press Daddy had prayed out loud for God to take him out of his body suddenly and quickly and not let him suffer like his brothers. I saw the sadness in each loved one's eyes that day as they departed for their home, each going home to grieve in private and try to keep it all together and move forward. Four very close relatives had died in such a short period of time. We had all stood as one unit to get through them all but the pain lingers long after the funeral we also knew. Our hearts were heavy and our minds couldn't hold the thought of losing another family member any time soon. Phone calls and cards were promised as the last one departed out of my door and drove off. I sat and rung my hands as I heard Tommy say he had to leave also and get back to Carol. She was pregnant with Lil Tommy and due in a month or so and couldn't make the drive up to attend the funeral. Aunt Virginia wanted us to come up on Monday and get Daddy's personal things. She said she wasn't in good health and couldn't promise it would be there if she passed away. Tommy decided to stay and go through Daddy's things as asked. Daddy had taken care of the businesses and everything so these were just a few personal items like his watch, ring, pictures, clothes and three little green books beside his bed he read every night.

I felt Daddy took my place that day. The dream had showed my death and funeral before my 31st birthday which would have been September 30, 1980. I believe Daddy thought it was easier for us to give him up than it was for him to give up any one of his children. It almost killed him when Tommy had his near death experience in 1970.

My First Grandson, Michael

You can read about the three dreams of Michael's
birth in my book; *MICHAEL AN ENDTIME SIGN.*
His conception, birth, and move to Virginia
was announced by The Archangel Gabriel.
Watch for my book *Michael 2* in 2011.

My First Granddaughter, Michelle

**Michelle in the pink dress she wore in the dream sitting
in Daddy's lap in heaven Christmas 1990.
She was born October 1st 1991.
Dreams, visions and visitations are healing tools.**

Chapter 10:

Dreams, Visions, Visitations Are Healing Tools

Monday was more painful than the funeral getting Daddy's things packed up and knowing Tommy would be leaving soon. Aunt Virginia sat and shared stories in between tears. When she couldn't control her emotions she would go in the kitchen and cook something, preparing lunch, she said but by the time we ate she had a feast. We all got a big laugh out of that. She said eating alone wouldn't be any fun she had already tried that after Wade died. The house looked so big and carrying out Daddy's things gave her a sickening feeling she said. Aunt Virginia had been mother to Daddy and companion after his full retirement. I knew Shirley and I both would help her each day by visiting her from now on but it would never be the same.

By the time Tommy left and I drove home I wanted to be in Daddy's car all alone. That car was drawing me like a magnet is the only way I can explain the pulling. I hadn't gone near it since Johnny parked it and locked it up. Since February 13, I had no desire at all to touch or see the place where Daddy died. But this day, February 17, it was drawing me. I asked BC to watch Penny and be home when the school bus ran for Tammy and Jay. I was going riding in Daddy's car. I needed some answers from God and felt I would get them in Daddy's car. At first it was scary to sit in the exact spot Daddy's spirit had left his body, but I got in and drove away crying. In the past when I was upset and not ready to talk to Aunt Ellen or Daddy, I would drive down to Aunt Annie's. I guess my subconscious knew where we were going and headed in that direction. As I drove down 360 it was as if I wasn't there but somewhere else. Then suddenly I felt a presence driving the car and putting on brakes. I actually felt the Presence's foot on mine as it put on the brakes. When I woke up from my trance or whatever it was a tree stared right at me. The car had stopped so close to it I could reach out and touch it but the presence drawed me to stay in my seat.

I screamed, Dear God, why did you take my Daddy? I beat my fist against the dash and poured my heart out to God as the tears flowed. Talk to me Dear God I beg you. You showed me so many things in dreams why didn't you show me my Daddy was leaving me. The Presence sat in the silence and allowed me to pour out every emotion I had in me. Once I felt empty the Presence reached over and touched my right shoulder and said, *"My child, my child, why doest thou cry? Where he is, is where I am, and where you shall be also."* All the emptiness in me filled up with pure joy and peace. My tears stopped as I smiled back at my Heavenly Father. For what I thought was an angel at first, then as Jesus, was actually Father-God. He filled every cell, emotion, organ, and place within my whole being. I wanted to hold onto that joy and peace for the remainder of my life and wondered how I could hold onto it. As Father God sat in His silence filling me, He said, "Remember, I told you, when you see me, you see my Heavenly Father." Then He smiled again and said, *"I AM THAT I AM have come to comfort you this day.*

Suddenly in the silence of those spoken words I felt an urgency to drive home and tell BC, call Tommy and Shirley, Aunt Ellen, Johnny and everyone in the family. I wanted the world to know that Father God had come unto me and said, *"My child, my child, why doest thou cry? Where he is, is where I am, and where you shall be also."* I backed the car out of the ditch filled with over powering zest and drove home with Father's Presence sitting in the passenger's side. I turned once and asked, "Don't you want to drive?" He smiled and replied, "Not yet." I said well okay, like a child in driver's training as my Daddy sat to guide me and give me pointers. I knew that day my physical Daddy had gone to heaven with God but he left us something more precious, my Heavenly Father who would never leave me. I wanted to scream it from the housetops. Sure we have read it in the Bible and by faith had believed it. But this day I experienced Father God. I couldn't help but ask if I had a Heavenly Mother? I'm sure Daddy was laughing as he waited in heaven for me to ask a question. He and Aunt Ellen both had gotten many laughs over the years about me asking so many questions rather than being content with the present answer. I saw Father God smile all over Himself as His Presence glowed brighter than the sun just like Daddy would have done except greater light and warmth. I couldn't stop myself from laughing as Daddy's memories danced in my head. He filled Daddy's car up with His Glorious Presence as He smiled and laughed with me. How long we sat in Daddy's car laughing I haven't a clue but it makes me smile from inside out as I share the experience with you even now. He laughed so hard that he made me laugh at my own curiosity.

"Sure my child," He answered. "Remember the story of Adam and Eve? How I made them in our image and likeness. Remember Abraham and Sarah. Remember Jesus' mother Mary and Mary Magdalene? In all my examples I have showed you your Father and Mother. Soon you will come to know Her as you know Me. For just as sure as there's a physical daddy and mama, there's a Heavenly Father and Mother."

About that time I noticed how awesome it felt to experience God in such an intimate way and hear him. I also noticed I was turning off of highway 501 onto my road. To close I thought for I wanted this moment to last forever. As I pulled up in the driveway, turned the motor off I just sat in God's Presence. I didn't want to leave but the same power that had pulled me in Daddy's car in the first place was now pushing me out of it. I smiled all the way in the house and as BC saw me he asked, "Where did you go? Who did you see that made you that happy? You look like you've seen an angel."

"Better," I replied. "I have been in the Presence of Father God. Yes. In my Daddy's car, Father God appeared and made Himself known to me. Do you want to know what else He said, but before he answered, I continued. He said Daddy is with Him and so will I be with Him from this day forward. He also said I would come to know my Mother God. Now I've got to call Shirley and Tommy and everyone in the family."

BC looked as if I had lost my mind as he shook his head and went down the hall. Who cares what he thinks I thought? I had just about had enough of his unbelief anyway as I dialed Shirley's number. I know it was Father God I yelled at him. He kept walking to the bedroom. My joy was bubbling over as I waited for Shirley to answer. She answered and could hear the joy in my voice but my experience didn't cheer her up at all. I quickly got off the phone not wanting her depressed state to steal my joy. I called Tommy and he was excited about the good news. He said just knowing that Daddy was in heaven made it sweeter. I was still excited when Tammy and Jay came home from school and couldn't wait to tell them. Like all children they loved the story and asked questions but soon ready to go play outside. I called Aunt Ellen and she was real excited about the news and as we shared she reminded me to be careful who else I told. After the way BC had reacted I decided not to share the experience with anyone else unless God told me who, when and where.

Within a week I was back at work and a regular routine had begun again. Before the funeral I had no idea what to do or how to move forward. After God's Presence in Daddy's car I knew I was going to be alright. Each day that passed Father God gave further understanding to that Presence. I knew I had a Heavenly Father who would never leave me and Daddy was with Him so my Daddy would never leave me either. And so would I one day be with God just without the physical body. I knew all that exist comes from the planning and purpose of God and summed up in the Word of God (Jesus Christ-Yahweh) and the very will of God. I knew God's plan is to share His understanding, His wisdom, His very Word within mankind. At this point I knew the Way to this life was first made manifest in Jesus Christ. Jesus is come in the flesh and Jesus was our Passover and Way to be in Elohim, (God Family). Jesus Christ was the very manifestation, the revelation of God to us. John 14:6 told me that Jesus Christ said, "I am the way. I am the truth. I am the life. No one comes to the Father except through me."

God was revealing oneness in unity and the very process that was at work in Jesus Christ was now working in us who believe. God was transforming our mind in order to come into unity and oneness with Him. To think differently we needed God's power and that power came in the name of the Holy Spirit. All that just by one visitation I wondered how much could we get in many visitations. Jesus told us in John 14: 7 that from this time you have known Him, (Father), and have seen Him, (Father). Physical minded people wouldn't see Father but once God transforms our mind to think beyond the physical we can see and know the Father and the Mother. Jesus took no credit for Himself and was revealing that he had the exact mind of God and walked in full agreement with Father God. Through Jesus paying for the sins of all mankind he fulfilled God's purpose as the Passover Lamb. After His resurrection He became our High Priest. Now mankind has access to the very throne of God which is God Himself. Freedom was what it was all about. Christ had come and gave us freedom from our own flesh natures and characters and had moved us in God's nature and character. What else Lord I asked? What else do you want me to know?

After Daddy passed and my experience in Daddy's car I had a hunger to know my physical mother in a more intimate relationship? That was strange I thought. We had always kept her at arms length since she left us but for some odd reason after Father God's Presence entered my life I had a hunger to know her and to know my Heavenly Mother. I knew now that whatever I sought understanding in, Father God would give it. I knew that God was working in me to enable me to experience understanding and growth on a spiritual level. My future looked positive and full of energy and I felt no matter what else that happened it couldn't top God's Presence in Daddy's car. .

My Broker wanted me to work in our Danville office and try to pull it out of the red. That was fine with me and gave me the opportunity to see and keep in touch with Aunt Virginia. She grieved alone and wasn't well. As the weeks passed I formed a habit of going over for lunch and if she had anywhere she needed to go I would take her. I remember one day she asked me what happened if you wrote a will and left everything to one person and that one person died before you did. I told her if he/she had children then it would go to them or she would need to change the will. She asked me if she made an appointment with her attorney would I take her over. I replied yes just let me know so I wouldn't set up appointments. She did make the appointment with her attorney the following week and all she told me when I picked her up was well that's taken care of. Let's get some lunch at the diner. I knew she meant Mary's Diner, hers and Daddy's favorite place to eat and it was just up the road from their home.

One morning as I drove to the Danville office I saw what appeared to be a huge television screen and Daddy was standing on the first balcony of what appeared to be the Holiday Inn. Daddy was just standing there leaning over the balcony looking down like he was looking at earth and smoking a cigarette. I thought what, what is this? Daddy is that you? I was so shocked to see him and wasn't even sure it was him since he was smoking. But before I could ask anything else without him saying a word it all vanished. For some reason I became concerned about Aunt Virginia. As soon as I got to the office I called her but she was fine and asked me to come over for lunch at noon. When I arrived I told her what I saw and she didn't seem surprised at all. She just asked me if she had to go in the hospital would I take care of her bills and house. When I asked her what was wrong she said she had colon cancer and needed surgery but her heart was too weak at that time. In my heart at that moment I knew then what Daddy was showing up to tell me. She said since Henry trusted you in his last breath to take care of his business and stated you would do it right and according to his plans she wanted me to take care of hers according to her plans. I agreed and we went up to the bank after lunch and she spoke with someone who had a paper for me to sign. I signed the document so I could sign her name to checks with my name underneath. Little did I know that I would take over that job a week later? But she had the surgery and it went well except her heart being weaker.

Christmas came and since Aunt Virginia was home from the hospital but not well we took Christmas to her. Her whole family showed up to enjoy the holidays and her brother Thornton and sister Grovine decided to take turns staying with her for awhile as everyone was leaving. Even though the day wore her out she loved it. It was too much just as I had thought for she landed back in the hospital by the next morning.

On December 28, 1980, I woke up from a strange dream almost too funny to be real I thought. I couldn't wait to tell BC and my Mama, who had come with us from the December 26 gathering at her house, as we stood around the fireplace. In the dream I saw Daddy standing on the third floor balcony of what looked like the Holiday Inn waiting. I immediately noticed he had moved up from the first floor to the third since the last vision and he wasn't smoking. He appeared to be brighter and more confident as he waited. I saw a greyhound bus traveling from earth upward towards Daddy. When the bus reached the third floor it changed into Aunt Virginia. They embraced and arm in arm walked in the hotel room and out of sight. All I saw after that was a beautiful bright white light as the door closed behind them. Then I woke up. We all were laughing as we stood around and they agreed it was a crazy dream. Mama said Aunt Virginia a greyhound bus she would kill me for comparing her to a bus. I shared that the only thing I could figure was after she had retired she worked as a waitress at the Greyhound Bus Station there in Danville for awhile to keep busy and I use to go and eat lunch with her.

BC knew Mama didn't know about the gift of discernment and played the joke up by agreeing with her and added he would help Virginia whip my butt. I told them if we were going to Danville to see Aunt Virginia I had better get breakfast started as I moved toward the kitchen. Suddenly the phone rang and I yelled back for BC to get it as I put the bacon on and Mama make biscuits. It was Shirley he yelled from the bathroom. As I entered the bathroom to take it and saw BC's face it was as if in an instant the dream flashed in my mind and I knew before she ever said a word. I heard, Carolyn, Aunt Virginia passed away around 8 a.m. as my mind showed me she was in Daddy's arms, she continued but the words were a blur. I heard Shirley sobbing as I asked, who was with her? She replied Uncle Thornton. She had received the phone call and was getting dressed to go over but they called back before I left and said she passed. She was peaceful Carolyn is what the nurse said. Her heart just stopped beating. The hospital called me but she passed before I got there. She's with Daddy now, Carolyn, as she heard my sobs. A few minutes later as I drawed a breath, I said, we will get dressed and meet you at the house. Did you call Tommy? Again the words blurred as my mind showed me Daddy and Aunt Virginia embracing with a smile walking in the heavenly light as the door closed behind them. I heard the door slam and like a flash I caught my breath and made some kind of a noise as I landed back to earth when I heard Shirley say, do you want me to call Tommy? I said please. I don't remember if she did or I did or both of us, Carolyn the zombie had appeared and just moving with the motions. My mind was consumed with Daddy and Aunt Virginia and heaven so there wasn't any room for decisions. Thank God BC knew how I was and finished breakfast as he saw me sit down at the table and asked what do we need to do. He replied Geneva and I will finish breakfast then we will eat while you sit and enjoy your coffee. Then we will all get dressed and go to Virginia's house. Mama didn't say a word she just watched and did as BC told her. She had never seen me like that, in fact she had never seen me upset at all to my knowledge. I got through Aunt Virginia's funeral quite well knowing she was with Daddy.

What had I learned from those visions to date? The most notable for me was the fact we keep growing spiritually after we depart our physical bodies. The Seed of Almighty God is planted within us when we accept Jesus as our sacrifice. At first no one knows he's in us. The Seed has everything God is and His Living Words are the food and water it needs to develop. The more we cultivate the Seed and feel it grow from a Seed to a twig to a tree the more we see and understand with our spiritual mind. It is growing in our darkness until the development is full term and comes forth to share and enjoy with others. Just like a woman who conceives a seed and is pregnant. She carries the seed while it grows within her and at full term if she is lucky she gives birth. The work is being done on the inside and one day manifest in the light for all to see, hear, hold, touch and behold. Jesus Christ is the foundation and our job is to carry it full term and bring it forth. We just sit in the silence and quiet of our mind as the Seed does its work. Also with the greyhound bus changing into Aunt Virginia at a certain time told me only God reveals His meanings in His own time. Some things are symbols in dreams and visions and God has to give us the understanding and does. We can live in the spiritual while still in physical bodies I learned. There really is life after physical death and the decision should be made while on earth as to where you want to go when you leave your body.

From 1980 until 1990 my life became more tensed, and more painful as God increased the dreams, visitations, visions, and revelations. I was still in my darkness in my mind for it hadn't been transformed into light or even the dawn of the morning yet. The only light my mind saw was from the dreams and visions. The Seed was growing inside but still had no power on the outside. It felt like it didn't have much on the inside either at times but that's where faith came in to remind me the power is there and coming forth. I had no spiritual peace within or without, only what I made for myself. No truth for myself or anyone else except what I read out -loud from the Bible itself. I didn't own the word yet and I knew there was more. Searching diligently on how to use this Jesus Holy Spirit power, while I battled with my know it all ego who always left me holding the bag. What a coward our egos are? They talk us into many mistakes and then leave us to fix the mess. I couldn't even fix the mess I had gotten myself into so I had no choice but to surrender it to God for him to fix. I read my Bible daily and quoted it, confessed my sins, went to church, paid my tithes and judged every motive like every other Christian that confessed they were born again. On the outside I looked just like anyone else but on the inside I was a messed up little girl locked in a dark prison at the bottom of a dungeon screaming to be set free. I felt so powerless as events, circumstances and loved ones left my life and my life as I knew it changed right before me and nothing I said or did worked. Before I could finish and survive one circumstance another one appeared. For every dream, vision, visitation there was a consequence to walk through. God showed me in a constant vision when I prayed and cried out why. My own darkness as God took one inch of my mind at a time and transformed it into light. During those seven years of pure hell within and without God gave me daily visitations of angels to comfort me and bring understanding. I also noticed the dreams and visions were manifested or came to pass much faster. Too many to mention at this time to give them the value they deserve. Some I have mentioned in my book, *Michael, An Endtime Sign.* In this book I am trying to stick to just the ones daddy appeared in. I will say the visions became more beautiful and manifested more peace, joy and beauty around me started the eighth year. Eight being an endtime sign from the Bible viewpoint also.

It was Christmas Day1990 when I saw Daddy again in the spirit or early morning of the 26th. He was sitting in a beautiful decorated room very cozy and warm feeling, almost like a Christmas scene, rocking in a rocker. In his lap he held a beautiful baby girl in the most beautiful pink laced dress I had ever seen. She had blue eyes and weighed about seven pounds with blonde hair. I asked whose baby is that you're holding Daddy. Thinking it was a baby already in heaven from earth. Making me aware of how involved our minds are in the spirit world. Daddy looked up and smiled as he said, *she is my granddaughter and yours.* I asked whose? He said, *by this time next year you will have a granddaughter to buy Christmas for and Michael will have a sister.* Then as he rocked the dream slowly vanished from my sight and I woke up suddenly. Usually the visions or dreams would leave suddenly but this time I noticed it vanished very slowly from my consciousness. Why Lord? What does that mean? I asked with all the fullness in me overflowing in outward joy as I got up dancing to make coffee. A baby girl by next Christmas to buy Christmas for and Michael a sister, I shouted to the housetops for I knew just like Michael had come from God in 1989 so would his sister come with the same spirit. Isn't God good I shouted? Yes He is so good I answered as I danced around the room just God and me. I knew Tammy, Tony and Michael would be over soon to pick up all the gifts from Christmas Day and to eat lunch. I couldn't wait to tell them and see their faces. When they arrived all happy to load the car with gifts I shared the dream. By next year at this time we will have a baby girl to buy Christmas for I said real calm looking for their expressions.

"Who?" Tammy shouted "Jay or Penny?" I looked straight at them as I picked up Michael and said you and Tony. What do you think about that Michael? You are going to have a baby sister to play with next year at this time. Tammy and Tony both looked surprised and Tammy said well I know that's not going to happen because I am on my period right now. I just smiled and said what is of God will come to pass. If not of God it will come to nothing. Time will tell which it is as I helped them load the car with the remainder of the gifts.

October 1, 1991, Tammy gave birth to a beautiful baby girl. They named her Michelle Ann Johns after Michael and me. I had a granddaughter and Michael had a sister just like Daddy had said last Christmas Day. Tammy's step-mother had found the pink dress that she wore in the dream without even knowing about the dream. Surely God's word does not return to Him void but accomplishes what He sends it to do. When the manifestations come for us to enjoy it was like God allowed time between dreams, visions and visitations so we could mediate on all that we saw and heard before the next one arrived. With each dream or vision there was always more than what I saw or heard at the time that in time would unfold as I studied the Bible with each word that I did hear. Always hidden treasures that would be revealed with I just looked for them.

One evening in September 1992, around 9 p.m. sitting in the dark, crawled up on the sofa in front of the fireplace, talking on the phone to Brenda, a friend from Georgia. We would get on the phone and talk for hours about God, his plans and purposes and our problems. At that time neither of us understood how God could get glory out of us suffering with finances and husbands that just didn't want to walk in the ways of God and why we were even with them. So many problems and so much drama at that time and we would search the Bible to see what God's word said about it. She and her husband had already divorced but far from being over. I was considering divorce at the time and looking for one reason why I should stay. Feeling caught between a rock and a hard place we would comfort each other with the Bible and memories from past ministers meetings. Talking about God gave us the peace in the midst of the storm. Every Friday night my husband would go to play poker and drink all night so that was our quiet time together with God, to ask him questions, and discuss our options. We had shared our prayers, concerns and hopes for over six months with no hope in sight for either of us. But curled up on the sofa in the soft, warm light feeling very romantic, I was ready for a break through or a change and God knew it as we laughed at what we were thinking about doing. Pay back was sounding sweeter and sweeter as we talked when suddenly a beautiful lady in a flowing ice blue gown appeared. I sat in total shock starring at this heavenly being standing ten feet tall it seemed in my living room. The whole house was lit up with her radiance. After a few minutes of pure silence I heard Brenda asking if I was still there. I replied yes but you won't believe what is standing in my living room. What she asked? I said a beautiful female angel in a glowing flowing ice blue white gown. Who is she Brenda asked? I don't know as I answered her ever so softly afraid I would upset this magnificent being just by talking yet my eyes never leaving her sight. Well ask her, Brenda said. I said okay. "In Jesus Christ Son of the Living Almighty God's Name, who are you?" I could hear Brenda laughing her butt off on the other end as I said it. She knew I was scared to death at what I was witnessing just by the way I said it. While I sat frozen to the sofa and not laughing at all for I knew this was the hugest being I had ever witnessed.

Suddenly this huge magnificent being smiled and her smile felt like it opened up my whole being. Brenda said what is she saying or doing? I said smiling at me. Smiling Brenda asked? Yes, smiling at me. Just listen and let's see what she wants. I will put you on the speaker and if I go to heaven tonight know that's God's will over a divorce and tell the kids. Brenda agreed and we sat in silence for a few minutes when this huge magnificent light being spoke and it was like Brenda was a million miles away as I listened with full attention. "I am Mother God. Some call me Wisdom. Others call me Counselor, while still others call me Daughter of Zion. Say to Wisdom, "You are my sister." I repeated back to her out loud, "you are my Mother God. Some call you Wisdom. Others call you Counselor; while still others call you Daughter of Zion. Say to Wisdom, You are my sister."

Then Mother God continued, "Call understanding your kinsman; they will keep you safe I have poured out my heart to you and made my thoughts known to you, accept my words and store up my commands within you, turning your ear to wisdom and applying your heart to understanding, look for it, search for it, as for hidden treasure, then you will understand the fear of the LORD and find the knowledge of God. For the LORD gives wisdom, and from his mouth comes knowledge and understanding. Wisdom will enter your heart and knowledge will be pleasant to your soul."

I felt her words enter my being like a refreshing spring as it traveled through my inner being and settled. I heard Brenda asked, what did she say. Is she still there? I said yes, she said, "Call understanding your kinsman; they will keep you safe. I have poured out my heart to you and made my thoughts known to you, accept my words and store up my commands within you, turning your ear to wisdom and applying your heart to understanding, look for it, search for it, as for hidden treasure, then you will understand the fear of the LORD and find the knowledge of God. For the LORD gives wisdom, and from his mouth comes knowledge and understanding. Wisdom will enter your heart and knowledge will be pleasant to your soul."

Brenda sat in silence on her end as if she was soaking up every word within her being. As we sat in this calm silence Mother God spoke again, "Wisdom is Supreme. My LORD has wisdom like that of an angel of God. He knows everything that happens in the land. But now the ones that have hurt you or may hurt you in future times do not consider him innocent. You are of wisdom; you will know what to do to him. God gave you wisdom and very great insight, and a breadth of understanding as measureless as the sand on the seashore, which you possess. You desire truth in the inner parts; you will hear joy and gladness; in wisdom we made them all; the earth is full of our creatures. I will teach you to walk in wisdom; I will teach you to attain discipline; I will teach you for understanding words of insight; let the wise listen and add to their learning, and let the discerning understand. Now repeat what I say."

I spoke out loud for Brenda to hear it again as Mother God had requested. "Wisdom is Supreme. My LORD has wisdom like that of an angel of God. He knows everything that happens in the land. But now the ones that have hurt you or may hurt you in future times do not consider him innocent. You are of wisdom; you will know what to do to him. God gave you wisdom and very great insight, and a breadth of understanding as measureless as the sand on the seashore, which you possess. You desire truth in the inner parts; you will hear joy and gladness; in wisdom we made them all; the earth is full of our creatures. I will teach you to walk in wisdom; I will teach you to attain discipline; I will teach you for understanding words of insight; let the wise listen and add to their learning, and let the discerning understand. Now repeat what I say."

As soon as I finished her words she smiled and vanished from my sight. The living room returned to its normal way and I felt a cool breeze pass by me like someone had just refreshed me with a cool glass of lemonade. I caught my breath and asked Brenda if she was still there. She answered yes and asked if Mother God was still there. I said no, she just vanished like a cool breeze. Brenda said I felt a cool breeze. You did I asked what do you think it all means? Brenda said I don't know but I know it was for both of us and you better cancel that appointment with your attorney and not get a divorce at this time. Why I asked? Because we need to study out her words and wait, for she said she would teach us wisdom, discipline and understanding. So we better wait and listen and learn. We discussed the vision and visitation until after 3 am and couldn't explain anything any better than when we started discussing it. We gave up and blessed each other, hung up and went to bed.

Early Saturday morning she called back and asked how I slept. Like a baby I said and feel so clean. Isn't it a beautiful September morning? Brenda said yes it is. I'm going and get Mama and go shopping or do something. Heck we might end up in Virginia. I replied come on. I was going to get Michael and Michelle and keep them this weekend. Brenda said do you think it would be alright if I went and shared this experience with Sister Ruth? I said I think so she didn't say keep it a secret, besides Sister Ruth may have already had the experience since she is an old prophet and we are just babies. Call me when you're back and tell me what she said.

From that time until present I have spent my every waking hour looking up every word Mother God had spoken and searched out all the verses on discipline, insight, discernment, knowledge, and daughter of Zion, along with all the 'she's and hers'. With my Bible computers and

Strong's computer on words and their meanings along with my Dake Bible, {The Bible God led me too and told me to purchase years ago}. I wrote pages upon pages and then some more pages, books and more notebooks of every verse. I asked God questions as I went through each one and lost much sleep being so excited with the expectancy of this new revelation any minute coming forth. I attended every church I was invited too just to learn what God wanted me to know and then move on as God led me to the next place. I asked preachers, teachers and any human being I came in contact with if they ever studied Mother God. I discovered that most people won't talk about it or afraid of the subject or just think it's a cult to believe God is male and female. I discovered how male the world really is and how big a male's ego really was. So big most men couldn't bring themselves to even think it was possible to have an eternal God who was, is and always will be male and female. I learned the ignorance by listening to most of these male preachers over the years and nothing had really changed. Yes, we have Gloria Copeland and Joyce Meyer and others and even had women running as president but underneath all those smiles was still a huge male ego that God was about to knock down with one wave of the Holy Spirit glory. I had to learn to keep my discovery a secret like all the Holy Spirit gifts in the past. Most people will read God's word like a book, not digesting any of it but just tasting it or judging it to fit their belief as long as it doesn't interfere with their lifestyle or fun. I try to remember and keep seeking out the few that want more of God and found them in every church I visited. Some people study the Bible the way I experience the ocean just walking on the sand with the ocean flowing over my feet. Then some of us aren't satisfied until we understand what God meant in every word, gesture and attitude.

I assume most of you like my self grew up in one form of religion or another and Mother God wasn't taught or grew up with a church where all the focus is upon the Mother God. I remembered what Aunt Ellen and Daddy had taught me for years not to judge anything or anyone but learn from every experience and encounter. Therefore I kept my focus on just that.

It wasn't until August 12th 1993 when I saw Daddy again. I was on my way to Danville when the heavenly television showed up as I drove. I saw Daddy standing on the third floor balcony watching and waiting. This time I asked, In Jesus Christ Name, Daddy, who are you waiting for? Remembering the last time I saw him on a balcony Aunt Virginia went to him. He said, "El". I immediately began to cry and asked when. He said soon. I went onto Shirley's and spent that day with her sharing the vision and walking down memory lane.

When I left Shirley's I decided to go the Chatham Road route and straight to Aunt Ellen's. She was sitting up in her chair and smiled when she saw me. After I stayed awhile asking how she felt, just small talk avoiding the vision, fighting with myself not to say anything since she was always the first one I shared it with. This vision I didn't want to share with her because I didn't want to believe it or accept it. I played over it in my mind coming down the road from Danville how hard life had been for me since Daddy left and just the thought of losing her actually made me sick to my stomach as the tears flowed. Aunt Ellen talked about how good Betty had been to her since Johnny died. She bragged as if she was praying or prophesying over Betty, Brandy and Presley. She said it was time for her to move on and let Betty live her life and enjoy her children. She shared how she hoped Betty would marry again since she was so young and even though Larry had stepped in to be a father to Brandy and Press it wasn't the same. I just sat and listened thinking this may be the last time I hear her soft voice and she was spending her last hours bragging on her family. She said JP and Wanda her other two grandchildren had been so good to her. It was so sweet of Wanda and Phil to open their home and allow her to stay with them but she hoped they understood she had to come back to her home. She wanted to be in her home when she went to her heavenly home and felt it was soon.

As soon as she said the word soon I knew she knew she was passing soon. She knew me so well and had figured it out that I had had a vision or dream or she had had the same vision. For some odd reason I felt she knew she was leaving her body and the last people on her mind were JP, Wanda, Betty, Brandy and Presley. She talked about them more and bragged more on how proud she was of them more than she ever had. It was time she said to depart to her God, the God she had devoted her whole life too. All she could do for her family now was hope that God would answer her prayer and they all accept Jesus in their heart and serve him as their master. But she would be waiting in heaven to hear that answer. Then as she bowed her head and her voice lowered almost in a faint she said, *Cowtail, do you think Press is in heaven?* I rose from the chair and sat on the floor near her on my knees to take her hand before answering. Aunt Ellen I don't know but you will soon find out. She said I know I will see Johnny and Henry and all of my family but I don't know about Press. She squeezed my hand and smiled at me. With that smile I knew she knew she was passing. I sat on my knees holding her hand near her rocking her and just cried. She reached over and placed her hand onto my head and said, *"Cowtail, you've been like a daughter to Press and me. Johnny couldn't have loved you any more as a sister if you had been mine. I want you to promise me you will continue to study the Bible and prepare people to walk into the light of heaven. Sometimes it's hard and people are cruel but you know how wonderful heaven is with God and you need to never give up on people. When they won't listen you just pray. Will you do that for me?*

I promised I would and thanked her for being my mother and most of all teaching me the Bible. I thanked her for showing me how to study the Bible and all she did for Shirley and Tommy. I asked her to give Daddy a big hug and kiss for us all and Johnny too. I thanked her for teaching me how to love children, all children, and look at them as precious gifts from God to love, protect, spoil, cherish and encourage. As my nose ran from the tears that flowed and my voice weakened I looked up to kiss her and she had fallen off to sleep. I sat near her until Betty came in and asked me to help her to put her in her hospital bed there in the den. Once she was tucked in like a baby she opened her eyes and smiled as she took my hand and smiled, *I will be seeing you. More importantly you will be seeing me. You're not alone Carolyn Ann. You'll be the strength the family needs now. In time you will see how important you are to the family. Just as important to them as you have been to your Daddy, Johnny, Press and me.*

I left around 7:30 p.m. and she was fast asleep. My drive home was full of her words. Sublimed grace she passed to me as she healed my hurting heart and allowed me to accept her departure. I witnessed a miracle that day. She healed my heart and prepared me for her passing. She gave me hope that I would see her again and I would never be alone even though that day I felt so alone in a family and world that didn't understand the gift of discernment at that time. You're not alone Carolyn Ann rung in my heart, mind and ears as I drove home with every intention of returning the next morning. I wanted to spend as much time with her as I could before she departed not realizing they were her last words to me, her last bit of advice, her last hope, and her last prayer for me.

Early the next morning I received the phone call that she had passed during the night. The person said she went peacefully while her family stood around her. My heart was sad as I heard her family stood around her. I was part of that family. Who decided at the last minute I wasn't worthy to be called? Who was so jealous of our relationship that they wouldn't call me to come and be with her in her last hours or minutes? I was sad because I knew the Smith family had lost one of the greatest spiritual teachers on this planet. I was sad because I was selfish and never wanted her to leave me. I was sad because I knew she had left behind grandchildren that wouldn't grow up with this lady of wisdom by their side to teach them by action as I had been or have the intimate relationship we had. I was sad because I didn't know how many members of the Smith family hadn't confessed their sins and received Jesus in their heart as savior. I was sad because I didn't think I could fulfill her wish for me and that was to continue writing and publishing books about how marvelous our God really is. I was sad because like my Daddy she was my pillar of strength and my anchor when I drifted to far away from God. I was sad because she was my rope to remind me not everyone has a personal intimate relationship with Christ like we did. Now I needed to learn how to throw out the rope like she had done for me so many years and lead them to the lighthouse on the shore before they were loss for all eternity.

She had a way about her in every project she tackled to bring out a spiritual lesson in such a way you wouldn't forget or get mad. She had a way about her that glowed like the sun when the Holy Spirit was speaking through her. She had a deep concern for people who lived like the devil she called it and just kept going around and around that fool's mountain. She had a deep prayer life that touched your heart even a thousand miles away that was so strong you just had to call her to hear her voice. To think I wouldn't hear that soft spoken voice again in this lifetime just made my heart overflow with tears. Little did I know at that time that love really is all we take with us to the other side and I would continue to hear her words of wisdom? I was grateful she wasn't suffering in her body any more but sad and selfish because she left us on earth. Who would I run too now to share my dreams and visions with? Who would sit and talk with me for hours or carry me places to give me a family history lesson? It was all about me and how I felt and I immediately knew she would disapprove but self pity had visited me that day.

Suddenly her words rang loud in my ears as she spoke, *me, what did I teach you about denying self and thinking of others? What about my grandchildren? They need you now. Betty needs you now. Many people need your strength and all you want to do is sit her and feel sorry for yourself.* Boy was that a wake up call. She wasn't kidding when she said I would be seeing her and more importantly she would be seeing me. To make a long story short I got up, prepared food, called in flowers and called the rest of the family, maybe not in that order but it all got done before I left to go to Aunt Ellen's home smiling. I thought how hard it was going to be to enter her home and she not be there. I laughed as I thought she only gave me about ten minutes to be full of myself before she intervened and put me back on the right track.

To my surprise she was there in spirit and everyone could feel her. The house was filled with the smells of food and laughter, like a family home coming and heavenly home coming at the same time, there were so many spirits in that house that day and for days up to the funeral and days past the funeral. For Aunt Ellen it was a glorious time and she made sure I saw and heard it to share it one day in a book and to her grandchildren.

Then there was a time period where I couldn't feel her at all and the place was lonely and sad. But once JP her oldest grandson whom she had left the home house too started remodeling the house and talking about his grandmother she returned. Now I can go up to the home house almost anytime and feel her or be flooded with rivers of wisdom she pours into me. Every room has a happy story for us who grew up there. Every family event leads to laughter when we all sit around and share our memories. We know we are healed from the hurts of childhood when we can share those as well and laugh at ourselves or the person who hurt us. Aunt Ellen said life on planet earth was a bed of thorns and it was our job to find the roses and make perfume for the entire world to enjoy. She loved roses and had a rose garden where she worked in for many hours and prayed for family and community concerns. She had flowers of all kinds where she sung or hummed *I come to the garden alone while the dew is still on the roses, and the voice I hear ringing in my ear is God Almighty, my savior. And He walks with me and He talks with me and He tells me I am His own. And the joy we share as we tarry there, none other has ever known.* As you can see she didn't sing it the way it was written. She sung it or hummed it based on who she needed to pray for. She hummed many a prayers while she worked during the day and only a few even knew she was doing it. When family drama was going on you could see her at the stove cooking and humming some hymn and in truth she was humming a prayer over the situation. At times I would sit and time it just to see how long before God answered and everyone would be laughing over the drama. She didn't like fussing or negative in her home and if her prayers didn't change the situation real quick she would exit outside to work in flowers or the garden or on the front porch shelling peas or something. She didn't hang around and listen to much negative. When people said hurtful things or did hurtful things against her or God she called him, rather than getting mad and fussing she would hum out a prayer or sing a gospel hymn, that their minds and hearts would be opened to love and peace. She said a home without peace and joy was also a home without love regardless what they told. She taught me to do the same. As I sing or hum some of her favorites even today I can feel her close by. She loved the Smith family and wanted every one saved from them-selves she called it and surrendered to do God's word, will and work.

We can only hope our future generations will grow up and discover the love, which is God. Like Aunt Ellen said you only know lust, selfish love she called it until you come to know Love and that is God through our Lord Jesus Christ. You can only discover the spirit of respect when you first learn how to respect yourself, your family, and co-workers and people in general then you are truly respecting God. You can only honor your earthly father and mother when you remember they make mistakes but never stop loving you. You can't forgive others until first you forgive yourself. You must own your true self and never sell it to anyone. Then and only then can you be truly happy with others regardless of what they say and do. For you know where you came from and why you are here and where you are going when you leave this old world. She said we would discover that not all families grow up and love each other the way the Smith family does. They won't have the relationships we have and we must be patient and teach them and like all families we have a few bad apples too. But remember rotten apples make good wine she would laugh and say.

I thought she should have been concerned about leaving us when she was passing. But No, her last thoughts were about the man she had spent her life with and where he was spending eternity and about the younger generations that was going their own way instead of God's way. She felt she had failed God because she didn't know for sure if her beloved Press was saved or not. She was concerned because of the lifestyle he chose to live. He went to church and played the religious part she said but was he truly saved was her question. Her last years were sad more than happy because of her concern over Press's soul and where it was and if her own grandchildren would find Christ for them selves. She didn't carry the joy she always had. Those of us that knew her could feel her sadness after Johnny died. She put a front on many times to not share her sadness with everyone. But in her letters to Peggy and me she shared her love, sadness and concerns about the generations she would be leaving behind when she passed. In her letter writing she was connecting Peggy and me to stay close and help one another after she passed. She would say you know Cowtail she has the gift you have but she won't share it with everyone so be there for her. You and Peggy stay close and remember me sometimes and the happy years we all had here in this old house. When I'm gone stay close to the other cousins and keep them coming to the reunions. Tell them, all that have crossed- over will be here and they need to be here too.

She passed with another concern on her heart that we discussed in her last years and that was for all her grandchildren blood born or adopted born to accept Jesus in their heart, read his words and come to know Jesus for them selves, not to depend on what man says. She knew if they all accepted Jesus as Lord she would see them all now and in eternity.

I was told she didn't like my first book *A Daddy But No Mama,* but when I asked her about it after moving back to Virginia in 1990. She said, it was a little to truthful but God would forgive me. Then she laughed and said maybe you will write a book about me someday but don't tell all of my secrets from my youth as she hugged me laughing. I replied you say it as a joke but I will write about you. She pushed me back and looked me eye to eye and said, well wait until I'm dead and gone and don't tell my secrets from my youth. I believe I have kept that promise in this book. Why wouldn't I write a book about Aunt Ellen Tune Smith? She was the one who taught me how to write at age six; how to write letters with feeling and how to love and forgive. I only wish I had disobeyed her and wrote about her before she passed. She filled me with volumes of books of down to earth common sense and wisdom. .She taught me that love heals, love inspires and love triumphs.

For years her words haunted me each time I shared. I could only hope Uncle Press confessed of his sins before he passed. God certainly gave him enough time to do so. I can only hope he asked Jesus into his heart those last few minutes he had and both of them are together in eternity. It was different with Aunt Ellen we all knew she was with the God she had served, taught and lived with on earth all of her life. Our cousin James use to say he knew Aunt El had a mansion or special place in heaven just for her, after all the hell the Smith's put her though.

From that date when Daddy showed up for Aunt Ellen to this one I haven't seen Daddy in dreams or visions but one could happen before I finish this book. It doesn't always mean he is waiting for a loved one to cross over sometimes he just shows up to remind me love is all that counts. Not to forget. I have felt his presence many times when I went through hardships and the loss of loved ones just like I have felt Aunt Ellen's each time. When Lil Tommy passed in 1998 and the funeral was over his mother asked me to cook an old fashion Smith breakfast.

Standing there stirring the milk gravy and my butt in tune with the stir (a family memory of how I learned how to cook mild gravy) Aunt Ellen showed up and told me not to forget the bacon. About that time Carol asked if we felt Aunt Ellen's presence. I replied yes, she just reminded me not to forget the bacon. She said, you didn't think you would have an old fashion Smith breakfast and I not be there, did you? Suddenly a huge laugh broke from each of us for we all knew our loved ones who had crossed over were here to help us through all this pain and lost. That's just one gift love gives us when we stay close and intimate with our families. They live in a to and fro realm with Christ and can show up where they will to be at any time.

The dreams, visions and visitations increased and multiplied and became more real or understandable with dates and names after Daddy passed. Aunt Ellen knew that fact those last years of her life and asked me to teach her. What an honor to share with her and show her my research on the word as to what the Bible says about a certain dream or vision? What an honor just to sit with her and she ask me questions only for her to add more insight to it? Sharing my dreams, visitations and visions was easy and like a game we played for she had such an opened mind and heart and knew the Scriptures so well herself.

They multiplied even more after she passed but I keep most of them to myself and God now. I share only what my Heavenly Father will allow me to share with people because so many are coming about the end of times and all the changes taking place. But oh how I love it when I hear a preacher, teacher or prophet speaking and teaching what God showed me and we haven't connected on earth except by the spirit. They are paving the way for God's people. Let him who hears continue to hear. Let him who sees continue to see.

Learning to know God better and His plans and purpose for us being on earth has been and will be a lifetime study. A life time process and time is so precious and wonderful. Spending it with God each day is heaven my friend and heaven is in God. How do we move forward when the past is so present in our daily lives? How do we heal from the past when we're searching for that innocence, that pure love we had in our youth before sex ruled and tossed us here and there? Love comes in so many forms, receive it regardless of what form it is, grasp it and hold onto it with all your strength. Never allow fear to stand in your way or block your view. Never allow sex to rule your life but know it is only one of God's gifts once we come to know Love for who it is. With each form love came to me in Johnny, James, Jesse, Daddy, Shirley, Tommy, Joyce, Aunt Ellen, Mama, grandparents, my husbands, children and grandchildren, all my aunts, uncles and cousins, friends and co-workers, school mates, dogs and church family, each has left a lasting memory that will go with me when I leave this body. There are to many to name from over the years but each deposited a little love in me and withdrew a little from me. How rich is that?

Why would anyone want to spend their days in negative, fussing, complaining, judging and condemning and all that stays behind us when we can enrich our lives with love, Aunt Ellen would say? Some more than others but staying surrounded with love has carried me through many trials and hardships and will continue. For love will never let me down. Cherish it; cherish your family that knew you before that mate. That knew all your faults yet loved you anyway. Appreciate their love. Learn to hum a prayer when someone hurts you until your heart can sing for joy again. Learn to walk away and plant a flower or tree and pray to the God within you until you can feel that innocent love within you again. Be ready to meet your Creator with a smile every day. A clean pure heart overflowing with love for God, parents, brothers, sisters, children, mate and all of life in every form will fill you with the most loving memories. Focus on happy, loving memories each day and don't allow anyone to rob you of the love you deserve from every form whether it's parents or siblings. Then and only then will you be a healthy soul. Love will heal every wound in your soul and you will be able to say as you feel, all is well in my soul. In every trial, hardship and problem there is a love lesson. Look for it and move forward with your past.

Someone asks me if our loved ones could take on a different form after they crossed over? To answer the simplest and most truthful I would have to say usually forty to fifty days after a loved one passes is the time frame they make themselves known to me in the spirit. Others may have a different experience or a longer stay but for me I usually stay in the spirit more than the flesh right after a loved one crosses just to be in God's intimate presence for my own healing. So it only stands to reason that they would come to me more at that time in the last form I remembered them in. But there have been some that came to visit to warn me or ask me to help a spirit cross over into the light that was only spirit energy. And some showed up after years of being in the eternity. I had one spirit Paul was his name, a dear friend for many years while in his flesh body, which had crossed over, appeared to me one morning in my secret place and asked me to help someone live for it wasn't his time yet and he wasn't ready. His mind was full of death yet he was one of God's children, one that walked away from God years ago to go his own way. It was some one that turned his back on God, love and family for another woman; someone that wasted his gifts, time and money on drinking and negative thinking. It was some one who had hurt me to the core of my soul and beyond. He cut such a pain into my whole being that only God and time could heal me. He was someone I couldn't stop loving even though I tried for years to stop. He had been sent to me by God and left me because of God. Yet it was a time of testing for me, a time to put into practice all my Christian teaching on forgiveness and help a soul come back to God. I remembered Aunt Ellen's words as I sat and pondered over my answer. She had told me when he left that he would return to God and when that time came I had better be prepared. That God would test my forgiveness since I allowed him to control my emotions for so long. I never figured it would happen after all it had been over thirty years. Yet here I sat on my commode with Paul's spirit staring at me asking me to help his soul and help save his physical life.

That morning came just like Paul had said it would. God was at work and went to James my cousin and woke him up and told him to get up to Carolyn's that morning at 7 am. James thought something was wrong with me as he rushed up from Drakes Branch Virginia. God also used Penny my daughter as well to save him from a deadly stokes that morning confirmed by the doctors. God needed all three of us in obedience that morning with our hearts tuned in. Then once this man was out of danger we were to tell him about the visitation from Paul asking me to help save his life and to tell him it was time to return to God. He did come back to God and he lived with Jesus and for Jesus for seven years before he passed. So you see sometimes God uses dreams or visions or visitations to save our physical lives or the life of another. What a reward to see a soul that wandered away from God over thirty years ago come back to God and die with a great testimony. The years he wasted are between him and God. What a joy to see James, a cousin and brother in Christ walk with such joy after God woke him up and used him to save a soul? It's no telling how many people he shared that experience with and helped others. It changed Penny that day and reminded her God still loved her, and cared about her. She has a testimony to pass down to her children.

Two other times during that seven years God wanted me to pray for him to live when doctors had given up. God also showed me his departure date, what time, where and who he wanted with him at the time of his departure and who to tell. I saw that on a Sunday before he passed on a Wednesday. With him in the spirit from the spirit world was his daddy, his mother, his brother Ray, Uncle George, Aunt Rachel and many others. I told only his oldest daughter Tammy and niece Tonia at his request. I called his cousin Doris in Bedford Virginia and told her and who all was with him knowing she would be so grateful and pray as well. They were free to tell whomever they felt to share the information with. I told Penny and Jay they needed to stay with their daddy for the next three days but not about the vision from his loved ones waiting for him. When I saw his sister Ruby smiling and glowing as she waited with her loved ones for her brother I knew he was ready and was actually leaving. He and Ruby had words years back and he hadn't forgiven her even though she had forgiven him. I knew his time had come and God had honored my words and Aunt Ellen's from years past. God says two or more witnesses and I had my two witnesses and didn't need another.

In another book I will go into greater detail concerning this and other experiences because it is seven wonderful years romancing with God as we led him backwards to where he turned his back on God. You see wherever you leave God is where you must return to pick him up. The Reverse is what some call it. Never give up on your loved ones. Keep them ever before God's face, reminding God of His promises. But for now let me say, God is releasing greater revelations in this hour on what it means to be in an intimate relationship with Him, He has always desired intimacy with His people. From Genesis to Revelation we read the story of this God seeking a people who would love Him above everything else. He is calling us from simple intimate devotion into divine union where we become one with him. This is this Oneness generation if you can see that. Greater revelations began in 1988 and started manifesting themselves in the physical realm in March 1989. There are not three Gods but only Oneness. There's One love, One joy, One peace all which comes from the ONE GOD. Waves of the Holy Spirit are flowing all over the earth now as he moves upon the waters and getting stronger by the day.

Allow me to share just a few more golden nuggets from the kitchen of Aunt Ellen: When you decide to be rebellious you hurt God's heart and the people all around you. God is reaching into souls in these last days and healing all the wounds at once in our souls. What does it mean when people say last days? It means the end of sin ruling God's planet just that simple. God is pleased when we are open and honest even with our doubts and fears. It's okay to fall down just don't allow yourself to stay down. Be like a child and make yourself get up. When people put you down and speak badly about you, walk away and pray for them. Ask yourself is any of that true? If so, repent and ask God to help you in those areas but don't get mad. Only people that truly care about your soul will take the risk and correct you. Don't justify or make excuses but be a real mature adult and apologize and tell them you will try to do better. Then thank them for caring about you. Remember a man will live on a housetop or one room apartment alone before he will live with a negative, complaining woman. Confessing your weaknesses and not putting forth the effort to change them is you yourself lying to yourself? Remember when Jesus cross got to heavy for him to carry it God sent someone to help him. He will do the same for us for he is the same God, he knows how we feel. Also honor the way you dress. Your presence carries an awesome message, gestures, silence, and words are all being sent out all the time by you whether you are aware of it or not. As your daddy use to say if you wear a top that exposes your breasts he will pinch them to answer your silent prayer and craving for attention. So don't preach 'respect and honor me' and dress like a whore for there's always a man who will see and hear your silent cravings for attention and look and pinch. People pick up your energy and can read you like a book for we are a living book or a dead one. Ask yourself what message are you sending out to others? Let your words and actions be one and the same.

What is God doing and saying now in 2010-2011? God is revealing a higher level of His secrets in 2010-2011. What is our job? First to obey for it is better than sacrifice. Rebellion has taken many children whether you believe it or not. There is a price for rebellion and we don't always know what that price is until we lose it. There's also a reward for obedience and we don't always know what that is either. Secondly there are secrets in God that He hasn't revealed to mankind before and He is revealing His secrets to all willing to listen now. Third the blinders and deafness is coming off His bride the church for all seeking to know God. Forth we must get back to Biblical honor and honor all our leaders and pray for them. Fifth is wisdom manifold wisdom of God. God is revealing Himself and His angels in such awesomeness to all willing to receive Him. Sixth is creative, God is awaking all religions to His Creation and Purpose. Seventh God is using the media, movies and all to get His message out to the world until His church learn some lessons in real love. Some churches will continue to preach gloom and doom for they are warning churches. Others will teach dreams, visions and visitations while others will show what the scientists have proven as the word of God. Eighth is fear. God is removing all fear from His people and showing them it's only an illusion. Ninth is holiness and God is speaking all over the world for the people in the earth to clean themselves up. He is speaking to the people in the pews and on the streets. People who have lost hope in churches and religion. People who have sought him and cried for him yet waited for years for answers and understanding. And tenth are dreams, visions, and visitations like the world has never seemed before. It will be reported all over the world of people of all religions and some that have no religious backgrounds. God is back in the streets of America now very strongly and American people's focus should be on America and Israel now more than anytime in history. People of all ages especially the youth has God's attention. You will hear testimonies from youth about gold dust anointings and other anointings that haven't been manifested in over two thousand years coming upon whole groups of people at once. They will be dreaming spiritual dreams, dreams of guidance, specific known facts to solve problems and inventions. Dreams of warnings of coming dangers and storms; warnings to people and visitations to people that have been hurt and abused in so many ways that they can't find any reason to believe we have a loving God who cares. Three- fourths of the dreams for 2010-2011 will be warning dreams showing us how to avoid danger. What God is revealing to you or in any area where God wants His will, He will reveal to you. It's a dangerous place to live out-side of God's will at this time. People will begin to discern the spirit behind situations and know how to tell it to go. The prophecies we speak over people will come to pass quickly now. Suddenly God shows us things to fix, parts of the body that needs healing and when we lay hands and allow God to do His work or speak a simple word they will be healed and know it's God. Some people we will hug or shake hands with and we will see their past, present and future. We will see the truth behind their words or complaints. God is proving He is with His people in such strong ways that multitudes will serve him. Multitudes will be drawn off the streets of America and around the world to follow God when they hear him for themselves. Just as the oil poured out so mightily upon our waters in one hundred days or more will the Holy Spirit oil pour out among the peoples? The focus will be off church buildings and preachers and put it where it belongs on God and His work.

In Ephesians 5:31-32 Paul relates the union of a man and a woman to Christ and the Church. It is a mystery how God and man can become one but this is the inheritance of every believer who will lay down there selfish lives for this great King. The Lord is longing for a people who perfectly reflect His character and nature in God's eyes on the earth as His ambassadors. But before that can happen with each individual, people must get a hunger to learn what the character and nature of

Christ is so they will recognize it when it appears in themselves and in others and give credit where it belongs with God. Be prepared for it will appear. There is none righteous no not one upon the earth. We all need God looking at the perfect Jesus in us. Be prepared to see beyond the flesh person and really see and hear the God within. That which is within has been hidden from most people but the time has come for it to come forth for all to see who really is ruling in each person. Whether God or selfish self it will be revealed, for the veils are coming off by the hands of God. People all over the world will begin experiencing God the way only a few have for the past two-thousand years.

In Dreams Visions and Heroes, you took a journey of intimacy with the King. You pulled from my personal relationship with God for your own personal relationship with God and gave yourself keys on how to love God more. Jesus pulled people to him just like he pulled God to him. We are to be pullers not pushers. God is a magnet and is constantly drawing people to Him. He pulls at our hearts and comes to us in our dreams. He smiles at us through little children and praises and encourages us through people that have no motive but love. That seeks no motive or reward other than to show you God. The ego lovers love to push but the God nature loves to pull people into the Kingdom of Life. In God is life eternal. It's not about me but our Lord Jesus Christ. Then our Lord Jesus Christ says it's not about me but all about our Creator God. God speaks to me about me. God speaks to you about you and the people you love. God speaks to us about our country and world affairs. He's not looking for preachers but for people with an experience with life to give a testimony everywhere they go.

We all need a now God, a right now God, in this season where all are confused and afraid of losing everything they have spent their life getting. When God says money is coming to me. It's coming. God works at both ends. Sometimes all we can see is the middle, the bill that just arrived. Learn to ask God to show you the answer and believe He will. God is the beginning and the end so who is in the middle? We and the Holy Spirit that's who's in the middle. I remember when Uncle Early asked me what was in between the space in words. At that time I didn't know but now I do the Holy Spirit Power Himself. His will is simple: good health, prosperity, and eternal life. It's like having a baby. You know you are pregnant so you tell the world before the baby gets here even before the body shows. We dream about the nursery, the sex of the baby, his/her education, and the clothes you will be buying. You spend your whole time even working to make money preparing for this arrival. Now learn to expect that job or next book written and published or movie or reaching a goal or starting a business you always dreamed about. Whatever we need or want that lines up with God's will after we ask God to provide it we need to know its coming and start preparing. Can we be content while we wait? Yes, content where we are until God moves us and only you and I can practice that daily. All the prayers in the world and all the hands can be laid on you won't bring it any faster, only daily patient contentment and practice. Know God loves you so much he will never deny you anything that is good. Some things are some people we lose we think God is cruel but if it was truly ours and intended to stay to build us up and help us grow spiritually it couldn't leave us ever. Not in a million years could anyone ever walk away from us; but if the lesson is learned and its time for you and I to grow up in another area of our life there's another teacher coming to teach and help us. You see our comforter never leaves us and our love is secure. You won't just talk about this subject, but live it as a way of life.

When you realize God is the husband, the wife, the boy friend, the girl friend, the gardener, the provider and protector you will be bold in your relationship with Him. When you see God in your doctors, bosses, servants at Wal-mart, everywhere you go, you will walk in a secret place. When you can't see God in a person then you will give them some of yours. You will have walks with him and you will be invited into His bed chamber for that intimate relationship and pillow talks that only you and He can have. You will enter the secret place in your own mind and heart and romance God. You will discover God's love, joy and peace that is above understanding and only by being inspired by the Holy Spirit could you share with another. You will magnify God and vibrate him all the time.

Don't look for or expect perfection from yourself or anyone else. Just know the perfect one lives inside and is coming forth and is molding us himself into that perfect image and bringing us forth with him. You will have an every day, every night life style where you are always consciously aware of God all around you, consciously aware of angels and loved ones in the spirit all around you after reading this book so expect it. You will listen for groups' of people fellowshipping, studying or singing about your Jesus, your God and drive for hours if necessary to get there just to be around happy people talking about your Jesus, your God. I whole heartily recommend this book to you and everyone you know. It will draw you and your family into this divine romance with the King and Queen where it will overflow into the lives of all around you. Who is the King and Queen? They are the Image and Likeness of God Himself or put another way, the Mind and Heart in the

Oneness of God Himself, working together to transform a Spiritual Body that is eternal and like Jesus.

If you didn't have a childhood or family like the Smith family you can decide now to make your family as loving and caring as we were, as we are, as we shall be as long as we want it. When you hear of a loved one that is dying, you will put your life on hold just to sit in their presence and talk to them about God and let the God in you flow into them. You won't spend their time or yours with speaking of the problem but speaking about the solution. God is our Solution every time so lets talk about the solution. The Lord is saying, "May I have this dance for eternity?" With a whole heart you say, Yes Lord you may have this dance and every dance from now on. When you dance with someone from this day forward say to yourself, "Lord I sure do enjoy dancing through life with you."

I've shared my childhood secrets and friendship with God in hopes to see more people dancing with the Lord. I spend time reevaluating scriptures that have become too familiar to us, highlighting how it's all about the heart. I hope you are stirred by the efforts. Don't tune the WORD, WILL, and WAY out but instead tune it in. Then fine tune it to hear ever so clearly what the Lord is saying to you. He is talking to every person are you listening? Dance with the Lord through life. When you see the word ADD in the Bible and they are God's character and nature, ask God to add those to your character and nature He already knows they are there inside of you and will bring them forth for growth. Be strong for living in love is a painful road, a truth most people won't tell you and some will tell you they don't want to hear the truth. Oh but the rewards are well worth all the suffering. Remember what Jesus said, even a sinner, which means an unbeliever, can love those who love them back. But it takes God love to love those who don't love you back. Ask any mother and she will tell you she has loved her children even when they screamed in her face I hate you.

If I had only one wish for my life it is leaving people with the tools, the personal experiences to dance with Jesus Christ. To be romanced by our LORD. To know the intimate relationship with a real visible God like my family and God taught me. He is all around and He is listening and watching us all the time. Neither He nor His angels will stop you from being rebellious but neither will they stop the consequences Satan brings by worshiping him. God is not a mystery only parts you don't understand and if we live a million years we won't understand all of God but we can understand ourselves. Why would we want to understand ourselves? To know just how perfect and loving you really are. To know how much you are created in His Image and Likeness. Once you know yourself you won't worship Satan, negative or rebellion. Who is Satan? Rebellion! Why would I want you to romance and dance with God Who is Love? Because once you have had the best you won't ever settle for seconds again. Cheap sex will turn your stomach and fifty words your ears will tune out and protect you from. You will know a person by the spirit rather than by the flesh. You won't hang around and listen to negative people. You won't think and talk negative any more yourself. You will truly discover that the glass is you and really is half full and God is working every second with what you give him to fill you up completely with love, joy and peace.

What do I miss about Daddy in the physical realm? Daddy's boldness in standing for what was right because it was the right thing to do; His calmness and loyalty to his children and family, and his willingness to expand his heart to add more people as they entered the family in his love circle which was our security. The family would say if Uncle Henry liked you, you had to be alright. His appreciation to God, family, neighbors, customers, and country; His smile, joy and peacefulness; our breakfasts together and talks; His taste testing when I made rolls with so many encouraging words as he reached for another fresh out of the oven.

What do I miss about Aunt Ellen the most from the physical realm? Her calling me every time someone was sick, a death or just needed prayer or a visit; If she was worried about JP or Wanda she would call to share and investigate her own motives before saying anything. The freedom to drop in any time and see her big smile as I entered and a meal if I needed to eat; Her mealtimes around her table; the trips we took together and our visits to others as I received a family history lesson. Her family and Bible stories and her cute little examples to get a point across; walking with her around that big farm, helping her with her flowers or garden, canning and cleaning or doing whatever. What do I miss the most about Daddy and Aunt Ellen in the physical realm? THEM!

I would like to close by leaving a few keys I would like for you to have about our God and hope something I say will draw and pull at your heart until you ask our Lord Jesus Christ into your heart and life. Religion put Jesus on the cross, his love kept him there and the Holy Spirit Power raised him from the dead or we wouldn't be saved from ourselves and our sin today. Everything revealed from God is by the Holy Spirit. True salvation from our sins is revealed in Matthew 16 of the Bible and understanding comes by revelation from the Holy Spirit.

Matthew tells is there are four things we need to be saved from sin and they are: a face to face encounter; Revelation from the Holy Spirit; Confessed and said you are Christ. If you have experienced and accepted those publically on the basis of love and not to keep from burning in a hell fire you are saved. Then you have a pulling, a hunger to know what God said and read and study the Bible. You are not afraid to listen to other beliefs because you are secure in your love. We don't have to ask for power we know we already have it. We know we are in God's will even when others see us as a mistake or a sinner. We know all of Jesus came from God and was God in the flesh and Mary was a carrier. We know how powerful the Holy Spirit is when he turned God into a man and made flesh the living word. (John 17). Eternity lives in him so what can the Holy Spirit do to man, woman, and child? He has given his angels charge over us why not use them for God's glory? God will reach us anyway he has too, whether through dreams, visions, visitations, people, books or tapes. He will encourage us and build us up the same way. He's not in a box and it's not the law that saves us but God himself who is the law. Learn to avoid people and things that stop your joy. Don't fight fear just relax in God and be content. Remember negative words draw the opposite of God. Opposite of love, joy and peace within and without; Practice being a blessing daily to everyone and soon it will be automatic or just learn the lessons and accept the consequences of your choices without burdening others with your judgments and complaints. We're not promised tomorrow so set a goal to make each day a good memory to leave behind. Soon you will have volumes of happy memories that you can recount when sickness, layoffs, appliances or whatever breaks down and deaths come. You will have a storehouse of good memories to fall back on to remind you how blessed you still are. Ephesians 4:29 says be a blessing in word and deed to others and yourself. Start telling yourself what God says about you. Realize there's power in the words of God when you repeat them from the heart. Then when others speak negative to you or gossip about you with bad words you will stay calm for you will know what God says about you. Isn't He the only one you need to please anyway? God says in Proverbs to let all your words be upright and pure. That alone will take a lifetime to practice. Learn to encourage yourself with the words of God and you won't depend upon others to do your job. Psalm 91 is the supernatural secret room where you learn to speak and live a supernatural life. God is supernatural shouldn't that be our goal?

You say well that's just too hard following God. Eating an elegant is taking one bite at a time is what I heard. Learning to walk takes one step at a time with many missed steps and you end up on your knees but you didn't give up did you? It's a daily process with great rewards but it's also up to you. After all, it is your life to be used or to be wasted. God will love you whichever you decide, but will you be satisfied when you get to eternity?

The Brothers and Sisters

**Henry the baby, Uncle Press, Uncle Thornton the oldest,
Aunt Virginia and Aunt Grovine.
Missing is Uncle Jesse, Aunt Mae and Aunt Ruby.
We lost all of these back to back.**

The Queen of the Smith Family

Aunt Ellen Tune Smith
My hero!

Daddy World War II and Purple Heart Medal Hero

Henry Smith Our Hero!
Daddy's Life and Heroes

Carolyn, Tommy Shirley

Aunt Ellen's Porch

My Grandson Michael and JP Smith on Aunt Ellen's porch

**Clarence, Larry, Jesse Jr. James
Cousins**

**1977: Daddy and Aunt Virginia kept this picture
by their bed until they passed**

Chapter 11:

Life Goes On

I want to close by saying that this book mostly explains the spiritual side of our upbringing according to the way I received it. None of us are perfect or any thing to look up to, but just a southern country family that loved a loving God and appreciated a family. I feel after Aunt Ellen passed she was the one that had prayed the most over Daddy is why he came for her and to help me accept God's decision. She had the greatest spiritual connection with Daddy. She had planted many words of life in him like she had all of us is why I believe Daddy was connected to her. I could assume many things and even believe or ask why Uncle Press didn't greet her but I won't because I don't know. Aunt Virginia was like a mother to Daddy after his parents passed at such a young age. He waited for them on that heavenly balcony because his heaven wouldn't be complete until they arrived I believe. I also know her son Johnny and many loved ones were there to greet her into the light to many to name but a fact nevertheless. I learned from Daddy's visits that there are many levels or consciousness in the heavenly realm and we keep growing spiritually after we cross over.

I want to take the time to answer a few questions I have been asked over the years. The first and most asked question is if I believe in death. I don't believe in death but life abundance. I believe our real self which is spirit and soul created in the image and likeness of God just leaves the physical body. But I also know from the Bible there are some who will carry their physical body with them and it will be changed as they ascend. I have seen many of my loved ones over the years after they left their physical body is why I believe that. Jesus, Enoch, Elijah and Elisha are the ones I have seen that carried their body with them. I have seen Cousin Johnny and Cousin Elizabeth playing kick ball in a huge green meadow up in heaven. Also Aunt Annie came to me in a dream with instructions about a necklace she had and described that necklace in great detail in her son James possession. When I told him we looked in her jewelry and there it was and he sent it to the person she had instructed him to send it too. In my second book on my dreams and visions I will tell all that God allows me to tell and there are many. All but a few in the past two years have already come to pass. They may have come to pass by the time the second book comes out.

How could I believe they are just sleeping like some people believe after seeing that in the spirit world? There are loved ones I haven't seen or felt at all that may be sleeping as they say and some I didn't see until years after they passed from this physical life. I do believe the closer the relationship you have with a loved one the easier it is to see them in the spirit. I understand there are many who do believe in death and death does exits I just don't believe in it. Death was created and anything created can be destroyed. Jesus said the last enemy to overcome is death. So why would he say that if it wasn't real? It feels real when we lose a loved one just like fear feels real. But just as soon as you replace death with life, death disappears. Just like when you replace fear with faith fear disappears. I have seemed too many loved ones cross over or step out of their bodies and still be very much alive to believe in death in Jesus Christ realm. I know there are many who believe there are many paths to heaven and there may be but for me I only saw and see one path, Jesus Christ the living son of the Living Mighty God our Creditor.

Some people say I use God as a crutch or sugar daddy. I agree. What better sugar daddy can you have that gives to you all the time, all of his goodness and mercy with no strings attached, no motive except unconditional love. Some say I am just ignorant or live in a fancy world. I say, maybe so, but it's a nice world to live in, in my opinion. You have the right to believe as you wish and go wherever you desire but just suppose I am right. Wouldn't that be a better place then not to know where you or your loved ones may end up?

I believe each spiritual experience was a clue for my life and some I missed. I believe Daddy and Aunt Ellen, my dreams and visions were willing instruments surrendered to God to be used by God to teach me and others. At my birth someone decided that I needed to live and so I did. I had nothing to do with it so my ego can't get any credit. I wasn't raised with preachers but a family that valued honor and respect; People who believed in honest work and took pride in what they did to do their best. Either we loved them so much we wanted to please them or we were too afraid to disobey. But truth be known I wouldn't trade my childhood for any one else's. I've heard many of my cousins say the same. Sure it was hard times right after World War I and II but that drawing appreciation made hard work fun. They taught us how to make work fun.

We were taught to respect and cherish responsibility as a valuable gift. If I had my choice my Mama wouldn't have left us and if she had she would have come back. Heck I probably would have been rebellious and arrogant because even being raised as a Christian I owned both of those. But like Daddy said her leaving us was divine intervention or she would have come home or never left. I believe the dream about my own death like all the others that have come to pass were divine intervention to teach. The death dream threw the fear of death which held me in bondage out of the window and gave me hope of a life after physical death. Leaving the door opened to hear and see God, His angels and spirits and learn from them so I could be a witness and a testimony. It showed me in that dream that death consists in the ego mind only, in Christ realm there is no death. Why else would God give me such dreams and visions if it wasn't for teaching and being a testimony to such facts? That's when I learned I could have an intimate relationship with my God also. So maybe it was a three-fold lesson or more.

From age eight until I had the dream about BC my future husband God had groomed me and molded me into the bride he wanted me to be not what some man wanted me to be. The husband was supposed to be an added delicious gift like adding frosting onto an already delicious chocolate pound cake. That dream also taught me that even when God gives you a mate that mate still has the free choice to live his life, spend his life his own way. That person must choose whom he will serve and give his life too. You see, we are spending our precious time on earth either surrendering to the flesh carnal selfish side of ourselves or we are spending it surrendering to God's will, way and work within us, that God part of us.

I learned we serve God with a sincere heart or serve the devil. It was better to do our best than it was to half way do anything. I think the Bible calls it luke-warm. My family called them wannabes just like Satan, the evil one. Daddy would say I brought you into this world I can take you out of it too if you don't want to obey and be sincere in whatever he had asked us to do. Today some people call that a threat but for us it was love. Daddy desired the best from us just like God desires it from His children. Daddy was a big sugar daddy when you obeyed him and kept him pleased. We knew the house rules and it was our choice but we never liked the consequences they called it when we disobeyed. We loved the rewards so it was the rewards that drove us to obey I believe. Aunt Ellen and Daddy helping us to make good habits each day was a precious gift in our eyes. You might ask how? What was so precious about obedience and sincerity? Well it has kept us all out of jail so far. It protected us from drugs and alcohol habits. It gave our own homes a place of peace and love, honor and respect, an attitude of speaking and doing our best at any project we took on. Just to name a few.

We learned that being surrounded by love was a choice not a feeling. The feeling showed up only after the choice of which thought we were going to surrender too was made. Each member of the Smith family appreciated the other so much they vibrated appreciation for everything. Appreciation is just one grain within the seed of love that we see and enjoy when God love is present. When times were hard financially or illness in the family or community showed up it wasn't just saying a few words, call it a prayer but love in action. Real love is an action word. It drives us to get up each day and do our work. It drives us to study and do our best, to belong and be accepted. It drives us to live in a clean conscious and always aware God is watching and listening. Those holy angels are all around us and if we need help just cry out and it's there. People are called angels sometimes because they give over and above the human giving level. I learned not to put one person upon a throne or pedestal and look to them as if they were God, not even preachers and teachers. They will disappointment you every time. We learned that all children are gifts from God and have an angel assigned to them that report back to God every detail. When adults allow children to disrespect their elders the angels report that also to God. Accountability is coming God makes sure of that I don't need to worry.

The secret room taught me how to enter the secret room or chamber of our own heart. The heart beyond the flesh heart where God lives; it taught truthfulness and it isn't always an easy pill to swallow. Sometimes it looks sweet and delicious only to be bitter and mean. Knowing the darkness within ourselves and how to remove that darkness requires daily work and much practice. It requires much study in the word of God. Sweet victory comes and fills the space where darkness once dwelt. Greater is God within even if he is only the size of a mustard seed than he that is in the world.

The marriage code taught me how much I didn't know about people and relationships. It wasn't about emotions and feelings or me. It taught me how to be impersonal which means, not involving human personality or emotion. It taught emotional pain that is involved and how painful it feels when you try to change another person instead of just going with the flow. If you don't like the flow it is better to be separated from it than to stay and lose your own self. That it was more important to be characterized by honesty, justice, and freedom from improper influence and stand up for what was right because it was the right thing to do when I did I was called cold-hearted. The human heart taught me all of the above plus purity and how valuable it really is. The Bible says, only the pure in heart will see Jesus. That was my goal from the first day that verse was read to me as a child. When I got older and realized Paul and all the apostles saw the resurrected Jesus and none of them had a pure heart from my viewpoint, I knew it meant something different. Even as a child I sought this pure heart and what it meant. Oh how simple it was once learned. Giving up the flesh emotional heart to God and receiving Christ heart was the pure heart I needed to see Jesus, for he was the pure heart. All I needed to have a pure heart was God's only begotten son living and moving and having his being in me. How simply is that? Get out of here ego confusion and don't come back for as you can see I am not my own any more. You will now deal with the Master of the house is my attitude. What's yours?

Thank you again for choosing to take this journey with me. I hope something in this book will change your thinking to God's thinking. I pray you will be forever blessed with a pure heart and see God your creator. I pray you understand God is the law and when we learn the law and live by them we learn God and live in HIM! I pray all of you who want it will come to dreams, visions and revelations of God and have spiritual experiences. I hope you have a personal intimate relationship with Jesus and the Holy Spirit and come to know your true Father and Mother if you want it.

Now until we meet again to take another journey in life I pray you all be blessed with the manifestation of prosperity, divine health, a sound mind, restoration and transformation.

Now to the God who inspired me to write this book I humbly summit to your will as to who will read this and understand the message they are to receive and be blessed forever more in Jesus name. LORD now bless Yourself with all the credit and success. For your name sake be gloried in me and in this and all books you write through me forever according to your will. Amen and so be it! I love you LORD. Thank you!

May God bless the reading of His word and everyone who reads any of my books? May you and your family be blessed when you read my books and may you receive all God intends for you to receive. Thank you for your time and for purchasing my books. I'm not writing for the money but it sure does help pay my bills so you have blessed others already. That's a good start. You can't finish a race until you start so you have already taken the first step. I write because God woke me one morning and said write, publish and keep writing. God has planted many books in me to be published and shared with people all over the world but it's up to God to get it in their hands once I finish my part. He wants to bless you with His Greater Presence and purpose. Just Receive HIM!

I hope you will watch for my next book, *Michael 2 Unsolved Mystery.* The goal for that book will be, *can you solve this mystery? The girlfriend claimed he killed himself over her. Why would he kill himself over someone he had decided to break up with over a month prior?* If you haven't read *Michael An Endtime Sign,* I suggest you read it so you will be half way in solving the mystery of Michael's death. His conception, birth and move to Virginia were announced by the Archangel Gabriel himself. The same angel that announced Isaac and Jesus announced his birth. A boy born with the Holy Spirit and appeared in spirit at his own funeral and many witnesses saw it so nothing is impossible with God. It's a must read if you want to know how a child born full of the Holy Spirit lived his life. If you have children, teens or grandchildren you will be inspired. Whether you believe it or not has no affect on God or His plans but it does have an effect on you and your life.

Some of my future book titles God has inspired me to write and publish after Michael 2 and before I leave my body if Christ tarries are: Dreams, Visions and Revelations 2; Me And My Chihuahuas; Consider Me Dead. I hope you watch for them.

Again thank you readers and you are blessed more than you were before you read this book. That I know!

Chapter 12:

The Total Sum

Copied and Pasted as it was written without any changes with permission. This teaching and others can be found on their website. I hope you enjoy it as much as I did.

Yeshua Jesus said, "I tell you these things BEFORE they happen so when they come to pass you will know that it is I who gave you truth."

Yeshua Jesus also said, ""No one can come to me unless the FATHER who sent me DRAWS him, and I will raise him up at the last day. It is written in the prophets: 'They will ALL BE TAUGHT BY GOD.' *Everyone who <u>listens to the Father</u> and <u>learns from Him</u> comes to me.* No one has seen the Father except the one who is from God; only he has seen the Father. I tell you the truth, how who believes has everlasting life already." (John 6:43-47)

Again Yeshua Jesus said, "What do you want me to do for you?" "Lord, I want to see," he replied. Jesus said to him, "Receive your sight; your faith has healed you."

What are the birth pains according to Jesus? (Mark 13:6-"Many will come in my name, claiming, 'I am he,' and will deceive many. When you hear of wars and rumors of wars, do not be alarmed. Such things must happen, but the end is still to come. Nation will rise against nation, and kingdom against kingdom. There will be earthquakes and famines in various places. These are <u>the beginning</u> of <u>birth pains.</u>

Robert Moment put it this way: Even when things go wrong, we need to have faith. The Bible says, "He causes his sun to rise on the evil and the good, and sends rain on the righteous and the unrighteous." Belief in God does not create a protective bubble around us. We see crime. We see cancer. We see war. We see these things, and we ask ourselves, why? We ask God, why? We wonder how we can ever be happy in a world so torn. But Romans 8:28 tells us, "And we know that in all things God works for the good of those who love him." All these things happening in the world, all these things that hurt us and confuse us, all these things are somehow going to work for good. How do we know? We have to have faith. We're back to the mustard seed. When something bad happens, we have to believe that it is for a greater good, that it is all part of God's plan.

Sometimes, we even feel guilty for our happiness. This is the world talking, not the Holy Spirit. We should never feel guilty for our joy. Our joy is a gift from God, and by letting the world see our joy, even in the midst of so much pain, we let the world see our faith. By showing the world our faith, we show them our God. Our happiness glorifies Him. Our happiness is a gift from Him. All we have to do is reach out and accept it. Robert Moment is an innovative forward-thinking "throw the box away" inspirational life coach, marketing expert, speaker and author of highly acclaimed book, *God Will Always Be There For You.* Robert is passionate about empowering individuals on how to experience God's love, power, joy, peace and prosperity. Visit his site at http://www.ChristianInspirational.org and sign-up for the FREE online Bible study titled, Christian Living. Copyright © 2010 by Robert Moment. All rights reserved. You may forward this article in its entirety to anyone you wish. (He is glad to share God's wisdom with you.)Thank you Mr. Moment!

Now I would like to share a lesson from Ray C. Stedman: Stedman sums up the guts of this book and the teaching from my Daddy and Aunt Ellen. We would be wise to learn from these powerful teachers. I hope you see the meaning behind the decisions, the discipline and the choices the Smith family made for three little children that could have damaged them for life by the abandonment of their mother. I choose The One Commandment, The Gospel of John because my Daddy lived his life and raised three children according to the book of John, the book Psalms and the book of Proverbs.

Title: The One Commandment
By: Ray C. Stedman
Series: The Gospel of John
Scripture: John 13:18-38

At times I grow tired of the ugliness of our world. Sickening reports of violence, rape, murder, drug traffic, and pornography and child abuse are flung at us constantly by television and newspapers. It's enough to make you want to either fade out or blow the whole mess up. In our local paper last week there was a story that President Reagan,

Constantin Chernenko of the Soviet Union and Prime Minister Margaret Thatcher of Britain were each given one wish they could have fulfilled. Reagan wished that a flood would cover Russia; Chernenko wished for an earthquake to swallow the United States; but, asked what she wished, Margaret Thatcher replied, "Well, if those two wishes are granted I would like a nice relaxing scotch and soda!" Many would probably join her in that wish.

The world is well supplied these days with naive and simplistic solutions to some of the terrible problems that grip us. Every day we see bumper stickers that suggest easy ways to solve our problems. "Make Love Not War," "Arms Are For Embracing," "Ban the Bomb." Once I even saw one that said, "Abolish Hate." Well, these are perfectly proper goals, but I confess I grow weary of such mindless solutions. Yet, when we turn to the wisdom of Jesus, as he is teaching his disciples in the Upper Room on the very night on which he was betrayed, it sounds as if he too is suggesting the same kind of futile advice when he tells them to "Love one another."

In the section for today, found in Chapter 13 of the Gospel of John, our Lord sends the traitor out from the midst of the disciples to do his dirty deed; then gives the disciples a new commandment that sums up all ten of the old ones in one commandment; and he reveals to Peter his coming denial of his Lord -- in that order.

I am not going to follow that order, however. But I want to begin with the new commandment, in Verses 31-35. We will understand what has happened to Judas and what is happening to Peter only when we see these in relationship to that central thing that Jesus talked about, the new commandment:

When he [Judas] had gone out, Jesus said, "Now is the Son of man glorified, and in him God is glorified; if God is glorified in him, God will also glorify him in himself, and glorify him at once. Little children, yet a little while I am with you. You will seek me; and as I said to the Jews so now I say to you, "Where I am going you cannot come." A new commandment I give to you, that you love one another; even as I have loved you, that you also love one another. By this all men will know that you are my disciples, if you have love for one another. {John 13:31-35 RSV}

This is a very important moment in our Lord's life. He introduces it with these rather mysterious words about glorification: "The Son of Man is now glorified." He refers to the exodus of the traitor from the midst of the disciples. It is important to see that Jesus does not say this, nor does he give the new commandment, until Judas is gone. When

Judas leaves Jesus says, "Now is the Son of Man glorified." That is, now (by this means) is God's purpose advanced and fulfilled. Not only the Son but the Father too is glorified. Further, Jesus says the Father will glorify himself again and he will do it immediately, which is clearly a reference to the cross. We know from the Scriptures that the whole universe exists for the glory of God, and, since Jesus himself tells us that here is a moment when God is glorified, we must see this as a very significant and profoundly important moment.

This is also indicated by the new name, "Little children," by which he addresses the disciples for the first time in his ministry. That is a tender word, a family word. Most commentators agree that it was at this moment in the events of the Upper Room that our Lord began to institute the Passover Supper (and what we call the Lord's Supper), which immediately followed the Passover. Throughout the cities of Judea and Galilee and all through the length and breadth of the land that night, Jewish families were gathering to eat the Passover lamb. It was traditional then, as it still is today, for the father to act as the host for the family and invite the children to ask questions that revealed the meaning of what was going on. The littlest child was the one who began by asking, "What do these things mean?" and the father explained.

Clearly this is what our Lord is doing here in the Upper Room. He sees himself as the head of a family of whom the disciples are the children. That is how he addresses them, "Little children," and they break in with the questions that children ask at times like this. Also our Lord here clearly states to the disciples that the time of his departure has now come. "Where I am going," he tells them, "you can not follow me." Within twelve hours he will be hanging upon a cross. Less than twenty hours from this he is cold and dead in the grave. This, then, is a time for last instructions.

Here they are: "A new commandment I give to you, that you love one another, even as I have loved you, that you also love one another." Those simple words, "Love one another," sound like a first-century bumper sticker. Imagine all the little donkeys of Israel with a sign on their rumps saying, "Love one another"! It looks very much like the same kind of rather futile advice that bumper stickers give to us today. While it's good advice, no one can carry it out. Yet the whole world has always agreed that this is exactly what we need to do to solve our problems. All this terrible array of evil that haunts us and sickens us today would disappear if we could teach people to "Love one another." All the ugliness, the child abuse, the broken marriages, the violent crime, the senseless destruction, the terrible drug traffic that is destroying our children, the awful pornography, the sex mills that grind continually in every big city -- all this would disappear if we learned to love one another.

I was interested to read in the volume *Caesar and Christ,* in Will Durant's great history *The Story of Civilization.* His description of the ministry of Jesus. Will Durant was not a Christian, but, as these words make clear, he understood the power of our Lord's ministry:

The revolution he sought was a far deeper one, without which reforms could only be superficial and transitory. If he could cleanse the human heart of selfish desire, cruelty, and lust, utopia would come of itself, and all those institutions that rise out of human greed and violence, and the consequent need for law, would disappear. Since this would be the profoundest of all revolutions, beside which all others would be mere coups d'etat of class ousting class and exploiting in its turn, Christ was, in this spiritual sense, the greatest revolutionary in history.

Will Durant recognized that if Jesus could teach people to love one another it would dramatically and drastically change the history of the world.

But is this merely futile advice, first-century bumper sticker wishful thinking? No, for in the wonderful way God has of hiding truth, hidden within this sentence of Jesus is a dramatic secret, the answer to the question we all ask, *"How do you do this?"* We all know how difficult it is to love unlovely people. Here is how one Christian writer described his problem in this area:

Loving people is about the most difficult thing that some of us do. We can be patient with people and even just and charitable, but how are we supposed to conjure up in our hearts that warm, effervescent sentiment of goodwill which the New Testament calls "love"? Some people are so miserably unlovable. That odorous person with the nasty cough who sat next to you in the train, shoving his newspaper into your face, those crude louts in the neighborhood with the barking dog, that smooth liar who took you in so completely last week -- by what magic are you supposed to feel toward these people anything but revulsion, distrust and resentment, and justified desire to have nothing to do with them?

We can all identify with that. How do we "Love one another"? Jesus tells us in these simple words, "As I have loved you." What the Greek, literally, says is, "As I have loved you in order that you might love one another." One is the cause and the other is the effect. As in many places in Scripture, the word "as" here can better be translated "since": "Since I have loved you in order that you might love one another." Here our Lord is saying that his love for us will stimulate and awaken within us the ability to love other people; his love will be the measure, the cause and the identifying mark of authentic love from him.

Our love, if we understand this and relate to it, will be like Jesus' love. I do not need to detail for you what that is. It takes the whole of the gospels to tell of the marvelous, wonderful love of Jesus. I see at least three characteristics that were unusual (and inimitable) about his love:

- First, it was without respect of persons. He did not love people who were nice to love, as we do. He chose to love the unlovely: people who were rejected, difficult to love, looked down upon, and held in contempt by society. He loved them, not because he wanted the good feeling of love, but simply because they needed love and his love responded. This is the characteristic of his love. It goes out to people who need love regardless of what they are like, no matter how dirty, leprous, hurtful, proud or arrogant they may be. It goes out because they need love, without respect of persons.

- Secondly, that love will be expressed in deeds, not just words. It will not be mere talk about love, singing songs about love or calling oneself loving and not showing it. Love will be expressed in deeds. Remember the Lord's words at the scene of the last judgment when the sentence is pronounced to those on the right hand of the judge: "Enter into the kingdom that has been prepared, because when I was sick you visited me, when I was hungry you fed me, and when I was naked you clothed me..." {cf, Matt 25-34-35}. Deeds, not words.

- Thirdly, it is a love without end. This is how John describes that love where he introduces the whole chapter in these words, "Having loved his own, he loved them unto the end." He never gave up on them. He loved them as long as his love could do anything to reach them. And his love included even Judas. The love of Jesus reached out to all.

Henry Drummond, who was a contemporary of D. L. Moody (and an associate of his for a while), has written a tremendous message, a classic, on the "love chapter," First Corinthians 13, called *The Greatest*

Thing In The World. In it he says that if a piece of ordinary steel is attached to a magnet and left there, after a while the magnetism of the magnet passes into the steel so that it too becomes a magnet. He points out that this is an example of what staying close to Jesus does. Earlier we sang,

Turn your eyes upon Jesus; Look full in His wonderful face. And the things of earth will grow strangely dim In the light of His glory and grace.

This is what our Lord is teaching. It is those who learn to enjoy his love, who reckon on it, rejoice in it, feel the warmth of it and remind themselves of it; those who remember the fact that they do not deserve it, that they in no way have earned his love but they have it anyway; those are the ones who become magnetized with his love and are able to pass it on to others regardless of whether they respond in kind or not. That kind of dramatic, life-changing love is authentic Christian love. For two thousand years our Lord has been demonstrating that he can do this with people. Not everybody who calls himself a Christian displays this kind of love. (We will see why in a few moments.) Nevertheless there are hundreds of thousands, even millions, who through the course of the centuries have found this secret and do display a dramatic change of life. Rather than hard, arrogant, proud, contemptuous people they have become softened, loving people. Rather than violent, angry, injurious people who strike back at everyone who comes in their path they have become tender, loving, gentle people, changed by the love of Christ. That is what Jesus means by "as I have loved you."

Now we are ready to look at the other two figures in this drama. *How do the actions of Judas and Peter relate to this new commandment?* Here we will learn the answer to why some people who call themselves Christians -- even some who unmistakably are Christians -- do not always manifest this kind of love. Let us take the case of Judas first.

Remember both Judas and Peter were disciples. Both of them were close companions of Jesus, having been with him for three and a half years. They both teach us something very valuable.

The account of Judas begins in Verse 18 of Chapter 13, and proceeds in three movements which record dramatically how Jesus sought to reach and change this man. In Verse 18 Jesus begins to speak of Judas by quoting the passage of Scripture that predicted that a betrayal would occur.

I am not speaking of you all; I know whom I have chosen; it is that the scripture may be fulfilled, "He who ate my bread has lifted his heel against me." I tell you this now, before it takes place, that when it does take place you may believe that I am he. Truly, truly, I say to you, he who receives any one whom I send receives me; and he who receives me receives him who sent me. {John 13:18-20 RSV}

Jesus is quoting Verse 9 of Psalm 41, written by David 1,000 years before these events we are looking at took place. Here, in but one sentence out of that psalm, Jesus describes what is happening right at this very moment among the disciples. The psalm had said that one who ate bread with the Lord -- one of the ones whom he himself had chosen to be his disciple -- would not only fellowship and eat bread with him but would "lift up his heel against him." That is a dramatic picture. It is as though you met an old friend and, as you reached out your hand to greet him he responded by giving you a karate kick in the face. It is a picture of a reprehensible, dastardly, unexplained and unexplainable reaction to a proffer of love and friendship. That is what Jesus declared the psalm said would happen: The traitor would be a disciple, who would betray him in a reprehensible manner.

Judas did not have to be that traitor. There is evidence all through this account, even in the very verses we are looking at, that Judas could have turned. How God would have worked out the fulfilling of the prediction I do not know. I do not have to know. There was a time when John the Baptist said to the Pharisees, who claimed to be the children of Abraham, "God is able from these very stones to raise up children of Abraham," {cf, Matt 3:9, Luke 3:8}. God has a thousand and one ways to fulfill his purposes. We never need to say that Judas was forced into being a traitor. He chose to be the traitor by the day-to-day choices which he made.

But the psalm said that the act of treason would be a heartless, reprehensible thing, done in the face of the friendship that was offered him, like a heel lifted up to kick someone in the face. Our Lord says the event will be certain and it will be literal: *"I have told you these things before they happen, that when it happens -- because they will happen -- you will know that I am the one of whom that psalms was speaking."*

Then, in very important words introduced in Verse 20 by that *formula of focused attention,* "Truly, truly," Jesus declares that the reason why Judas refused to believe was because he had never received our Lord. He had never yielded to his Lordship, never opened up his will to Christ, but had always pursued his own course in the midst of the disciples, regardless of what the Lord wanted. He outwardly went along with many things. He, too, was sent out with the twelve to do outstanding miracles. The Scriptures report that, when they came back, all twelve of them recounted how they had seen devils cast out by their word, people were healed, and the dead were raised. etc. Judas was one of the twelve. The Lord gave him power, even though he knew what his heart was like.

But, Jesus said, the reason why he failed was "because he did not receive me. He who receives me, receives him who sent me" In the first chapter of his gospel, John says, "As many as received him, to them gave he power to become the sons of God, even to them that believe on his name," {John 1:12 KJV}. So it is possible to be a member of a church, a visible disciple, called a Christian, and regarded as a Christian by other Christians, and still not have your heart respond to Jesus and surrender to his will. This is the case with Judas.

Our Lord goes on to announce this betrayal to the disciples.

When Jesus had thus spoken, he was troubled in spirit, and testified, "Truly, truly, I say to you, one of you will betray me." The disciples looked at one another, uncertain of whom he spoke. One of his disciples, whom Jesus loved, was lying close to the breast of Jesus; so Simon Peter beckoned to him and said, "Tell us who it is of whom he speaks." So lying thus, close to the breast of Jesus, he said to him, 'Lord, who is it?" Jesus answered, 'It is he to whom I shall give this morsel when I have dipped it." So when he had dipped the morsel, he gave it to Judas, the son of Simon Iscariot. {John 13:21-26 RSV}

According to this account it was very difficult for Jesus to do this. He was "troubled in spirit." It bothered him greatly. Here is compassion of his heart going out to Judas. We can sense the hurt, the terrible pain and sense of loss he felt, that one of his own should be involved like this. Jesus was deeply "troubled in spirit," emotionally stirred, hurt and upset by this.

It was difficult also for the disciples to believe that it was Judas. That is amazing? They were stunned and shaken by the revelation "One of you is to betray me." The other gospels tell us they began to look at one another and say to the Lord, "Lord, is it I?" *That is one of the greatest signs of spiritual health among the rest of the disciples.* They did not look at the Lord and point to one another, saying, "Is it him?" That is a marvelous commentary on the fact that we do not know ourselves very well. All of us at times have done things that shocked us, things we did not know we were capable of doing, or said things we did not realize we could have said. The disciples feel this. Filled with self-distrust they ask, "Lord, is it I?"

But this also indicates the smooth deceit of Judas, for he too said, "Lord, is it I?" He had so hidden <u>his motives</u> that none of the other disciples had the slightest idea that it was he. After three and a half years of living with these men he, had never said anything to the other disciples to tip them off that he did not agree with what the Lord was doing with them; that he had a different objective and a different purpose than they. He had hidden and covered it all.

As this account makes clear, when Jesus identified him, he did so only to John. John, "the disciple whom Jesus loved," was lying on his side on his couch, his head close to the breast of Jesus. Simon Peter, who evidently was across the table, in his impetuous curiosity wants to know, "Who is this?" He signals to John to find out, and John asks Jesus, "Who is it?" Quietly, out of earshot of the others, Jesus replies, "It is the one to whom I will give this morsel." And he dipped the bread in the dish. It was a mark of friendship for the host to dip a piece of bread into the crushed fruit and wine that constituted one of the dishes of the Passover supper and then hand it to an honored person. Since Judas was on the other side of Jesus, our Lord simply dipped the bread in and passed it to him.

The other disciples were still unaware of what this meant, but when Judas took the morsel a sinister thing happened.

Then after the morsel, Satan entered into him. Jesus said to him, "What you are going to do, do quickly." Now no one at the table knew why he said this to him. Some thought that, because Judas had the money box, Jesus was telling him, "Buy what we need for the feast"; or, that he should give something to the poor. So, after receiving the morsel, he immediately went out; and it was night. {John 13:27-30 RSV}

It is obviously a very profound word that John adds at the end, a word which refers more than simply the darkness of the night. It's really remarkable that here in the very presence of the Son of God himself, the Lord of Glory, the One to whom all power in heaven and on earth had been committed Satan, also present, entered into the heart and life of Judas.

There is a teaching around today that Christians ought to "bind" Satan before they do anything. Some groups mistakenly "bind" Satan by prayer before they begin a service. *But our Lord does nothing of the sort. He knows Satan is personally present, and yet he does nothing to stop him, because he understands what we must come to understand -- that it is the will of the individual alone that determines the outcome.*

Let me share with you the comment on this scene by the great Bible scholar, Dr. F. F. Bruce:

Satan could not have entered into him had he not granted him admission. Had he been willing to say "No" to the adversary, all of his

Master's intercessory power was available to him there and then to strengthen him. But when a disciple's will turns traitor, when the spiritual aid of Christ is refused, that person's condition is desperate indeed.

That is the problem. Judas consistently refused the help that Jesus offered. He consistently refused to open his life, surrender his will and let Jesus in. As a consequence, Jesus' power to give the gift of love that would change his heart could never reach Judas. *After this, as John tells us, Jesus made no further effort to change him.* "Get your business done quickly!" he told him. Judas went out into the Judaean night, and as John infers, into the darkness of Satanic gloom.

Have you ever known anyone named Judas? Isn't it remarkable that children are still named Adolph, or Benedict, but no one who has known the biblical story has, to my knowledge, ever named a child Judas? (I'm sure somebody is going to tell me that he grew up with a boy named Judas, but I have never met anyone with that name.) It has become the symbol of everything dishonorable and treacherous in human relationships. The gift of love that Jesus came to give can never help those who persistently refuse his life. That is one reason why many people who calls themselves Christians, who regard themselves as such, and are regarded as such by other people, <u>do not</u>, and <u>cannot,</u> manifest the love that Jesus is speaking about.

Now, what about Peter? We get his story at the end of the chapter. Apparently Peter never heard what the Lord said about the new commandment. All he heard was, "Yet a little while I am with you. You will seek me; and as I said to the Jews so now I say to you. 'Where I am going you cannot come.'" Like a child in school, Peter immediately shoots up his hand and says, "Lord, where are you going?" I am always amazed at the patience of Jesus. If I had been there I would have said, "Peter, when are you going to get the message? I have told you a dozen times where I am going. I am going to a cross. I am going to a tomb. I am going home to the Father." But Peter never heard.

Jesus does not rebuke him because he knows that what he meant to ask was not "Where are you going?" but, "Why can't I go with you?" Have your children ever asked you that? "Why can't I go, Daddy?" Jesus answers, "You can not follow me now! But afterward, you shall." It was a long time afterward. Probably 30 or more years went by before Peter, then an old man, imprisoned in Rome, was led out and, according to the traditional account, was condemned to be crucified. So moved was he by the fact that he was to share the manner of his Lord's death, he insisted on being crucified upside down. Thus our Lord's words were literally fulfilled. "You can not go with me now, Peter, but afterward you shall."

But there is another reason why Peter cannot follow the Lord now: His love is the wrong kind of love.

... Peter said to him, "Lord, why cannot I follow you now? I will lay down my life for you." Jesus answered, "Will you lay down your life for me? Truly, truly, I say to you, the cock will not crow, till you have denied me three times. {John 13:36-38 RSV}

Peter was perfectly sincere when he said these words. He was thoroughly committed to Christ and his cause. He felt right down to his toes that he would lay down his life for his Lord. His loyalty mounts to the fore here, and he declares he is quite willing to die for him. Jesus knows he means it, but he also knows that it is a totally unreliable commitment. He knows that it comes from purely natural affection, and natural affection is never strong enough to handle the demands against love in this life.

That is what we too must learn.

Peter's affection was the kind that he would have had for anybody close to him. Before he was born again he loved his wife, his mother and his father, his brothers and his sisters (if he had any) with a purely natural love. Under certain circumstances he would also have laid down his life for them. Natural affection can do this. Many a person has laid down his life out of a natural love. But it was not yet love born of the Spirit within, and capable of effecting a bold witness instead of a dramatic self-immolation.

Here is the primary reason why Christians do not often manifest the unique quality of love that Jesus is talking about when he commands, "'Love one another." We feel that our natural affection is fulfilling that demand; that if we love those who are dear to us, and near to us, we are loving one another. But we are not. Natural affection, natural zeal can not do God's work.

New Christians, their faces aglow and their hearts aflame with love for the Lord, oftentimes dream up grandiose plans to win the world for Christ. Some of them have great gifts of organization and they set up programs designed to win the world for Christ in this generation. They mean it. Fired with zeal they go out to buttonhole people on the streets, riding roughshod over personal rights, offending their own families (and slowing down their conversion for several years). That is what natural zeal does. People filled with that kind of zeal are always exciting to be around. It looks like they are going to get something done, but it always falls apart because, like Peter, they don't understand the weakness of the flesh.

It's a great period of hope, because, as he did with Peter, our Lord is quite willing to teach them; it will be a process of pain and hurt, rejection and failure. I don't know any Christian who has ever been used of God who hasn't had to go through that same process.

We must learn that our zeal for Christ will not do what he wants done. We have to learn through failure, hurt, and rejection, to glory in his love for us -- not our love for him -- then our own hearts will begin to burn with his same love.

Peter is an example of this. After the Day of Pentecost, when the Spirit of grace had fallen upon him, and began to impart to him an inner awareness of the love of Jesus for him, he was able to tell what had happened to the many people who had shouted for Christ's death on the cross. With boldness and plainness, he preached so powerfully in the strength of the Spirit that three thousand people were converted on that day.

This is the lesson that will be taught us precisely and plainly by our Lord here in the Upper Room.

Here is the first hint that the secret of changing the world is teaching people how to love one another -- and that when we manifest that kind of love, either as individuals or as a group, we become a loving community.

The world may not always agree with us, they may not always come and join us -- although many of them will -- but they will know one thing: Such people have been with Jesus. "By this shall all men know that you are my disciples, that you have love one for another."

Message No: 37

Catalog No: 3867

Date: March 10, 1985

I have shared the above *The Total Sum* because it covers the whole theme of this book. To understand why good people suffer, why they keep on loving, praying and why it takes courage to be a real Christian and why so many people are turned off with religion would be too simple. To understand the words and deeds of (Yeshua) the real Jesus Christ, our Lord, I learned at a very young age that following Christ can and is a painful yet most joyous road and requires God's strength and courage daily. The easy road is the world's way but it won't give you intimacy with God. It won't give you self-respect, honor, inner peace and joy and in the end you have nothing to take with you to the other side if you believe there is life after this physical life. There is life after physical life and death whether you believe it or not.

With each gift from the Holy Spirit comes responsibility. Understanding that every person has the gift of discernment, prophecy, dreams and visions within and it needs to be received, believed, cultivated and used for the glory of God once awakened by God. Some choose to call it by a different name and use it for selfish gain, but however you choose to use it; it is still a gift from God. This book is not to determine what you use your gift for or to judge anyone on the choices they make but only to enlighten you about dreams and visions from my personal experiences, both good and bad. Also how important the people are, you choose to share your gifts and life with, and the chances you take when you do share. Not everyone will believe it is from God and we are not here to change their mind. I hope the journey has entertained and educated you just a little in a different way that you may understand our great Creator God and how he uses children, teens, anyone who is willing. All is required is your willingness. What you focus upon you become as some people say it. So why not focus on a God who is all love forever and ever?

The Smith Home

09/04/2007

After JP Smith remodeled it I'm sure his Grandmother Ellen is smiling upon him from above. I know those of us who were raised there and still call it home smile.

I want to thank you JP for allowing me to use this picture and Joann for taking the picture. Also I want to thank you Cousin Peggy for encouraging me to write about Aunt Ellen and continue to write. I hope you know how important your encouragement has helped me over the years. And especially my Granddaughter Michelle for all the work and time she puts into my books. I hope you know how much I love and appreciate YOU.

Thank all of you for taking this journey with me!

Believe God for He has said, "I have blessed you!"

"Love one another as I have loved you."